Edward Backhouse

Witnesses for Christ And Memorials of Church Life From the Fourth

to the Thirteenth Century

Edward Backhouse

Witnesses for Christ And Memorials of Church Life From the Fourth to the Thirteenth Century

ISBN/EAN: 9783337005351

Printed in Europe, USA, Canada, Australia, Japan

Cover: Foto ©ninafisch / pixelio.de

More available books at **www.hansebooks.com**

WITNESSES FOR CHRIST

AND

MEMORIALS OF CHURCH LIFE

FROM THE FOURTH TO THE THIRTEENTH CENTURY.

A SEQUEL TO "EARLY CHURCH HISTORY."

BY

EDWARD BACKHOUSE

AND

CHARLES TYLOR.

IN TWO VOLUMES.

VOL. I.

LONDON: HAMILTON, ADAMS & CO.
1887.

The Madonna di S. Luca, or Black Virgin of Bologna.
Copied from the original by Edward Backhouse.

Ipsam tamen religionem, quam paucissimis et manifestissimis celebrationum sacramentis misericordia Dei esse liberam voluit, servilibus oneribus premunt, ut tolerabilior sit conditio Judæorum, qui etiamsi tempus libertatis non agnoverunt, legalibus tamen sarcinis, non humanis præsumtionibus subjiciuntur.

(That very religion which the mercy of God designed to be free, with very few ceremonial sacraments, and of the plainest kind, is oppressed with slavish burdens, so that the condition of the Jews is more tolerable, who, although they knew not the time of their deliverance, are yet subjected to the yoke of the law, not to the weight of human assumptions.)—AUGUSTINE.

There is but one Divine element of life which all believers share in common; but one fellowship with Christ which proceeds from faith in Him; but one new birth. All who possess this, all who are Christians in the true sense, have the same calling, the same dignity, the same heavenly blessings.—JOVINIAN.

TO THE READER.

THE title "Witnesses for Christ" was originally chosen by Edward Backhouse for the entire work, of which these volumes form the second instalment. It seemed however more appropriate to designate the former volume, the second edition of which was published in 1885, *Early Church History*. In the two volumes now presented there is little attempt at a consecutive history of the Church, and the original title is therefore reverted to.

With regard to the authorship of these volumes it should be stated that the idea and inception of the whole belong to the late Edward Backhouse, who had collected much material (extending even to the seventeenth century), and whose artistic taste supplied many of the illustrations. For the remainder of the work Charles Tylor is responsible.

A cordial acknowledgment is due to several friends who have rendered aid in various ways in the preparation of this work; especially to Joseph Bevan Braithwaite and Thomas Hodgkin. Valuable assistance has also been received throughout from R. Hingston Fox.

The hymns at pages 74, 75, 109, and 174, from *The Voice of Christian Life in Song*, are reprinted with the kind leave of the authoress; and those in Vol. II., pages 247 and 248, are taken by permission of the publisher from Dr. Neale's *Hymns of the Eastern Church*.

CONTENTS OF VOL. I.

PERIOD I.

FROM THE DEATH OF CONSTANTINE, A.D. 337, TO THE DEATH OF AUGUSTINE, A.D. 430.

CHAPTER I.

	PAGE
The Arian Epoch	3

CHAPTER II.

Athanasius	25

CHAPTER III.

The Cappadocian Bishops	41

CHAPTER IV.

The Cappadocian Bishops (*concluded*)	76

CHAPTER V.

Ulfilas	116

CHAPTER VI.

Martin of Tours	136

CHAPTER VII.

Ambrose	154

CHAPTER VIII.

Chrysostom	175

CHAPTER IX.

Chrysostom (*continued*)	199

CHAPTER X.

Chrysostom (*concluded*) 229

CHAPTER XI.

Jerome 257

CHAPTER XII.

Jerome (*concluded*) 280

CHAPTER XIII.

Augustine 301

CHAPTER XIV.

Augustine (*continued*) 328

CHAPTER XV.

Augustine (*concluded*) 345

CHAPTER XVI.

The Spirit of the Age :—
- I. Public Worship 367
- II. Baptism and the Eucharist 373
- III. Virginity 376
- IV. Fasting 382
- V. Almsgiving 385
- VI. Saint-Worship 386
- VII. Relics 395

CHAPTER XVII.

The Spirit of the Age (*concluded*) :—
- I. Monachism 400
- II. The Church and the World 413

CHAPTER XVIII.

Jovinian and Vigilantius 419

ILLUSTRATIONS TO VOL. I.

THE MADONNA DI S. LUCA, OR BLACK
VIRGIN OF BOLOGNA .. .. ..   *Chromo-lithograph.* *Frontispiece*
FAC-SIMILE OF A PAGE FROM THE CODEX
ARGENTEUS (GOTHIC VERSION OF THE
GOSPELS), REDUCED .. ..   „   *page* 134
EPISCOPAL CHAIR OF AMBROSE, OF WHITE
MARBLE, IN THE CHURCH OF ST. AMBROSE,
MILAN .. ..   *Woodcut* ..   „   154
DOORS OF THE BASILICA OF ST. AMBROSE,
MILAN, CONTAINING A PANEL OF THE
GATES WHICH AMBROSE CLOSED AGAINST
THE EMPEROR THEODOSIUS .. .. ..   „   „   169
BAPTISTERY OF S. GIOVANNI I FONTE,
RAVENNA .. ..   *Chromo-lithograph*   „   373
MARBLE FONT IN THE BAPTISTERY OF THE
CATHEDRAL AT VERONA .. ..   „   „   374

ERRATUM.

Page	Line	For	Read
399	6	Gregory VIII.	Gregory the Great.

PERIOD I.

FROM THE DEATH OF CONSTANTINE, A.D. 337,
TO THE DEATH OF AUGUSTINE, A.D. 430.

CHAPTER I.

The Arian Epoch.

From the time of Constantine the history of the Church becomes the history of the world. To continue the subject in the historical form of the previous volume would lead us far beyond our limits. The purpose of the present work is rather to seek out true WITNESSES FOR CHRIST, whether amongst those upon whom the Church has bestowed the title of saint, or amongst the rejected and proscribed, whom she has branded with the name of heretic. The former, however great and good, were for the most part contented with the Christianity by which they were surrounded; and if they made any attempts at reformation, did little more than aim at the correction of abuses in discipline and manners. They left the fungus growth of superstition untouched, and in some cases even more rank than they found it. The heretics, such of them as are worthy of memorial, are those who, not always it is true in its completeness, discovered the truth through the mist which hid it from the eyes of the many, and who ventured the loss of character, liberty and life in order to persuade others to embrace it.

Per. I.
Chap. 1.

At the close of the first century we found Christianity numbering but few followers, little known and despised, yet steadily permeating the great Roman Empire, and wherever it came effecting a marvellous change in the dispositions and conduct of men. From age to age the Church grew, and asserted her reality and her power in the teeth of all manner of calumny and opposition. In spite of adverse laws and cruel edicts, she won her way, step by step, even before the days of persecution ceased, to a recognised place of influence and honour.

When Constantine declared himself her nursing-father, a new era opened before her. Suddenly her relations with the world were changed; her implacable enemy was cast under her feet; she ceased to be persecuted, and, alas! she became a persecutor. From this time we look upon the Roman Empire as no longer pagan, but Christian; the laws are Christian; the magistrates are Christian; the Emperor is Christian. Pagan temples and sacrifices, if they do not at once disappear, are gradually replaced by Christian churches; and paganism soon begins to hide itself in the corners of the earth.[1] The wholesale admission of the people into the Church after the accession of

---

[1] The name *pagan* is derived from the Latin *pagus*, a canton or country district, because it was there the old idolatry survived the longest. In like manner, *heathen* signifies one who lives on the *heath*, that is, in the open country. For a fuller account of the etymology of the word pagan, see Gibbon, iii. p. 84, note (?).

Constantine brought with it a crowd of abuses, and powerfully accelerated that declension which, in spite of the purifying effect of persecution, had been going on for several generations.

Another point of difference between the history of the Church before and after the edicts of Milan (A.D. 313, 314) must be noticed. The historic materials, which before were scanty, now become abundant. A host of Church writers appear at once upon the scene. Homilies, orations, lectures, commentaries on Scripture, controversial treatises, confessions, epistles, histories, biographies of saints and hermits, hymns, poems, are poured forth in such volume that only a few amongst modern scholars have patience enough to master the folios in which they are preserved. This brilliant era of Christian literature lasted but little more than a century; it did not survive the irruption of the barbarian hordes. After the Goths, Vandals, Franks, and Huns had swept over the empire, trampling down civilisation, the lamps of knowledge became few and dim, and were soon all but extinguished.

It will be convenient to divide the present work into chronological epochs, the first of which will embrace the period from the death of Constantine, in 337, to that of Augustine, in 430. A brief outline of events between these two eras may serve as an introduction to our biographies of the Witnesses of this age.

On Constantine's death he was succeeded by his three sons, who divided his empire between them. Constantine II. received the Western provinces, Constantius the Eastern, and Constans had Illyricum, Italy, and part of Africa, for his share. Constantine, whilst invading the dominions of Constans, was killed in battle, A.D. 340. Constans was slain A.D. 350 by one of his generals, who was in turn overcome by Constantius, in 353. Constantine and Constans favoured the Catholic or orthodox party; Constantius, like his father in his later days, espoused the cause of the Arians, but with a more blind zeal and greater intolerance. The nature of the Arian error has already been explained in *Early Church History*. Arius, whilst ascribing to our Lord divine honour, taught, contrary to the plain testimony of Scripture, that He had a beginning, and is not of the same substance or essence (homo-ousion) as the Father. Partly from the Oriental love of speculation, partly from an honest dread of sensuous ideas and unscriptural terms, a great portion of the Eastern Church became his followers. The chief opponent of Arius was Athanasius. The whole life of this remarkable man was devoted to the defence of our Lord's proper deity, the cardinal truth which it was the object of the Council of Nicæa to settle and confirm.[1]

---

[1] *Early Church History*, 2nd ed. pt. ii. c. 11.

We have seen that at Constantine's death Arianism was in the ascendant. That Emperor, in the part which he took in theological controversies, never lost sight of the interests of the State. It was otherwise with Constantius, who entered the polemical lists as if he had been himself a bishop.[1] His reign, with those of the succeeding Arian emperors, was a period of intense agitation in the Church. "Council was held against council; creed was set up against creed; anathema was hurled against anathema."[2] "As many creeds exist as inclinations," wrote the orthodox Hilary of Poictiers in his exile, "as many doctrines as modes of life. . . . Whilst we are disputing about words, searching into novelties, catching at ambiguities, anathematizing one another—scarcely one belongs to Christ . . . We make creeds every year, nay every month; we repent when we have made them; we defend those who repent; we anathematize those whom we defended; we condemn either other people's opinions in our own, or our

A.D. 337–361.

---

[1] "He accepted with complacency the lofty title of 'bishop of bishops.'"—Gibbon, iii. p. 40. The reign of Constantius is described by a living author as "one of the most peculiar of which history has preserved a record; the reign of a man deeply dyed in the blood of relatives and friends, who used the obsequious service of eunuchs instead of entrusting the affairs of the State to honest and capable ministers, whose feeble haughtiness and cowardly ambition bear no trace of the influence of Christianity upon his life, but who, nevertheless, plunged into theological discussions with an eagerness, and continued in the same with a patient endurance, such as we should scarcely find nowadays in a salaried professor of Divinity."—T. Hodgkin, in the *Edinburgh Review*, Oct. 1877, p. 373. Like his father, Constantius deferred baptism till shortly before his death.

[2] *Dict. Christ. Biog.*, art. Arianism, i. p. 158.

own in other people; mutually devouring one another we are at length mutually consumed."[1] "The posting service of the empire," says Ammianus Marcellinus, "was thrown into confusion by the troops of bishops galloping hither and thither to the assemblies which they called synods."[2] And Athanasius rebukes "the restless flutter of the clergy, who journeyed the empire over to find the true faith, and provoked the ridicule and contempt of the unbelieving world."[3] But it was not the clergy only who took part in the strife. The points of the Arian controversy were the fashionable topics of conversation amongst all ranks, from the highest to the lowest. "Every corner and nook of the city" (Constantinople), writes Gregory of Nyssa, "is full of men who discuss incomprehensible subjects—the streets, the markets, the dealers in old clothes, the money-changers, the hucksters. Ask a man how many oboli it comes to, he will dogmatize on generated and ungenerated being. Inquire the price of bread, you are answered: 'The Father is greater than the Son, and the Son subordinate to the Father.' Ask if the bath is ready, and you are told: 'The Son of God was created from nothing.'"[4] The war was very far, however, from being confined to words; the in-

---

[1] Roberts' *Church Memorials*, p. 104. Compare Eph. iv. 14.
[2] *Roman History*, b. xxi. c. 16, § 16.
[3] Schaff's *Nicene Christianity*, p. 632.
[4] Neander, iv. p. 41, note; Socrates Scholasticus, *Eccles. Hist.*, b. ii. c. 2.

tolerance of the age showed itself in innumerable acts of violence, in which the Arians seem to have far outdone the Catholics. The great cities of the East especially were the frequent scenes of confusion and bloodshed.

A.D. 337–361.

At the Council of Antioch, A.D. 341, although in a minority, the Arians with the Emperor's help obtained the victory. Athanasius was condemned, and Gregory of Cappadocia, a man of coarse and violent character, consecrated bishop in his stead. At this council also four creeds were adopted, in all of which the Homo-ousion, or orthodox formula, was set aside.[1] In 343,[2] Constantius, alarmed for the peace of the empire, agreed with his brother Constans, who befriended Athanasius, to hold a general council. A numerous body of Eastern and Western bishops met at Sardica.[3] At this council the Nicene doctrine prevailed; but the Arian bishops, disgusted at the admission of Athanasius to the council, stood aloof, and held a rival synod in the neighbouring city of Philippopolis, where the decrees of the Council of Antioch were confirmed. The death of Constans, in 350, left Constantius free to pursue his own course. He summoned three successive synods of the Arian party—namely, at Sirmium, 351; Arles, 353; and

---

[1] Robertson's *History of the Church*, i. p. 216; *Dict. Christ. Antiq.*, art. Antioch, Councils of, i. p. 93. Nevertheless, the Canons of the Council of Antioch have always held a place of authority in the Catholic Church.

[2] Or 347.   [3] Now Sophia in Bulgaria.

Milan, 355—the result of which was that Athanasius, who had been twice before exiled, Hosius of Cordova, Liberius of Rome, Hilary of Poictiers, and other eminent bishops of the Catholic party were deposed and banished. At Milan the Emperor himself propounded an Arian formula which he professed to have received by revelation, and attempted to quench all freedom of debate by saying, " Whatever I will, let that be esteemed a canon."[1]

The Arian party, which comprehended within it men of great diversity of opinion, now split into two camps—the Semi-Arians, or Homoi-ousions (so called from the word which they adopted in contradistinction to Homo-ousion, to express that the essence of the Son is *like*, but not the *same* as that of the Father), and the thorough Arians, who held more distinctly than Arius himself that the Son is essentially a creature, unlike the Father not only in substance but in will.[2] These dissensions gave

---

[1] Schaff, pp. 634, 635; *History of the Christian Church* by Philip Smith (*Students' Eccles. Hist.*), pt. i. p. 262.

[2] Hence they were called Anomoians (*Unlike*). The subjoined table may help the reader to distinguish the chief schools of thought which prevailed during the Arian ascendancy. We are indebted for it to the kindness of Thomas Hodgkin:—

Name of Party.	Chief Promoters.	Theological Formula.
Sabellians or Patripassians.	Sabellius. Marcellus of Ancyra. Photinus.	The Son is the same as the Father. (Confounding the persons.)
Homo-ousions (Catholics).	Athanasius, &c.	The Son is of the *same* essence as the Father, but a different person.

rise to a succession of synods—two at Sirmium, A.D. 357, 358; one at Antioch and one at Ancyra, 358; and two simultaneously in 359. 160 Eastern bishops in this year met at Seleucia, in Isauria; whilst the Western bishops, to the number of 400, gathered at Ariminum,[1] in Italy. At the former council the Homoi-ousions prevailed over the thorough-going Arians; at the latter the orthodox party would have been victorious over both, if it had not been for the arbitrary conduct of the Emperor. The West had always in reality been faithful to Athanasius; and when a Semi-Arian Creed was proposed by the Imperial Commissioners it was rejected, the Nicene Confession was confirmed, and the Arian errors anathematized. But Constantius was determined to carry his point, and protracted the sittings of the council

	Name of Party.	Chief Promoters.	Theological Formula.
Arians.	Homoi-ousions or Semi-Arians.	Eusebius of Cæsarea. Eusebius of Nicomedia. Emperor Constantius during most of his life.	The Son is of *like* essence with the Father. (Dividing the substance.)
	Homoians.	Acacius. Eudoxius. Ulfilas.	The Son is like to the Father "in all things" or "according to the Scriptures." (The terms essence and substance being rejected as unscriptural.)
	Anomoians.	Aetius. Eunomius.	The Son's essence is entirely *unlike* that of the Father.

[1] Now Rimini.

so long that many of the bishops, impatient to return to their dioceses, and dreading the approach of winter, began to waver. Entreaties and threats on the part of the court prevailed with others, until at length the entire council was brought to abandon the Nicene, and put their hands to the Semi-Arian Creed. "The whole world," exclaims Jerome, "groaned in astonishment to find itself Arian!"[1]

This state of things, however, did not last long. On the death of Constantius, in 361, Christianity itself was for a time set aside by the accession of Julian, surnamed *the Apostate*, nephew to Constantine the Great. As soon as this prince ascended the throne, he declared himself in favour of the ancient idolatry, and restored it to its former place as the religion of the State. He sought to infuse new life into the dying creed by adopting the moral code of Christianity and introducing many of its forms. The laws which he enacted against the Church were indeed mild in comparison with those which his predecessor had issued against heathenism,[2] yet in the course of his short reign the Christians had to endure no little hardship, both from the government and the people.[3]

---

[1] Newman, *Arians of the Fourth Century*, pp. 356–361.

[2] When in 350 Constantius became sole Emperor, heathen sacrifices were forbidden under penalty of death.—Schaff, i. p. 38.

[3] Julian restored the banished bishops, but "stripped them of their honours and emoluments, 'that, being relieved from the weight and incumbrance of their temporal possessions, they might the more easily obtain

One form in which Julian's enmity to the Gospel showed itself was the attempt to rebuild the Temple at Jerusalem. He seems to have supposed that he could falsify our Lord's prediction of its perpetual ruin. At his call Jews from all the provinces of the empire assembled on the holy mountain of their fathers, and entered with fanatical zeal into the great national work. The rich used spades and mattocks and baskets of silver, and ladies carried the earth and stones of the holy spot in their silken aprons. But as soon as the rubbish had been cleared away, and the old foundations laid bare, " fearful balls of flame burst forth from the earth, burnt the workmen, and again and again drove them from the spot. The balls of fire raged up and down the street for hours." This singular phenomenon has occupied the pens of many modern historians, who, as might be supposed, suggest various explanations; few of them, however, denying the historical facts. To the Church it was nothing less than the interposition of the Almighty

A.D. 361-363.

---

the kingdom which was promised to the poor.'"—Roberts' *Church Memorials*, p. 93. In his efforts to resuscitate paganism, the Emperor found himself thwarted by the fidelity of the Christian women. He complains that the ladies of Antioch were ready to bestow anything they had in the house upon the Galilæans (Christians), or to give away to the poor, while they would not expend the smallest trifle on the worship of the gods. And Libanius, the celebrated heathen professor, in a letter to the governor of the same city, writes : " When the men are out of doors, they obey thee who givest them the best advice, and they approach the altars; but when they get home, their minds undergo a change, they are wrought upon by the tears and entreaties of their wives, and they again withdraw from the altars of the gods."—Stephens' *Life of St. Chrysostom*, p. 11.

Per. I.
Chap. 1.

Hand, which would not suffer prophecy to be made void, or presumptuous unbelief to triumph.[1]

The reign of restored paganism was short. Julian died in 363, and was succeeded by Jovian, a zealous upholder of Christianity, but who, from the critical nature of the times, left the pagans unmolested. At his death, after a reign of only eight months, the purple fell to Valentinian I. and Valens, under whom the final division of the empire was made, Valens taking the East and Valentinian the West. Valens trod in the footsteps of Constantius, and suffered himself to become the tool of the Arian clergy. His reign was in consequence a period of deplorable desolation in the Oriental Churches. "Worthy bishops were driven from their sees; worthless men, who had their patrons among the Imperial eunuchs and chamberlains, were imposed on the Churches as priests and bishops."[2] Many of the orthodox clergy were put to death. The following is one

---

[1] The facts are attested by three contemporary authorities—Ammianus Marcellinus, Gregory Nazianzen, and Rufinus. The first, a heathen historian, was at the time in personal attendance on the Emperor. Gregory, in Cappadocia, preached on the event the very year of its occurrence, and avers that the heathens did not call the prodigy in question; according to him, a luminous cross surrounded by a circle also appeared in the sky. Rufinus, who was at the time in Italy, went to reside in a monastery on the Mount of Olives about sixteen years after the event.—Amm. Marc., b. xxiii. c. 1; *Dict. Christ. Biog.*, art. Julianus, Emperor, iii. pp. 512, 513. Later writers speak of a whirlwind, an earthquake which preceded the fire and produced great destruction, and other prodigies.—See Socrates Scholasticus, b. iii. c. 20; Sozomen, b. v. c. 22; Theodoret, b. iii. c. 20, &c.

[2] Neander, iv. p. 76.

of the dark deeds which are laid to the account of the Arians during this period. In the year 370, eighty Catholic priests presented themselves to the Emperor in his palace at Nicomedia, to sue for redress of the intolerable hardships to which their party were subjected. Valens, dissembling his displeasure, gave Modestus, the prefect, secret orders to put to death the whole deputation. Apprehensive of a popular tumult, if so large a number of good and religious men were slain without the forms of justice, the prefect pretended that he had received orders to send them away into exile. They heard the tidings of their destiny with composure and resignation, and were embarked on board a ship. But when the vessel reached the middle of the Astacenian Gulf, the sailors set fire to it, and, leaping into a small boat which they had in tow, escaped. A strong easterly wind drove the burning ship towards shore, where it was utterly consumed, with all who were on board. On the death of Valens, in 378, the Catholics recovered their power, and the Arians in their turn were driven from the Churches, never to regain their former influence.[1]

The legal toleration of paganism continued in the first years of the Emperors Gratian and Valentinian II. in the West, and Theodosius in the East; until, in 381, Theodosius, whose character and military genius could brook no breach of

---

[1] Socrates, b. iv. c. 16; Sozomen, b. vi. c. 14.

uniformity, directed the whole force of his authority to its suppression. "Let no one," so runs one of his edicts, "in any station of life offer up an innocent victim to senseless idols; nor by a more secret sacrifice seek to propitiate the Lares by fire, the Genius with wine, the Penates with sweet incense; nor for such a purpose let any one kindle lights, throw frankincense on the fire, or hang up garlands. But if any one shall dare to kill and sacrifice a victim, or to derive auguries from the inspection of its steaming entrails, he shall be held guilty of treason . . . But if any man shall offer incense to perishable images, the work of men's hands, and shall present to others the ridiculous spectacle of a man fearing what he himself has fashioned, whether he hangs the tree with garlands, or piles his altar of turf in their honour—since religion is grossly insulted even by these more slender forms of devotion—he shall be condemned to lose that house or that property in which he shall be proved to have practised heathen superstition."[1]

The efforts of the Emperor were zealously seconded by the clergy and the Christian populace. The fanatical monks turned out and joined themselves to mobs of hirelings which the bishops had collected for the destruction of all that remained of the heathen sanctuaries. At Alexandria, A.D. 391, the bishop Theophilus, a violent and rapacious

---

[1] A.D. 392.—Hodgkin's *Italy and her Invaders*, i. pp. 185, 186.

prelate, undertook a crusade against the renowned shrines which were the boast of that city. He caused the temple of Mithra, in which human beings had been wont to be sacrificed, to be cleared out, and the tokens of its bloody mysteries laid open to public view. He exposed the fraud by which the priests were accustomed to impose on their votaries. The statues of the gods were made hollow with the back fitted against a wall, so that an easy entrance into them was secured. Secreting themselves within, the priests pronounced the responses and commands which the ignorant took for the voice of the divinity. When Theophilus came to the temple of Serapis, reckoned one of the wonders of the world, he found a colossal statue formed of plates of metal artificially joined together. The god was in a sitting posture, with a sceptre in his left hand, on his head a basket, and in his right hand the emblematic serpent, whose three tails terminated in the heads of a dog, a lion, and a wolf. There was an ancient tradition, universally believed, that "if any impious hand should approach too near to the statue, the heavens and the earth would instantly return to their original chaos. Theophilus commanded one of his soldiers to strike the image. A ladder was placed, and the man, armed with a weighty battle-axe, mounted, and aimed a vigorous blow against the cheek of the idol. The pagans were beside themselves with horror; an undefined

A.D. 381–395.

18   DESTRUCTION OF THE STATUE OF SERAPIS.

Per. I.
Chap. 1.

awe oppressed even the Christians, uncertain what might be the consequences of this audacious act. The cheek fell to the ground; no convulsion of nature followed; the heavens and the earth remained tranquil as before. The soldier repeated his blows; the huge statue was overthrown and broken in pieces," and a swarm of mice ran out of the head! The fragments of the body were burnt in the market-place, and the head was carried in triumph through the city for the inspection of those who had once worshipped the idol, and who now ridiculed its impotence. This victory was followed up by the overthrow of all the temples of that part of the Delta: some being levelled with the ground, some converted into chapels and cloisters. But the conquest was not achieved without desperate opposition on the part of the pagan inhabitants, and much blood was spilt.[1] In Rome,

---

[1] Socrates, b. v. c. 16; Theodoret, b. v. c. 22; Gibbon, iii. pp. 521, 522. The death of the celebrated pagan lady Hypatia took place some years later, viz. in 415, in the reign of Theodosius II. Of this lady, who was a teacher of the Neo-Platonic school in Alexandria, and lectured on geometry and the philosophy of Plato and Aristotle, the Christian historian Socrates relates that she excelled all the philosophers of her time, and that the cultivation of her mind had imparted to her such refinement and self-possession, that she was able to appear in public with perfect composure and modesty. Suspected by the populace of preventing the prefect of the city, Orestes, from being reconciled to the bishop (Cyril), a party of fanatics, headed by Peter the Reader, conspired to take her life. They seized her as she was returning home in her chariot, dragged her from it, and carried her to the church of Cæsareum, where they stripped her and killed her with oyster-shells. Having torn her body in pieces, they took the mangled limbs to a place called Cinaron, and there burnt them. "So inhuman a deed," remarks Socrates, "could not fail to bring the greatest opprobrium, not only upon Cyril, but also upon the whole Alexandrian Church. For

paganism still held its ground, especially among families of distinction.[1]

A.D. 381-395.

But Theodosius was not only a "*most Christian*," he was a "*most Catholic*" Emperor. Summoned by Gratian to deliver the East from the Goths, and baptized when dangerously ill into the Nicene faith, he set himself to combat with equal skill and success at once the enemies of the Catholic Church and those of the empire. To him was due the second general council (that of Constantinople, A.D. 381), by which the Nicene Creed was finally established with the addition of a clause stating in express terms the divinity of the Holy Spirit.[2] The soldier theologian thus makes known his Imperial will. The decree, directed in the first place against the Arians, was meant to reach all dissenters. "It is our will that all the nations who are subject to the rule of Our Clemency shall adhere to that religion

---

surely nothing can be further from the spirit of Christianity than murders and massacres."—*Eccles. Hist.*, b. vii. c. 15.

[1] It has been estimated that there were 152 temples and 183 shrines still devoted to idolatry in the city at the end of the 4th century (Robertson, i. p. 278). Prudentius, the Christian poet, relates that a debate was held in the senate on the rival claims of Jupiter and Christ, in which Theodosius himself, who had come to Rome as a conqueror, took part. The result was a vote in favour of the new religion, and 600 of the old families of Rome passed over to Christianity.—*Epistle to Symmachus;* Milman, *History of Christianity*, iii. pp. 91, 92.

[2] The creed as adopted at the Council of Nicæa will be found in the *Early Church History* (pp. 418, 419). As enlarged by the Council of Constantinople, it is with one exception the same as we find in the liturgy of the Church of England under the name of the Nicene Creed. In this liturgy the word *Filioque* (*and the Son*), denoting the procession of the Holy Ghost from the Father and the Son together, has been added.—See the two creeds in Schaff, pp. 667–670.

which the divine Apostle Peter handed to the Romans, as is sufficiently shown by its existence among them to this day ... We believe the One Godhead of Father, Son and Holy Ghost with equal majesty in the Holy Trinity. We order those who follow this law to assume the name of Catholic[1] Christians: we pronounce all others to be mad and foolish, and we order that they shall bear the ignominious name of heretics,[2] and shall not presume to bestow on their conventicles the title of churches: these are to be visited, first by the divine vengeance, and secondarily by the stroke of our own authority, which we have received in accordance with the will of heaven." This edict being found insufficient, another, more stringent, was issued the next year. "Let there be no place left to the heretics for celebrating the mysteries of their faith, no opportunity for exhibiting their stupid obstinacy ... Their crimes being made manifest, let them receive a mark of opprobrium, and be kept utterly away from even the thresholds of the churches. If they attempt any outbreak, we order that their rage shall be quelled, and they shall be cast forth outside the walls of the cities, so that the Catholic churches, the whole world

---

[1] Catholic, καθολικός (καθ' ὅλου, on the whole), general, universal. This term was employed by very early Christian writers in the same sense in which it is still used.

[2] Heresy, αἱρεσις, signifies—(1) a *choosing*; (2) an opinion which any one *chooses* for himself; (3) something *different* from the *Catholic* opinions.

over, may be restored to the orthodox prelates who hold the Nicene faith."[1]

These measures, although not in all cases rigorously enforced, were successful. "Neither heathenism nor sectarianism," observes Robertson, "had much inward strength to withstand the pressure of the laws which required conformity to the Church."[2] Expelled from the old Churches of the empire, Arianism found refuge amongst the barbarians, especially the Goths and Vandals, the latter of whom, when they acquired possession of North Africa, A.D. 429, cruelly persecuted the adherents of the Nicene faith.

But with the overthrow of Arianism its disastrous effects did not disappear. By this half-century of theological contention a severe blow had been dealt at the life of Christianity. "Whilst," observes Ullmann, "the sanctifying and beatifying doctrines of the Gospel which point to the conver-

---

[1] Hodgkin, i. pp. 183–185. Theodoret states that this enactment was due to Amphilochius, bishop of Iconium, whose zeal for orthodoxy exceeded even that of the Emperor. Disappointed in the request he had made, that the Arians might be prohibited from holding their assemblies in the cities, Amphilochius had recourse to an expedient. He went to the palace. The Emperor's son Arcadius, who had recently been created Augustus, was seated near his father. Amphilochius saluted the Emperor according to custom, but paid no attention to his son. The former, supposing the omission had arisen from forgetfulness, called him back. "Sire," said the bishop in a loud voice, "you see how any want of respect to your son arouses your displeasure; you may be assured that the Lord of the universe abhors the blasphemies uttered against his only-begotten Son, and turns away from those who dishonour him."—*Eccles. Hist.*, b. v. c. 16. A similar story is told by Sozomen (b. vii. c. 6), which, although the details do not entirely correspond, no doubt relates to the same occurrence.

[2] *History of the Church*, i. p. 284.

sion of the inner man were suffered to lie inactive, every one from the Emperor to the beggar occupied himself with incredible earnestness in the discussion of propositions, concerning which the Gospel communicates just so much as is profitable to us and necessary to salvation." "This contentious spirit," writes Gregory Nazianzen, "has torn asunder the Church; thrown cities into commotion, driven the people to take up arms, and excited princes against one another; separated the priests from the congregation, and the congregation from the priests. Everything which bears a holy name has been profaned; .. an insolent presumption has usurped the place of law; and we are divided, not merely tribe against tribe, as was Israel of old, but house against house, family against family, nay, almost every one is distracted within himself."[1]

The irruption of the barbarian nations has been already slightly alluded to. It is the grand political event of this period, and it influenced in the highest degree the future of the Christian Church. Already, in the third century, the Goths had broken through the barriers of the empire and settled themselves in some of its fairest provinces. They were succeeded by other tribes —Vandals, Sueves, &c., and continual wars with alternate success were waged until, in 402, Alaric, king of the Visigoths, invaded Italy, and in 410

---

[1] Ullmann's *Gregory of Nazianzum*, pp. 159, 161.

took Rome. For six days the Imperial city, which had stood for nearly twelve hundred years, was delivered up to the licentious fury of the barbarians. At the same time the Vandals and the Burgundians poured into Gaul, and the former, after establishing a kingdom in Spain, crossed over into Africa, A.D. 429, and made themselves masters of all the Roman dominions in that country.

In bringing this brief outline to a close we may notice an event which happened in the reign of the Emperor Honorius. Neither the attempt of Constantine to put an end to the combats of gladiators,[1] nor the protests of Christian writers renewed from age to age[2] could induce the Roman people to relinquish their favourite pastime. It seemed to require some act of heroic self-devotion to break the spell by which they were bound to these shameful barbarities. The Emperor Honorius, after the victory gained by his general Stilicho over Alaric and the Goths at Polantia in the year 404, was celebrating a triumph with the usual games. An Eastern monk named Telemachus left his cell and travelled all the way to Rome in order to protest against the unchristian spectacle. He entered with the multitude into the theatre of the Coliseum. Gazing with agonized heart upon the

---

[1] See *Early Church History*, p. 387. Constantine's edict seems only to have been local.—Milman, iii. pp. 344, 345.

[2] Tertullian and Lactantius (*Early Church History*, pp. 201, 440); Prudentius.

revolting scene, and seeing no other way of making his protest known, he leaped down into the arena and attempted to separate the combatants. A cry of execration arose. The spectators, "possessed," says the historian, "by the demon who delights in the effusion of blood, and maddened at the interruption to their sport, stoned him to death." The Emperor, struck with admiration at his self-devotion, and probably pricked in his own conscience, ordained that these sanguinary spectacles should be abolished, and that the name of Telemachus should be entered on the roll of martyrs.[1]

---

[1] Theodoret, b. v. c. 26. It was, however, only the combats of men with men that were discontinued. Encounters between men and wild animals, in which human life was often sacrificed, as well as unbloody spectacles of every kind, even on the highest festivals of the Church, were as largely and passionately attended as ever. To the disgrace of Christendom, the Roman games of the amphitheatre still exist in the bull-fights of Spain, France, and South America.—Schaff, pp. 124, 125.

CHAPTER II.

ATHANASIUS.

THE representative men whom we have selected from the ranks of the Catholic Church in this epoch were all contemporary; Augustine, the youngest of them, had nearly reached man's estate when Athanasius died. They are as follows:—

	Born	Died		Born	Died
Athanasius	296	373	Martin of Tours	316	396
Basil	329	377	Ambrose	340	397
Gregory Nazianzen	329	389	Chrysostom	347	407
Gregory Nyssen	331	395	Jerome	346	420
Ulfilas[1]	311	381	Augustine[2]	354	430

We have, in the former volume, followed the eventful history of Athanasius until the death of Constantine.[3] His course under that Emperor's successors continued to be of the same stormy and

---

[1] Ulfilas was not in fact a Catholic, but represents the Arian party.

[2] Other leading Churchmen of this century may be named: the learned Hosius, bishop of Cordova (A.D. 256-357), counsellor of Constantine the Great, and for a long period the most prominent figure in Western Christendom; Hilary, bishop of Poictiers (died 368), the great champion of the Trinitarian doctrine in the West ("a very Rhone of eloquence," as Jerome styles him); Ephrem, a deacon of Edessa, "the prophet of the Syrians" (308-373); Cyril, bishop of Jerusalem (315-386), celebrated for his catechetical discourses on the mysteries of the faith. Some of these dates, and of those in the text, are only approximate.

[3] *Early Church History*, pt. ii. c. 11, 12.

eventful nature; at one time a fugitive and exposed to hardship, at another returning in triumph to Alexandria and wielding his crozier with increased authority and vigour.¹ Inflexible of will, he alone, amidst the waves of party strife which during this time swept over Church and State, remained consistent to the one grand purpose of his life, viz., to preserve the orthodox faith pure from the taint of heresy. For this end he braved all dangers and withstood the mandate of the Emperor himself. He was five times driven into exile. His sufferings only augmented his fame, which extended to the extreme confines of Christendom.²

During his second exile (A.D. 341–346), Athanasius spent three years in Italy, a residence memorable for the introduction of the monkish life into the countries of the West. Two strange uncouth figures in cloak and girdle accompanied him to Rome. These were Ammonius and Isidore, youthful monks from the Nitrian desert.³ The former, one of four brothers called from their un-

---

[1] His return from one of his exiles (the second) is described by Gregory Nazianzen as a most imposing spectacle. "The vast population of the great city streamed forth to meet him like another Nile; innumerable faces gazed upon him; the air resounded with shouts of joy and was made fragrant with clouds of incense. Within the city the streets were spread with carpets of the gayest colours, and myriads of lamps lighted up the night."—Oration 21.   [2] Gibbon, iii. pp. 41, 42.

[3] Anthony, the first Christian hermit, was then living. Isidore afterwards became governor of the great hospice at Alexandria. He must be distinguished from the more famous Isidore of Pelusium, who lived in the succeeding century.

usual stature the Tall Brethren, was a learned man, and could repeat, it is said, the Old and New Testaments by heart, as well as passages from Origen and others of the Church Fathers; yet he cared nothing for the ancient monuments or magnificent works of the great city, but only to visit the martyr churches of Peter and Paul. The fastidious taste of the Roman people was at first offended by the appearance and manners of the strangers, but this feeling soon gave way to admiration and reverence, as they heard them dilate upon "that life of bodily self-mortification and spiritual exaltation of which Rome had hitherto only heard rumours."[1]

After the death, in 350, of the Emperor Constans, Constantius and the Arian prelates formed a new plot for the ruin of Athanasius. The chief obstacle to the accomplishment of their design was Liberius, the bishop of Rome, whom it was necessary to remove before a successful blow could be struck. Constantius was then at Milan. He sent his officers to Rome to seize Liberius and bring him by night to the palace. What passed between the Emperor and the bishop is recorded in the *Acts*, still extant, of the Imperial Consistory. The eunuch Eusebius, the Emperor's chief minister, and Epictetus, an Arian bishop, were also present.

Constantius. We have judged it right, Liberius,

---

[1] *St. Jerome*, by Dr. Cutts, p. 21; Socrates, b. iv. c. 23.

as thou art a Christian and bishop of our city, to send for thee and admonish thee to renounce all connection with the folly and wickedness of Athanasius, who has been condemned by the whole world and cut off by the sentence of the synod[1] from communion with the Church.

Liberius. O Emperor, ecclesiastical sentences ought to be enacted with justice. If therefore it please thy Piety, let the judges be assembled, and if it shall appear that Athanasius is deserving of condemnation, then let sentence be passed upon him according to ecclesiastical forms. No man ought to be condemned without trial.

The Emperor. The whole world has already condemned him.

Liberius. Those who signed the sentence were not eye-witnesses of what occurred, and were actuated by the desire of honour, or the fear of disgrace.

The Emperor. What honour did they desire? What disgrace did they fear?

Liberius. Those who prize thy Imperial favour more highly than God's glory have condemned a man unseen and unheard, an act which all Christians abhor.

The Emperor. Was he not present at the Council of Tyre,[2] when he was condemned by all the prelates of the empire?

---

[1] The second Council of Arles, A.D. 353.
[2] A.D. 335.—See *Early Church History*, p. 431.

Liberius. No, Sire, he was condemned unjustly after he had withdrawn. [A.D. 355.]

Here *Eusebius the Eunuch* broke in, most absurdly alleging that at the Council of Nicæa Athanasius was proved to be an enemy to the Catholic faith. No notice, however, was taken of this interruption.

Liberius. Of all those who were sent to trump up evidence against him, only five subscribed the papers. Two of these five are dead; the other three have entreated pardon for presenting a false accusation. Their memorial is still in our hands. Judge then, Sire, whom we are to believe, and with whom we ought to hold communion.

Epictetus the Bishop. O Emperor! it is not for the faith's sake, or in defence of ecclesiastical sentences, that Liberius is pleading, but only that he may boast before the Roman senators of having turned the Emperor from his purpose.

The Emperor. What portion of the universe, Liberius, dost thou reckon thyself to be, that thou desirest to destroy the peace of the world in order to shelter one vile person?

Liberius. If I stood alone in this matter, the cause of truth would be the same. There was once a time when only three were found to resist a royal mandate.

Eusebius. Dost thou compare our Emperor to Nebuchadnezzar?

Liberius. Not so. All that I desire is that, first, the Nicene creed may be ratified by universal subscription; and, secondly, that our brethren who are in exile may be recalled. If, when this is done, it can be shown that the teaching of those who now fill the Churches with trouble is conformable to the Apostolic faith, we will all assemble in synod at Alexandria, to meet the accusers and the accused, and having examined the cause, will pass judgment accordingly.

Epictetus. There are not public vehicles enough to convey so many bishops.

Liberius. Ecclesiastical affairs can be transacted without public carriages. All the Churches are able at their own charge to transport their bishops by sea.

The Emperor. A sentence once passed cannot be revoked; the decision of the majority of the bishops ought to prevail. Thou art the only person who maintains friendship with this impious man.

Liberius. O Emperor! it is a thing unheard of that a judge should accuse of impiety one who is not present to answer for himself, as if he were his personal enemy.

The Emperor. All men have been injured by him, but none so deeply as I. Not content with causing the death of my elder brother,[1] he never ceased to stir up Constans, of blessed memory, to enmity against me; and had not his aims been

---

[1] This allegation was totally unfounded.

frustrated by my invincible meekness and patience, he would have caused a violent contest between us. I account no victory I have ever gained so great as the ejection of this despicable man from the government of the Church. There is only one question. If thou wilt enter into communion with the Churches I will send thee back to Rome.

Liberius. I have already taken leave of the brethren; the laws of the Church are dearer to me than a habitation in Rome.

The Emperor. I will give thee three days to advise; subscribe and return to Rome, or choose the place of thy exile.

Liberius. Neither three days nor three months can change my mind. Send me whither thou pleasest.[1]

Liberius was banished to Berœa, in Thrace, where he remained two years, but at the end of that time he pined for Rome, his fortitude forsook him, and he purchased his recall by subscribing an Arian or Semi-Arian creed.[2]

The Emperor having again procured the condemnation of Athanasius at the Council of Milan (A.D. 355), proceeded by force to eject him. The bishop was presiding over an all-night vigil in St. Theonas' Church, in his city of Alexandria, when Syrianus, general of the army in Egypt, with a force of 5,000 legionaries, encompassed the

---

[1] Cave, *Lives of the Fathers, St. Athanasius,* ii. pp. 280-283, ed. 1840.
[2] Robertson, i. p. 227.

building. Athanasius himself has left an account of what took place. "I sat down on my throne, and desired the deacon to read the psalm of the day [the 136th] and the people to respond, 'For his mercy endureth for ever,' and then all to return home. Presently the doors were forced and the soldiers rushed in, sounding the trumpet, discharging their arrows, clashing their arms, and brandishing their swords in the light of the church lamps. Many of the people who had not time to escape were trampled down, others fell pierced with arrows; several of the virgins were slain, and the soldiers laid their hands on others, who dreaded their touch more than death itself." Athanasius himself had a narrow escape. "Seeing the soldiers ready to seize me, the clergy and some of my people present began clamorously to urge me to withdraw. I refused to do so until every one in the church had got away. Standing up, I called for prayer, and desired all to go out before me; and when the greater part had gone, the monks and the clergy who were about me came up the steps and dragged me down. Thus, under the Lord's guidance, I passed through unobserved, glorifying God that I had not betrayed the people."[1]

---

[1] Athanasius' *Apology for his Flight*, § 34 (24), and (Second) *Protest of the People of the Catholic Church in Alexandria*, §§ 3, 4; Oxford, 1873, pp. 206, 294. These two contemporary authorities and eye-witnesses differ slightly in the details. According to the latter, "The bishop was

When the Emperor Julian came to the throne A.D. 362. he restored, as has been already mentioned, the exiled bishops to their sees; and Athanasius returned for the third time to Alexandria (A.D. 362). But his energy in opposing paganism alarmed the new Emperor, and he had again to make his escape. His followers, full of grief, gathered round him. "Be of good heart," he said, "it is but a cloud, it will soon pass away." Finding a vessel lying near the bank of the Nile, he embarked to ascend the river to Thebes. But the Emperor had determined to take his life, and agents of the government were sent in pursuit. One of his friends contriving to outstrip the Imperial boat, brought him intelligence of the danger. His companions besought him to disembark and take refuge in the desert. He, however, directed the steersman to put the helm about, and return to Alexandria. They were met by the government boat, and hailed: "Where is Athanasius?" "He is not far off," was the answer, uttered perhaps by Athanasius himself. Suspicion was not excited, and the vessel passed on.[1] He reached Alexandria in safety, and remained concealed until the accession of Jovian in the same year, 363, restored him to his beloved flock.

The Emperor Valens, influenced by the firmness

---

seized, fell into a swoon, and was almost torn to pieces. We do not know how he escaped, for they were bent upon killing him."

[1] Theodoret, b. iii. c. 9.

of the Alexandrians and by fear of Valentinian, suffered Athanasius to remain for a while in his see; but in 365 he was once more compelled to fly, and it is said that he lay hid four months in his father's tomb at the gate of the city. He was finally reinstated in 366, and his long and chequered life was closed by his death in his own house in 373. He had occupied the see of Alexandria forty-six years. Athanasius was small of stature, somewhat stooping, and emaciated by fasting and many hardships. His countenance was handsome and expressive, and his eye piercing, so that his presence inspired even his enemies with awe.[1]

Gibbon, who seldom bestows eulogy upon Christian heroes, loves to extol the character of the great Alexandrian divine. "The immortal name of Athanasius will never be separated from the Catholic doctrine of the Trinity, to whose defence he consecrated every moment and every faculty of his being . . . His pastoral labours were not confined to the narrow limits of Egypt. The state of the Christian world was present to his active and capacious mind; and the age, the merit, the reputation of Athanasius, enabled him to assume, in a moment of danger, the office of Ecclesiastical Dictator."[2]

To this, Hooker's panegyric must be added.

---

[1] Schaff, p. 888; *Early Church History*, p. 430.
[2] *Decline and Fall*, iii. pp. 41, 185.

"In Athanasius there was nothing observed throughout the course of that long tragedy, other than such as very well became a wise man to do, and a righteous to suffer. So that this was the plain condition of those times: the whole world against Athanasius, and Athanasius against it; half a hundred of years spent in doubtful trial which of the two in the end would prevail—the side which had all, or else the part which had no friend but God and death, the one a defender of his innocency, the other a finisher of his troubles."[1]

A.D. 373.

The writings of Athanasius are numerous, and have always been greatly prized by the Church.[2] His great mission, as we have seen, was to uphold against the Arians the proper deity of the Son of God. "When the Arians maintained that the Son of God is only distinguished from other created beings by the fact that God created Him first of all, and then all other beings by Him, Athanasius answers: 'It is a narrow-minded representation that God should require an instrument for creation; it is as though the Son of God came into existence only for our sakes. By such a representation we

---

[1] *Ecclesiastical Polity*, b. v. c. xlii. 5.

[2] "When you meet with a saying of Athanasius," said Cosmas the monk in the sixth century, "and have not paper on which to copy it, copy it on your clothes."—*Dict. Christ. Biog.*, art. Athanasius, i. p. 202. The creed which bears the name of Athanasius was not composed by him, nor even in his lifetime, but seems to have originated about the middle of the fifth century.—Bingham's *Antiquities of the Church*, b. x. c. 4, § 18; Schaff, pp. 695, 696.

Per. I.
Chap. 2.

might be led to regard Him, not as participating immediately in the Divine Essence, but as requiring an intermediate agency for Himself . . . If we do not stand in connection with God through his Son, as thus conceived of, we have no true communion with Him, but something stands between, and we are not his children in a proper sense. For as to our original relation to Him, we are only his creatures, and he is not in a proper sense our Father; only so far is He our Father as we are placed in communion with Him through Christ. Without this it could not be said that we are partakers of the Divine Nature ' . . . The Arians believed that they ought, according to the Scriptures, to pay divine honour to Christ: Athanasius charged them with inconsistency, seeing that, on their own showing, they thus become idolators and worshippers of a creature. The Arians objected to the Nicene doctrine, that the idea of the Son of God cannot be distinguished from that of a created being, unless words are used representing Him with human attributes and affections. Athanasius replied that undoubtedly all expressions regarding the nature of God are symbolical, and have something of a human idea at their basis, and this we must abstract in order to come at a correct conception. This we do in the case of creation. In like manner we must abstract from the expressions Son of God, and Begotten of God, what belongs to human relations, and then there is left to us the idea of Unity of Essence."[1]

One word more. Devoted as Athanasius was to the defence of Christian doctrine, and great as was the license he allowed himself in denouncing those who maintained the Arian opinions,[2] he never used or counselled violent means to compel belief. In his high position, exposed to grievous persecution himself, it would have been easy for him to retaliate in kind, but he set herein an example which his successors would have done well to follow. The words in which he deprecates violence and persecution deserve to be written in letters of gold. "Nothing more forcibly marks the weakness of a bad cause than persecution. Satan, who has no truth to propose to men, comes with axe and sword to make way for his errors. Christ's method is widely different. He teaches the truth, and says: 'If any man *will* come after Me and be my disciple;'—when He comes to the heart He uses no violence, but says, 'Open to Me, my sister, my spouse.' If we open He comes in; if we will not open He retires; for the truth is not preached with swords and spears, not by bands of soldiers, but by counsel and persuasion. But of what use can persuasion be where the Imperial Ego dominates? Or what place is there

---

[1] Neander, *History of Christian Dogmas*, pp. 295, 296.
[2] He calls them "devils, Anti-Christs, dogs, hydras."

for counsel when resistance to Imperial authority must terminate in exile or death?"[1]

Allusion has been made to the life of Anthony the Hermit by Athanasius. It is the first of a long series of saintly biographies, held in the highest esteem by the Church of Rome. The work has probably been interpolated by a later hand;[2] but, allowing for this, it is marvellous that the sagacious and powerful mind of Athanasius should have given forth such a narrative, not indeed devoid of instruction, but mixed with so much of absurdity. It is only to be accounted for by the influence of superstition, even on the strongest minds, in an age when freedom of thought was not present to counteract it. Most of the biography is taken up in relating Anthony's encounters with the devil. The demonology of the monks was derived from the Neo-Platonists; and "when the solitary had reduced his hated enemy, the body, to a skeleton, and thus weakened his understanding and inflamed his imagination, he was in a fit state to hear strange voices, and behold fearful apparitions."[3] One of these encounters will suffice to relate.

When Anthony takes up his abode in a sepulchre, the devil comes one night with a whole troop of

---

[1] Athanasius, *History of the Arians*, c. iv. § 7; M'Clintock and Strong, *Cyclopædia of Bibl. Theol. and Eccles. Literature*, art. Athanasius.

[2] *Dict. Christ. Biog.*, i. p. 125.

[3] Ruffner, *Fathers of the Desert*, i. p. 182-185: ii. p. 28, note.

demons, and inflicts on him so severe a beating that he is as one dead. Recovering consciousness, he prays as he lies on the ground, and, his spirit returning, he cries aloud : " O ye demons, here am I, Anthony, ready for more blows. Try your worst, you shall never separate me from Christ." It was no hard matter for the devil to devise fresh schemes of malice. That night the whole troop came again, and raised such a hubbub that the walls of the sepulchre were broken down, and the demons rushed in, in all manner of fearful shapes—lions, bears, leopards, wolves, bulls, serpents, scorpions, asps—each setting upon the poor solitary, according to its nature. Still writhing from the whips and clubs of the day before, Anthony yet commanded himself, and mockingly said : " If you could do any harm, you would be satisfied to come one at a time ; it is a proof of your impotence that you put on the shapes of brute beasts. You have no power to hurt, for the Lord is my shield." Then the demons gnashed their teeth at him ; but were not permitted to do more, for (so runs the legend) Christ, who was watching the contest, came to Anthony's deliverance. Raising his eyes, the saint saw through the open roof a ray of light descending upon him. The demons vanished, his pains were assuaged, and the sepulchre became whole again. The appeal to his Divine Helper, put by the biographer into Anthony's mouth, is greatly wanting in reverence; and the answer attributed to the Lord shows how even the solitude of the desert cannot quench that universal passion of mankind—the love of fame. Anthony is made to ask, "Where wast Thou? Why didst Thou not appear for my relief at first?" The voice answered: "I was here, Anthony, but I wanted to witness thy combat. Thou hast accomplished it without flinching, henceforth I will be thy helper, and will make thy name famous far and wide."[1]

---

[1] *Life of St. Anthony*, c. 6, 7.

CHAPTER III.

THE CAPPADOCIAN BISHOPS.

SECTION I. The name of Gregory Thaumaturgus, bishop of Neo-Cæsarea in Pontus, is familiar to the readers of the *Early Church History*.[1] The fruit of his pastoral work is met with in the household of a Christian lady named Macrina, who, with her husband, concealed herself in the forests during the persecution under Galerius and Maximinus Daza. Their son Basil and his wife Emmelia had a family of ten children, and diligently followed in the ordering of their household and the bringing up of their family, the example set them by their parents. It is related of the eldest daughter, who was named Macrina after her grandmother, that she knew the whole of the Psalms by heart, as well as many portions of the books of Solomon.[2]

Macrina was beautiful, and, being also rich, her hand was sought by many. In accordance with the custom of the age, the choice lay with her father, who selected a young advocate of gentle birth. Before the time came for the marriage, the young man died. Macrina possessed a soul of no

---

[1] P. 337.   *Dict. Christ. Biog.*, art. Macrina (1) and (2), iii. p. 779.

common order, and regarding her betrothal as a virtual union, and her affianced husband as still living, though in a far-off land, to be joined to her again at the resurrection, she refused to listen to any further proposals of marriage. At her father's death, when she was about twenty-two years of age, the care of her widowed mother and of the younger children devolved upon her, and she even undertook the management of the family estates, which lay in three different provinces. She brought up her infant brother Peter, contracted eligible marriages for her four sisters, and, not disdaining household work, she baked the bread for the family, and prepared her mother's food with her own hands.[1]

BASIL, the first of the three subjects of this chapter, was next to Macrina in age, and was born A.D. 329. When a child, he was sent to the country house of his excellent grandmother, from whom he received the germs of Christian instruction. "She taught me," he tells us, "the words of the most blessed Gregory."[2] These early lessons and his father's teaching prepared him to enter into competition with boys of his own age at the grammar school in Cæsarea, the chief city of Cappadocia,[3] where he distinguished himself by

---

[1] Ibid.   [2] Basil, *Epist.* 204.

[3] In the time of Sapor the First, king of Persia, A.D. 240-273, who took Cæsarea from the Romans, the city is said to have contained 400,000 inhabitants. The modern town of Kaisariyeh, a little removed from the ruins of the ancient city, contains 8000 houses, and is situated at the

his brilliant talents and exemplary conduct. From thence he was removed to Constantinople, and studied under the sophist Libanius, one of the most noteworthy defenders of expiring paganism. The tutor has recorded his admiration of the eloquence of the young Cappadocian, and of his self-restraint amid the temptations of the New Rome.[1]

On leaving Constantinople Basil repaired to Athens to drink philosophy at that ancient fountain-head; and here also he had heathen preceptors for his guides, who still lectured under the colonnades or in the gardens where Plato, Aristotle, and Epicurus once taught.

At Athens Basil found a fellow-countryman of his own age, a native of Arianzus, a village or estate in the west of Cappadocia. This was GREGORY NAZIANZEN, the second of our Cappadocian worthies. Like Basil, he was the child of pious parents. His father Gregory was bishop of

---

northern base of Mount Argæus (the Arjish Tagh of the Turks) on the edge of a fertile plain. "No part of Asia Minor surpasses this neighbourhood for the quality and variety of its fruits."—Kinneir's *Journey*, 1813–14, pp. 99–103. The Arjish Tagh is the loftiest peak in Asia Minor, 13,100 feet. In winter the snow descends to within a few hundred feet of the plain; and even in summer the upper half of the mountain retains its mantle of dazzling white. A large proportion of the inhabitants of this district still call themselves Christians. They are more wealthy and luxurious than those of any other part of Turkey. They are divided into Old Armenians, Romish Armenians, and Greeks, who all despise one another as heretics.—Ainsworth's *Travels and Researches in Asia Minor*, 1842, i. pp. 220–225; Porter's *Handbook for Turkey in Asia*.

[1] Greg. Naz. *Oration* xx.; *Dict. Christ. Biog.*, art. Basilius of Caesareia, i. p. 283.

Nazianzus.¹ He belonged at the time of his marriage to a half heathen sect called *Hypsistarians* (worshippers of the Most High), and was won over to the Church by the persevering influence of his wife. This happened just when several bishops passed through Nazianzus to attend the Council of Nicæa, and he was baptized in their presence. The credulity of the age invested his baptism with miracles and prophecies. Gregory's mother was Nonna, a woman of a masculine character, in whom religion was all powerful, but it was the religion of the age, narrow and formal. She had unlimited confidence in prayer, and had attained such mastery of her feelings that when affliction came she never uttered a lamentation till she had given thanks to God. She carried her notions of almsgiving to such an excess as often to say that she would gladly sell herself and her children to provide money for the poor. She was so exclusive that she would never shake hands with or kiss a heathen woman, or eat salt with an idolater.²

Gregory the younger was born about A.D. 330, and was dedicated, even before his birth, to the service of the Lord. Not many days after his

---

¹ Texier describes Nazianzus, in its present state, as a ruined town in a hilly region abounding in stone quarries. The country to the south in the direction of Sasima (see below) is barren, the soil being strongly impregnated with nitre.—*L'Univers Pittoresque, Asie Mineure*. Arianzus was in the immediate neighbourhood.

² Ullmann, *Gregory of Nazianzum*, pp. 17-20.

birth his mother carried him to the church, and laid his infant hands on a volume of the Gospels. He used afterwards to compare himself to Isaac offered in sacrifice to God, and to Samuel, who was consecrated as a child by his mother Hannah. When old enough, he was, like Basil, sent to school at Cæsarea, where, probably, the friendship between them commenced; and from thence successively to Cæsarea in Palestine and to Alexandria. But his heart was set on Athens; and though the time of year was unfavourable for a voyage, he hastened to quit Alexandria and sail thither. When the ship arrived off Cyprus, a violent storm arose; the thunder, lightning, and darkness were accompanied by the creaking of the yards, the quivering of the masts, and piteous cries for help to Christ, even from some, as Gregory tells us, who had never before called upon his name. They had besides lost their store of fresh water, so that death from thirst or from shipwreck alike stared them in the face. A Phœnician vessel coming up, managed with great difficulty to supply them with water; still the storm did not abate, and for many days their fate hung in the balance. It was not the fear of death itself which tormented Gregory; but, in accordance with a frequent practice, his baptism had been deferred,[1] and death without baptism had come to be looked upon as the loss of

---

[1] See *Early Church History*, p. 132.

heaven. Overwhelmed with the thought, he dedicated himself anew to God, and prayed for mercy and deliverance for himself and the ship's company. The prayer, as he tells us, was answered; all on board were saved, and so affected by their deliverance that they received "spiritual as well as temporal salvation," which doubtless means that they underwent the rite of baptism.[1]

He arrived at Athens some time before Basil. The university, which had lost its ancient simplicity and freedom, was divided into rival schools, and it was the chief aim of the professors to spread their own fame and increase the number of their pupils. Fresh students were waylaid and fought for by the rival parties, and sometimes torn away from the very teacher whom they had come expressly to attend.[2]

The acquaintance between the two compatriots speedily ripened into an ardent friendship. Dissimilar in character, they were attracted to each

---

[1] *Dict. Christ. Biog.*, art. Gregorius Nazianzenus, iii. pp. 742, 743; Ullmann, p. 22; Neander, *Church History*, iii. p. 321.

[2] The proverbial jokes to which freshmen are subjected were of a mild character. Gregory says: "After being entertained at table, where he is made the butt of all present, the novice is conducted to the public bath, followed by all the students in procession, two and two. On reaching the doors, they raise a wild cry and command the procession to halt as if admission had been refused. Then they throw themselves upon the doors and, in appearance, force an entrance. Arriving within, their new companion is directed to take a bath; after which he is received into the fraternity and invested with all its privileges." By Gregory's good offices, Basil, who had no liking for such pranks, was exempted from this initiation.—Ullmann, p. 30, note.

other by their very dissimilarity: "Gregory, the affectionate, the tender-hearted; Basil, the man of firm resolve and hard deeds." "They occupied the same chamber and ate at the same table. They studied the same books and attended the same lectures." "We knew," says Gregory, "only two streets of the city: the first and more excellent, that which led to the churches and the ministers of the altar; the other, to the schools and the teachers of the sciences. The streets which led to the theatres, games, and other places of unholy amusement, we left to others. Holiness was our chief concern; our sole aim was to be called Christians, and to be such."[1]

Amongst the fellow-students of Basil and Gregory was Constantine's nephew, Julian, afterwards Emperor and well known by his surname of "the Apostate." The young prince attached himself to Basil, who responded to his advances. They studied classic literature, and even read together in the Sacred Scriptures. Gregory, however, regarded Julian with suspicion, discerning, as he tells us, his true character in his incessant restlessness and hesitating speech, and in every feature of his countenance; and he warned his fellow-students that that young man would one day bring evil upon the empire.[2]

---

[1] *Dict. Christ. Biog.*, i. p. 283; Newman's *Church of the Fathers*, p. 89; Gregory's *Funeral Oration on Basil*, c. 21.

[2] *Dict. Christ. Biog.*, ibid.; Ullmann, pp. 37, 38.

Basil spent five years at Athens (A.D. 351-356). He had won a name in the university, and it was with pain he tore himself away, yet a conviction of the emptiness of the world, even under its noblest aspects, seemed to have taken possession of him, and he described Athens as "hollow blessedness." Gregory remained there a short time longer.[1]

Returning to Cæsarea, where his father resided, Basil commenced practice as a rhetorician. The success he met with and his college reputation filled him with vain and ambitious thoughts. He looked with contempt on his superiors in rank; he adopted the airs of a fine gentleman; and began to indulge in the pleasures of the city. His sister Macrina perceived his danger. Her loving heart was deeply stirred at seeing her brother choose the broad way. But she was scarcely a wise counsellor for a young man in whose pathway the world had spread its snares. It is doubtful, indeed, if a wise counsellor was at that time anywhere to be found. The mistaken idea that in order to live above the world it was necessary to flee from it had been steadily gaining force ever since Paul and Anthony retired into the Libyan desert; and, although monasticism had

---

[1] *Church of the Fathers*, pp. 93, 94. The school at Athens, which had stood 900 years, the last refuge of heathen teaching, was abolished by Justinian I., A.D. 529. Its seven remaining professors went into exile and found protection with Chosroes, king of Persia.—Schaff, p. 68.

not yet been introduced into Asia Minor, the devout members of the Church were everywhere turning towards an ascetic life. It would have been a marvel if Macrina had escaped the general contagion. By her sisterly warnings she infused into her brother's soul the same disregard of earthly pleasures and distinctions, the same enthusiasm for self-mortification which ruled in her own breast.[1]

The idea of a recluse life was not new to Basil. He and his friend Gregory had already, when at Athens, pledged each other one day to turn their backs upon the world. Nevertheless, Basil describes himself as awaking, under the effect of his sister's admonitions, out of a deep sleep, and in the light of Gospel truth discerning the folly of this world's wisdom to which he had begun to devote himself. Interpreting literally our Lord's words: "If thou wilt be perfect, go, sell that thou hast, and give to the poor, and thou shalt have treasure in heaven; and come, follow Me;"[2] he at once resolved to give up his profession, and withdraw into solitude. Accordingly, about the year 357, he left Cæsarea to visit the most renowned ascetics of Egypt and Syria. "Their abstinence and endurance, their mastery over hunger and sleep, their indifference to cold and nakedness," excited in him the warmest

---

[1] *Dict. Christ. Biog.*, i. p. 284.
[2] Matthew, xix. 21.

admiration, accompanied by an ardent desire to imitate them. On his return he wrote to Gregory, reminding him of their mutual vow, and proposing they should withdraw together into the desert.[1]

Gregory had been two years at home since his return from Athens. His parents were advancing in age, and the duty which he owed to them weighed against the allurements of a life of prayer and meditation. He reflected also that the desert would not afford the opportunity which his studious disposition craved, for a critical acquaintance with the Scriptures. But, on the other hand, he longed to devote to God every faculty he possessed, and in his hours of contemplative abstraction the examples of Elijah and John the Baptist would present themselves, as most worthy of imitation.[2] Evidently he did not understand that it is in the New Covenant only, the Christian can find his perfect Exemplar; that Christians are called "to go into the world with Christ, not out of it with Elijah and the Baptist." For a while Gregory sought to reconcile the two conflicting influences, and attempted to live a hermit life in the midst of society. His food was bread and salt, his drink water, his bed the bare ground, his clothing coarse. Incessant labour filled up the day; prayers, hymns and meditations, a great part of the night. He condemned his former life; the mirth in which he

---

[1] *Dict. Christ. Biog.*, ibid.   [2] Oration 5.

used to indulge now cost him many tears. He even gave up music, as being a gratification of the senses. But he soon found that the abstraction of mind required by this mode of life was incompatible with his domestic duties. "Many cares," he says, "fretted me by night and by day; ruling servants was a very network of evil; and I could no more look after property with its attendant plagues of tax-collectors and law-courts, than a man can approach a house on fire without being blackened and scorched by the smoke." In this state of mind he replied to Basil's letter, by proposing that the latter should join him at Arianzus. Basil accordingly made him a visit. But the place disgusted him, for he found it cold and damp and intolerably muddy, to use his own words, "the very pit of the whole earth."[1]

A.D. 358.

By this time Basil's family had settled on the ancestral estate in Pontus, beside the river Iris,[2] the spot where he himself had passed his childhood. Here his sister Macrina and her mother converted their household into a religious sisterhood, to which the daughters of the noblest families in the province resorted. Basil was not slow to perceive the superiority of the monastic to the solitary life. "God," he writes, "has made us like the members of our body, dependent on one

---

[1] Ullmann, pp. 52, 53; *Dict. Christ. Biog.*, art. Gregory Nazianzenus, ii. p. 744, and i. p. 284.

[2] Near the little city of Ibora.—Ruffner, *Fathers of the Desert*, ii. p. 285.

another's help. What discipline of humility, of pity, or of patience can there be if there be no one for whom these duties are to be practised? Whose feet wilt thou wash; to whom wilt thou be as a servant; how canst thou be last of all, if thou art alone?"[1] Here unhappily he stopped. God, who made man to live in society, gave him also marriage, and set him in families; and has revealed Himself to us through that endeared relation of Father, which the Church of the fourth century presumptuously denied to her priests and her elect children. If, instead of placing himself at the head of a retrograde movement, and trying to give it a more practical direction, this man of commanding talents and unbending will had taken his stand on the New Testament, and withstood the popular current altogether, he might have conferred priceless benefits on his own and succeeding ages.[2]

The spot which Basil selected for his monastery was in the immediate neighbourhood of his mother's religious house, but on the opposite bank of the river. It was not a dreary wilderness like the Egyptian deserts, but a charming retreat, such as

---

[1] *Dict. Christ. Biog.*, i. pp. 284, 285.

[2] Basil was not actually the first to introduce monachism into Asia Minor; he was preceded by the Arian, Eustathius of Sebaste. On his return from the East, Basil joined himself to some disciples of this bishop, the counterpart of the ascetics whom he had seen in Egypt and Syria; but when he discovered they were the followers of a "heretic" he left them, concluding that they were "unsanctified hypocrites."—Ruffner, ii. pp. 282-285.

every lover of nature might covet. "God has shown me," he wrote to his friend Gregory, "a region which exactly suits my mode of life; it is in truth what in our happy hours we often dreamed of. That which imagination pictured in the distance I now see before me. At the foot of a high mountain, covered with thick forest, spreads out a wide plain, plentifully watered, and enclosed by a belt of many kinds of trees, almost thick enough to be a fence. On two sides deep ravines serve as a protection, whilst on a third the mountain torrent which breaks upon the wall of projecting rock, and rolls foaming into the abyss, forms an impassable barrier. From my cottage on the summit I overlook the plain and the windings of the Iris, which is larger and more picturesque than the Strymon near Amphipolis. Shall I go on to describe the fragrant smell of the meadows, the refreshing breezes from the water, or the vast numbers of song-birds and flowers? In all these another might take delight; but as for me, my mind is not at liberty to enjoy them. To me the greatest charm of this retreat is the quiet that reigns here. Remote from the tumult of the city, its silent repose is only now and then broken by a solitary hunter, who is in pursuit, not of bears or wolves, but of the deer, the roe, and the hare."[1] Even

A.D. 358.

---

[1] *Epistle* 14. The Iris runs through a valley some miles to the west of Neo-Cæsarea (now contracted into Niksar), with a fine mountain region between. Although the site of the monastery has not been identified, the

here, however, Basil could not escape from himself. In another letter he writes: "What I do in this solitude I am almost ashamed to say. I have abandoned my residence in the city, as being the source of a thousand evils, but myself I cannot leave behind. I am like voyagers unaccustomed to the sea, who, when attacked with sickness, leave the large ship because of its violent rolling, and descend into a little boat, but find no relief. Thus I, too, bearing about with me my inherent passions, have made but little spiritual progress by virtue of my solitary life."[1]

In the *Rule* which Basil instituted for the government of his monastery, and which still regulates the cloisters of the Greek Church, industry was combined with devotion. It was a common proverb: "A laborious monk is beset by one devil, an idle monk by a legion." By the labour of Basil's monks many a barren tract was converted into corn-fields and vineyards. His rule was severe. His monks wore coarse garments, seldom washed, a belt, and shoes of raw hide; their hair

---

description of the region by modern travellers answers to Basil's picture. Morier, who travelled in 1808-9 from Persia to Constantinople, writes: "At a pass between Isker-Sou and Niksar commenced a series of mountain scenery of the wildest and most romantic character. No description is adequate to paint the brilliancy and luxuriance of vegetation, and the picturesque forms of this region" (pp. 341, 342). The town of Niksar is situated among a forest of fruit-trees. The range of mountains to the east reaches an elevation of about 6000 feet.—See Porter's *Handbook of Turkey in Asia*.

[1] Ullmann, *Greg. Naz.*, p. 57

uncombed, their looks downcast.¹ One meal only a day was allowed, of bread, water, and beans without salt. "With us," wrote Basil to the Emperor Julian, "as is becoming, the cook's art has no place; our knives never touch blood; our daintiest meal is vegetables with coarse bread and half-sour wine."² The night, as well as the day, was divided into definite portions, and the intervals of sleep filled up with prayers and psalmody.³ Basil himself had but one outer and one inner garment; he slept in a hair shirt, with the ground for his bed, and never made use of a bath. But Basil's rule was more than severe. Like the pattern which he found in Egypt, it was an outrage against humanity. "It is the devil's craft," he says, "to keep alive in the mind of the monk a recollection of his parents and kinsfolk, so that under colour of aiding them he may be diverted from his heavenly course." And when some (for there seem to have been a few reasonable men still remaining) pointed to Paul's words, "If any

---

¹ Gregory's pattern of the true monk agrees with Basil's: "Vigils, fasts, prayers, tears, smitings of the breast, standing the night through, the mind going forth to God; disordered hair, feet naked in imitation of the Apostles, neglected clothing, unwandering eyes."—Ruffner, ii. p. 300.

² *Dict. Christ. Biog.*, i. p. 285; Ruffner, ii. p. 299; Basil's *Epistles* 41; Newman, p. 22. "Send me some fine pot-herbs," wrote Gregory Nazianzen to a friend, who, with Basil, was about to pay him a visit, "if thou dost not wish to see Basil hungry and cross."—Epist. 12.

³ "If any one is cross on being awaked, what punishment is he to have? At first, separation and deprivation of food; but if he continue insensible, let him be cut off as a diseased limb."—Shorter Rule; *St. Basil the Great*, by R. T. Smith, p. 224.

provide not for his own, and specially his own household, he hath denied the faith and is worse than an unbeliever," Basil, with perverse ingenuity, answered, that Paul speaks here to the living, not to the dead; whereas a true monk is, as regards all secular obligations, a dead man. The solitude of the cell was looked upon as the very essence of the Christian life. He declares with a singular ignorance of human nature: "Solitude puts to sleep the vicious motions of the mind, and leisure affords a way of extirpating them altogether." Intercourse with women was especially prohibited. It was forbidden to speak with, or even to look at them except in cases of extreme necessity. But the rule did not stop even here. "Shun the society of young men of thy own age" (such is Basil's injunction to the novice), "flee from them as from a burning flame; if thou leave thy cell thou leavest thy virtue." "What sort of virtue," asks Isaac Taylor, "is that which evaporates the moment it is exposed to daylight?" Girls were not allowed to profess before their sixteenth or seventeenth year; any irregularity fallen into by those who devoted themselves after this age, was punished with inexorable severity.[1]

Basil aimed at making the cloister a school for the priesthood. He held the strange opinion that the austerities of monastic discipline were

---

[1] *Dict. Christ. Biog.*, i. p. 285; Isaac Taylor's *Ancient Christianity*, i. pp. 415, 416; Ruffner, ii. p. 299; Newman, p. 22.

the best training for the Christian ministry; and when he became bishop he ordained scarcely any but monks, preferring those who carried self-mortification to the greatest extreme.[1]

A.D. 358.

The alluring picture which Basil drew of his retreat brought Gregory to his side. They prayed, toiled, fasted, and sang psalms together, and studied the Scriptures and Origen. Prior to Augustine, no one of the Fathers exercised so powerful a spell over men's minds as did Origen.[2] Admired by some as the first of Christian philosophers, shunned by many as a dangerous heretic, anathematized by councils, the shibboleth of rival theologians, it was at the copious well-spring of Origen's intellect that ardent, youthful spirits slaked their thirst for knowledge. Gregory and Basil culled from his works a selection of choice passages, which they named Philocalia (Love for the Beautiful).[3]

Possibly, however, at this time Gregory may have found Basil's cloister life somewhat severe,

---

[1] Ruffner, ii. pp. 288, 289. Chrysostom herein differed altogether from Basil. "The monk," he writes, "lives in a calm, where there is little to oppose him. The skill of the pilot cannot be known till he has taken the helm in the open sea in rough weather. Too many of those who have passed from the seclusion of the cloister to the active sphere of the priest or bishop, have lost their head; and often, instead of adding to their virtue, have been deprived of the good qualities which they already possessed. Monasticism often serves as a screen to failings which active life draws out, just as the qualities of metal are tested by fire."—Stephens, *Life of St. Chrysostom*, p. 53.

[2] See *Early Church History*, pt. ii. c. 4, &c.

[3] *Dict. Christ. Biog.*, i. p. 284.

for on his return home he wrote his friend a bantering epistle. "With Homer let us 'sing the garniture within,' to wit, thy dwelling roofless and doorless; the hearth without fire or smoke; walls nevertheless baked enough lest the mud should trickle down on us while we suffer Tantalus' penalty—thirst in the midst of water. And that beggarly fare for which thou called me from Cappadocia! I shall never forget the broth and the bread; bread so hard that the teeth made no impression, and when they did effect an entrance were set fast as in a paste. Unless that true lady-bountiful, thy mother, had promptly come to my help, I had been dead long ago. Nor can I omit that misnamed garden, void even of pot-herbs; or the Augean heap which we cleared off and spread over it; or how, in levelling a rugged bank, we dragged that heavy cart full, thou the gentleman, and I the vintager, with neck and hand which still bear the marks of my toil."[1]

Finding that Basil did not take his pleasantry altogether in good part, Gregory wrote again: "What I wrote before concerning thy Pontic abode was in jest, not in earnest; but now I write very much in earnest. Who shall give me back those psalmodies and vigils, those prayers which transported us from earth to heaven, that life which seemed to have nothing in it of material

---

[1] Epist. 8 (12).

or corporeal? O that I could live again the sweet time we spent in the study of the divine oracles, and enjoy the light which, through the guidance of the Spirit, we found in them. Or let me speak of lower things, the bodily labours of the day, gathering the wood and quarrying the stone, the planting and the draining. And especially of that golden plane-tree, more honourable than that of Xerxes, under which, not a pleasure-sated king but a weary monk did sit, planted by me, watered by Apollos (that is thy excellent self), and made by God to grow up to my honour, and as a monument of our mutual toil."[1]

Basil's reputation for sanctity attracted to him so large a number of devotees that his retreat had the appearance of a town. He also repeatedly made missionary journeys through Pontus, and everywhere there sprang up conventual houses of both sexes for the joint practice of industry and piety. In these institutions children were taken charge of, slaves protected, solitaries received, and (most mistaken charity!) a home made for married persons who imagined they were serving God by living apart. By his means also hospitals and other homes of beneficence were founded.[2]

SECTION II. In A.D. 360 the Emperor Constantius used all his authority to obtain the signatures of

---

[1] Epist. 9 (13).
Dict. Christ. Biog., i. p. 285; Smith, St. Basil the Great, p. 24.

Per. I.
Chap. 3.

the bishops to the Arian confession of faith, known as the creed of Ariminum (Rimini).[1] Gregory's father was one of those who yielded, but afterwards, through the influence of his son and of the monks of his diocese, who were devoted to Athanasius, he made a public confession of orthodoxy. Dianius, bishop of Cæsarea, also gave way. Basil, who regarded it as the great mission of his life to uphold the Trinitarian faith, was grieved beyond measure at his bishop's weakness, and refrained from all communion with him. When, however, two years afterwards Dianius was stricken for death, he entreated Basil to come to him and comfort his dying hours. The aged bishop expired in Basil's arms, protesting with his last breath that he had never intentionally departed from the Nicene faith, and had signed the creed of Ariminum in the simplicity of his heart.[2]

Shortly before the death of Dianius, Julian ascended the throne, A.D. 361. It was the desire of the new Emperor to surround himself with the associates of his early days; and he invited Basil to come at once to court. Basil was at first disposed to accept the invitation, but when he found that Julian had turned his back upon the Christian faith, and was preparing to restore paganism, he refused.[3] Julian was deeply offended, and deter-

---

[1] See *ante*, p. 11. [2] Id., i. p. 285, ii. p. 745.

[3] The student of history may recollect the two laconic epistles which passed between the Emperor and Basil. *Julian:* 'Ανέγνων, ἔγνων, κατέγνων.

mined to be revenged. Hearing that the citizens, so far from apostatising with himself, and building new heathen temples as he had commanded, had pulled down the only one still standing—the Temple of Fortune—he expunged Cæsarea from the catalogue of cities, and inflicted severe penalties on the clergy and the wealthy inhabitants. He even demanded of Basil a fine of a thousand pounds' weight of gold. Basil, in his reply, reminded the Emperor of the time when they two studied the Holy Scriptures together, and upbraided him with the folly of requiring so vast a sum from one who had not enough even to buy himself a meal. The Emperor was further exasperated by another occurrence. Eusebius, a distinguished layman, was chosen bishop in the place of Dianius, mainly through the exertions of Basil and Gregory. The choice, which was opposed by many of the neighbouring prelates, was offensive to Julian, who grudged the Church the possession of so able a citizen, and vowed that when he should return in triumph from his Persian campaign he would reserve the two friends, "as Polyphemus did Ulysses,"[1] for his latest victims. He did not live to return, but was slain in the expedition.[2]

A.D. 361.

Basil: 'Ανέγνως, οὐκ ἔγνως, εἰ γὰρ ἔγνως, οὐκ ἂν κατέγνως. "I have read, I have understood, I have condemned." "Thou hast read, but not understood; for if thou hadst understood, thou wouldst not have condemned."—Id., i. p. 285.

[1] *Odyssey*, b. ix.

[2] Sozomen, b. v. c. 4; *Dict. Christ. Biog.*, i. pp. 285, 286.

Basil had soon to repent of the part he had taken in the election of Eusebius. The new bishop, desiring to avail himself of Basil's theological knowledge and intellectual power to compensate for his own deficiencies, obliged him, against his will, to receive ordination as a priest. Shortly before, in 362, his friend Gregory had also been, by his father's authority and the will of the people, driven or entrapped into the priesthood. The perversion of the Christian ministry to a sacerdotal office, and the mistaken notions derived from the old Eastern religions, regarding the mortification of the body, made Gregory shrink with extreme dread from ordination. "I felt myself unequal to this warfare, and therefore hid my face and slunk away. My body of humiliation wages an eternal war with my passions. I toss to and fro through the senses and the delights of life; I stick fast in the deep mire; the law of sin wars against the law of the spirit, and tries to efface the royal image in me. Before we have subdued with all our might the principle which drags us down, and have duly cleansed the spirit, and have much surpassed others in approach to God, I consider it unsafe to undertake the cure of souls or the mediatorship between God and man, which belong to a priest." When to his conscientious scruples was added the forced manner of his ordination, which appeared to him nothing less than an act of spiritual tyranny, it was more than he could support, and leaving his new charge he betook himself to Pontus (A.D. 362), to seek consolation from his old friend. The Nazianzen Church was offended at Gregory's flight, and on his return demanded from him a public apology. He set himself to answer in a manner worthy of the occasion. The result was one of those eloquent discourses which have made his name famous as a master of Christian oratory.[1]

To return to Basil. A rupture soon broke out between himself and the new bishop. The latter was not only his inferior in worth, but was far less popular; and when, envious of his superiority, Eusebius treated Basil with coldness, if not with insolence, the latter might easily have wrested the episcopal authority out of his hands. Basil, however, had the prudence to withdraw from the contest, and shut himself up in his monastery in Pontus. Here he remained till 365, when the arbitrary measures adopted by the Emperor Valens for the spread of Arianism, brought him back to Cæsarea. Through Gregory's mediation he became reconciled to Eusebius, and gave him his powerful support in this hour of common need. The Arians assumed a threatening aspect, but Basil compelled them to leave the city. The in-

---

[1] *Dict. Christ. Biog.*, i. p. 286, iii. p. 745; Ullmann, pp. 67, 68; Oration 2, in Newman, *Church of the Fathers*, p. 123. The discourse is practically a treatise on the pastoral office, and is a storehouse whence Chrysostom, Gregory the Great, Bossuet, and other orators of various times have drawn their ideas.

surrection of Procopius at Constantinople, which just then broke out, prevented Valens for the moment from taking his revenge; and Basil had time to organise his defence. He also exerted himself to mitigate the suffering from drought and famine by which, in the year 368, Cappadocia was laid waste. He gave up the property which had recently come to him at the death of his mother, persuaded the rich merchants who had bought up the corn to open their stores, set on foot a public subscription, and himself superintended the distribution of bread to the starving multitude.[1]

In 370 Eusebius died. Basil saw that the cause of orthodoxy in the province depended upon his own elevation to the vacant see. The election of a bishop in the great cities had come, since the accession of Constantine, to be an affair of State, a matter of great political no less than ecclesiastical importance, and where parties ran high, it was often accompanied by tumults and bloodshed.[2]

---

[1] *Dict. Christ. Biog.*, i. pp. 286, 287; Ruffner, ii. p. 286.

[2] In the contest for the see of Rome, in A.D. 366, between Damasus and Ursicinus, a sanguinary street war was waged. Damasus, it is stated, followed by a furious mob, forced his way into the churches, and trampled down all opposers. After this, with a band of gladiators, he seized the Lateran Basilica, where he was ordained; and, having bribed the magistrates, caused his opponent to be sent into exile. The people would have hindered him from taking possession of the episcopal chair, but he cleared his way through them with blows; and then, with the ecclesiastics of his faction, joined by gladiators, charioteers, and armed rustics, besieged one of the churches where the adverse party were assembled. Setting fire to the doors, he forced his way in, slew 160 persons, men and women, and wounded many. "Notwithstanding all this," adds Roberts, "Damasus was a saint, and miracles were ascribed to him after his

In this instance the prize to be contended for A.D. 370. was of no common value. The bishop of Cæsarea was the possessor of power reaching far beyond the limits of the city itself. He was metropolitan of Cappadocia and exarch of Pontus.[1] In the latter capacity his authority, more or less defined, extended over more than half Asia Minor, and embraced eleven provinces. Basil, beloved and popular as he was, felt, nevertheless, that his election was insecure. The people generally with the clergy and monks were on his side, but the rich chafed under his ceaseless calls to charity, the authorities dreaded the displeasure of the Arian Emperor Valens, and the neighbouring bishops were jealous of his superior reputation and abilities. Instead of leaving the matter in the hands of Him who alone has the right to appoint his shepherds, Basil began to devise measures for the accomplishment of his purpose. He sent for Gre-

---

death!"—*Church Memorials*, pp. 202, 203. How widely the Church had departed from the apostolic rule in the election of its officers, even where such outrages were unknown, let Chrysostom declare. "The elections are generally made on public festivals, and are disgraceful scenes of party feeling and intrigue. The clergy and the people are never of one mind. The really important qualifications for the office are seldom considered. Ambitious men spare no arts of bribery or flattery to obtain places. One candidate for a bishopric is recommended to the electors, because he is of a noble family; another, because he is wealthy and will not burden the funds of the Church; a third, because he is a deserter from the opposite party."—Stephens, *Life of St. Chrysostom*, p. 48; Chrysostom, *On the Priesthood*, b. iii.

[1] As metropolitan he had fifty country bishops under him.—Ullmann, *Greg. Naz.*, p. 122. The term exarch was nearly synonymous with that of patriarch.

gory, but, fearing that if his friend were apprized of the real nature of the business he might shrink from undertaking it, he stooped to employ artifice. As though he were on his death-bed, he wrote, begging him to come and receive his last commands. The wretched maxim that deceit and falsehood are permissible when religion is to be promoted, was fast taking root in the Church.[1]

As soon as he received the letter Gregory prepared to go to his friend's help, but before he set out discovered the deception which had been put upon him. He protested against the fraud, refused to come to Cæsarea, and urged Basil to leave the city until the election was over. Such affairs, he told him, were not managed by men of piety, but by active and popular agents. But Basil was not thus to be deterred; he turned from the son to the father, the aged bishop of Nazianzus. Convinced that the cause of orthodoxy was involved in Basil's election, the old man roused himself for the occasion. Using his son as his amanuensis, he dictated two letters—one to the clergy and people of Cæsarea, calling on them to lay aside party feeling and choose Basil as bishop;—the other to the electing prelates, reminding them (as Basil's state of health

---

[1] *Dict. Christ. Biog.*, i. pp. 287, 288; Smith's *Basil the Great*, pp. 33, 34. In his *Rule*, Basil took a higher standard than in his own practice. He enjoined truthfulness to the exclusion of expediency even for a good end, adducing the words of Christ (John viii. 44).

had been made an objection) that they were not choosing an *athlete*, but a spiritual teacher. He also wrote to a bishop of wide influence, Eusebius of Samosata, urging him to visit Cæsarea and undertake the direction of this difficult business. Eusebius found the city in a state of distraction, but his influence and tact overcame all obstacles. Even the bishops yielded, or rather pretended to do so, for when the time came for the consecration, two of them only were found willing to join in it. The rule of the Church required three.[1] But if the adverse party hoped in this way to nullify the election, they were disappointed. The aged Gregory, though scarcely able to stand, caused himself to be lifted from his bed and carried in a litter to Cæsarea. With his own hands he consecrated the newly-elected prelate, and placed him on his episcopal throne.[2]

A.D. 370.

Basil's election filled the orthodox everywhere with exultation. Athanasius, then seventy-four years old, and nearing the end of his course, congratulated Cappadocia on possessing a bishop whom every province might envy. At Constantinople the news was received with far different feelings. Valens regarded it as a serious check to his designs for the triumph of Arianism. Basil was not an

---

[1] The fourth canon of the Council of Nicæa directs that, if possible, a bishop should be ordained by all the bishops of the province, but that in any case three, at least, should be present.

[2] *Dict. Christ. Biog.*, p. 287; Neander, iii. pp. 216, 217, note.

opponent to be despised; if he could not be made to bend, he must be got rid of.[1]

Basil had hoped that his friend Gregory would become his coadjutor in this new office, but he was disappointed. Gregory, whose affection appears to have been somewhat cooled by Basil's trickery, expressed satisfaction at his election, but excused himself from joining with him in public life; and although after a while he yielded to his importunity and went to Cæsarea, it was only to refuse all Basil's public attentions and marks of dignity, and soon to retire again to his quiet home at Arianzus.[2]

For some years Basil's episcopal rule was troubled by those bishops who had opposed his election. They withheld their sympathy and help, and delighted in thwarting his plans. One of them was his own uncle, who had filled a parent's place to him on his father's death, but who from some cause had left him and joined the party of opposition. Basil's younger brother, Gregory, distinguished by the surname of Nyssen, interposed his offices to effect a reconciliation; but the means he adopted were perhaps the worst that could have been devised. He, too, seems to have been imbued with the fatal error of the age, and to have supposed that a pious end justifies fraudulent means. He wrote forged letters to Basil in his uncle's name.

---

[1] *Dict. Christ. Biog.*, ibid.   [2] Id., p. 288.

The fraud, which was quickly discovered, only had the effect of widening the breach between the uncle and nephew. Neither would take the first step towards reconciliation; the former standing upon his prerogative of age and relationship, the latter on his rank as a metropolitan dealing with his suffragan. In the end, however, the more noble part in Basil prevailed, and he wrote his uncle a letter of affection and duty. The old man had only waited for this, and peace was restored between them.[1]

GREGORY NYSSEN is the third in our trio of Cappadocian bishops. He was two years younger than his brother Basil, and was of a retiring disposition. He had his brother's feebleness of constitution in a still greater degree, but did not possess the same strength of mind. As a youth, the observances of religion as then practised, had but little attraction for him. Martyrs' festivals were greatly in vogue; and his mother Emmelia having come into possession of some relics of the Forty Martyrs (soldiers who were said to have suffered in Armenia under Licinius, A.D. 320), appointed a solemn festival for the translation of the same to a chapel adjoining her nunnery.[2] High service, to which the whole country had

A.D. circa 356.

---

[1] Ibid.

[2] Some half-a-century afterwards, Gaudentius, bishop of Brescia, coming to Cæsarea, was presented by Gregory's nieces, who had a convent there, with some of the relics of the Forty Martyrs.—Du Pin, iii. p. 60.

been invited, was held in her garden throughout the night. She sent to Cæsarea for her son Gregory to take part in the ceremonial. He obeyed the summons, but with so little goodwill that he passed the night asleep in an arbour. Whilst thus sleeping, he had a dream in which he saw himself beaten by the martyrs with their rods, and almost shut out from the garden. Terrified by this vision, and full of remorse for the dishonour he had done to God's saints, he determined to devote himself to the Church, and undertook the office of reader. Soon wearying, however, of his new vocation, he relapsed into the world and became a professor of rhetoric. He also married, and his wife is described as a "very worthy lady, full of piety and good works." His friends were deeply grieved at his defection, and Gregory Nazianzen, who had extended the friendship he had for Basil to this younger brother, adjured him in the strongest terms to retrace his steps, styling his desire of worldly distinction, a "demoniacal ambition." Nyssen was not deaf to these entreaties. After some struggles, he resolved to quit the world, abandon his virtuous wife, and betake himself to his brother Basil's monastery. Here he passed several years, studying the Scriptures, and composing a treatise on Virginity, in which he laments most poignantly what he looks upon as the fatal error, by which, as by a wall or gulf, he

had for ever separated himself from that angelic A.D. 371.
state of perfection![1]

It was towards the close of his residence in the monastery, A.D. 371, that Gregory Nyssen so unhappily essayed to effect the reconciliation of his brother with their uncle. On the discovery of the deceit, Basil wrote him a letter of severe rebuke. He ridicules him for his simplicity, upbraids him with his unbrotherly conduct, and although, as we have seen, Basil himself had been guilty of the same thing, reproaches him with endeavouring to serve the cause of truth by deceit![2]

Basil's fame as a bishop spread far and wide throughout the East. Amongst those who came to visit him was Ephrem the Syrian, a learned monk, the author of many theological works in the Syriac language, and a successful combatant of heresy. He was also the first to introduce monachism into Mesopotamia. As Ephrem was ignorant of Greek, he took an interpreter with him. They arrived at Cæsarea on the eve of the Feast of Epiphany, and the next morning took their places in an obscure corner of the church. When Ephrem (so the story runs) saw Basil seated in a magnificent pulpit, arrayed in costly robes,[3] with a mitre

---

[1] *Dict. Christ. Biog.*, art. Gregorius Nyssenus, ii. pp. 761–763: and art. The Forty Martyrs, ii. p. 556.   [2] Id., ii. p. 763.

[3] By this time the episcopal insignia included the ring, crosier, and pallium or shoulder-cloth, a seamless mantle of white linen, with four red

sparkling with jewels on his head, and surrounded by a band of clergy, clad with almost equal splendour, he groaned in spirit, and said to the interpreter: "I fear our labour is in vain. For if we who have given up the world have advanced so little in holiness, what spiritual gifts can we expect to find in one surrounded by so great pomp?" But when Basil began to preach, it seemed to Ephrem as though the Holy Ghost, in shape like a dove, sat upon his shoulder, and suggested to him the words. From time to time the people murmured their applause, and Ephrem twice repeated aloud sentences which had fallen from the preacher's lips. Basil noticed this, and when the service was over, sent his archdeacon to invite him into his presence. This the messenger did reluctantly, and only after being twice bidden, for he was offended at the stranger's ragged attire. The two churchmen embraced each other with many compliments, and Basil asked Ephrem how it happened that, knowing no Greek, he had twice applauded during the sermon, repeating sentences of it to the congregation. Ephrem answered, "It was not I who praised and repeated, but the Holy Ghost by my mouth."[1]

A few words more about Ephrem before we continue the history of Basil. Shortly before his

---

or black crosses wrought in it with silk.—Schaff's *Nicene Christianity*, p. 265.

[1] *Dict. Christ. Biog.*, art. Ephraim the Syrian, ii. p. 138.

death, when the city of Edessa (whither he had withdrawn) was visited by a severe famine, Ephrem quitted his cell and made a powerful appeal to the rich not to let the poor die uncared for, lest their wealth misused should rise in judgment against them. They gave heed to the rebuke, and entrusted him with the distribution of their bounty. He himself attended upon the sufferers, both foreigners and citizens, until the calamity was at an end, when he returned to his cell, and a few days afterwards expired, about A.D. 379. Gregory Nyssen says of him that he desired "not to seem, but really to be good." But Ephrem did not escape the failings of the age. The interests of orthodoxy were preferred to truth and sincerity of conduct. In his dealings with Apollinaris, a noted heretic, he made use of a very unworthy artifice. Apollinaris had written a defence of his opinions, which he entrusted to a female friend. By feigning himself to be a convert to the writer's views, Ephrem contrived to get this work into his own hands; but, before he returned the manuscript, he glued the leaves together, so that no use could be made of it. The lady, unsuspicious, sent back the volume to the author, who wanted it for a dispute with a Catholic opponent. Great was his confusion,

A.D. circa 379.

---

[1] Schaff's *Nicene Christianity*, pp. 951, 952, and note.

when, on seeking to make use of his manuscript, he found it a sealed book.[1]

Ephrem is one of the sweet singers of the Eastern Church. His favourite theme was the lambs of Christ's flock. The following version of two of his choice pieces is by the authoress of *The Voice of Christian Life in Song*[2] :—

The Children in Paradise.

To Thee, O God, be praises
From lips of babes and sucklings,
As in the heavenly meadows
    Like spotless lambs they feed.

'Mid leafy trees they pasture,
Thus saith the Blessed Spirit;
And Gabriel, prince of angels,
    That happy flock doth lead.

The messengers of Heaven,
With sons of light united,
In purest regions dwelling,
    No curse or woe they see.

And at the Resurrection,
With joy arise their bodies;
Their spirits knew no bondage,
    Their bodies now are free.

Brief here below their sojourn,
Their dwelling is in Eden,
And one bright day their parents
    Hope yet with them to be.

---

[1] Roberts, *Church Memorials*, pp. 157, 158.
[2] Pp. 48, 54.

Lament of a Father on the Death of his little Son. A.D. 379.

Child, by God's sweet mercy given
  To thy mother and to me,
Entering this world of sorrows
  By his grace, so fair to see;
Fair as some sweet flower in summer,
  Till death's hand on thee was laid,
Scorch'd the beauty from my flower,
  Made the tender petals fade.
Yet I dare not weep nor murmur,
  For I know the King of kings
Leads thee to his marriage-chamber,
  To the glorious bridal brings.

Nature fain would have me weeping,
  Love asserts her mournful right;
But I answer they have brought thee
  To the happy world of light.
And I fear that my lamentings,
  As I speak thy cherish'd name,
Desecrate the Royal dwelling;—
  Fear to meet deserved blame,
If I press with tears of anguish
  Into the abode of joy;
Therefore will I, meekly bowing,
  Offer thee to God, my boy.

Yet thy voice, thy childish singing,
  Soundeth ever in my ears;
And I listen, and remember,
  Till mine eyes will gather tears,
Thinking of thy pretty prattlings,
  And thy childish words of love;
But when I begin to murmur,
  Then my spirit looks above,
Listens to the songs of spirits—
  Listens, longing, wondering,
To the ceaseless, glad hosannas
  Angels at thy bridal sing.

CHAPTER IV.

THE CAPPADOCIAN BISHOPS (*concluded*).

SECTION I. To return to Basil. In 371 the Emperor Valens divided Cappadocia into two provinces, making Tyana the capital of the new division. Anthimus, bishop of that city, choosing to consider that the ecclesiastical rule should follow the civil, claimed metropolitan jurisdiction over it in the place of Basil, and began to appropriate its revenues.[1] To such a course Basil was not the man tamely to submit. He summoned his friend Gregory Nazianzen to his side. Gregory wrote in reply, "I will come if thou wishest: if so be that the sea wants water or Basil a counsellor, I will come. At all events, I am ready to bear ill-usage in thy company." In the scene which followed, the parties on both sides figure in a manner unbecoming to the Christian ministry. As soon as Gregory arrived, the two friends set out together for a monastery on the Taurus range, situated in the severed province, to receive the produce of an estate which, up to this time, had belonged to the

---

[1] Du Pin says the point in dispute was as to the *limits* of the new province, ii. p. 123.

see of Cæsarea. As the rents were paid in kind they took with them a train of sumpter-mules. Anthimus, hearing of the expedition, hastened, full of wrath, to intercept the convoy. Notwithstanding his advanced age, he put himself at the head of a band of armed retainers, whom he stationed at a defile near Sasima, through which the train had to pass on its return. An affray ensued; Gregory was injured, and Basil had his mule taken from him.[1]

A.D. 371.

To strengthen himself against his rival, Basil determined to erect two new bishoprics as defensive outposts on that frontier of his diocese, and to fill them with the two Gregorys. The onerous duties of a bishop were, however, distasteful to them both, and so reluctant were they to abandon their retirement and enter upon public life, that in each case compulsion had to be used before they would suffer the ordaining hands to be laid upon them. But Basil was one of those men who, when they have a clear sight of their object, will make their way to it at any sacrifice; and when Gregory Nazianzen took to flight to avoid consecration, he even went so far as to pursue and bring him back. Gregory was deeply wounded. At his ordination he gave vent to his feelings, in these plaintive words: " Once more has the Holy Spirit been

---

[1] *Dict. Christ. Biog.*, i. p. 291, ii. pp. 748, 749; Ullmann, p. 122, note; Epist. of Gregory 25 (26).

poured out upon me, and once more I enter upon my calling, sad and dejected." [1]

The new bishoprics were Sasima and Nyssa. The latter, over which Basil placed his brother, was an obscure town,[2] so insignificant, that Eusebius of Samosata wrote to remonstrate against a man of such talents being thus buried. Basil replied that his purpose was to make the see famous by its bishop, not the bishop by the see. The choice of Sasima for the other Gregory was still more unworthy. It was a mean village or posting-station, situate within the new province of Tyana. The revenues of the Church were meagre, and it was a spot in the highest degree distasteful to the sensitive nature of Gregory, who, in one of his poems, has left us a description of it somewhat caricatured. " On a highway of Cappadocia, at a point where three roads join, is a halting-place where is neither water nor anything green, nor any mark of civilisation. It is a frightful and detestable village. Everywhere you meet nothing but noises, dust, waggons, howls, groans, chains, instruments of torture, and the executioner. The whole population consists of

---

[1] *Dict. Christ. Biog.*, i. p. 291, ii. p. 749; Ullmann, pp. 122-125. Surely we shall not believe that Basil's wilful action could confer the Holy Spirit on the unwilling Gregory. Very different were the feelings of the latter from those which the Apostle sets forth in his Epistle to Timothy : " God gave us not a spirit of fearfulness; but of power and love and discipline."
—2 Tim. i. 7.

[2] To the west of Cæsarea, and north of Nazianzus.

foreigners and travellers. Such was my church of Sasima."[1]

A.D. 371.

Basil was universally censured for appointing Gregory to such a place. Finding him slow to enter upon his office, he sent his brother of Nyssa to quicken his resolution. Gregory prepared to obey, but hearing that Anthimus had appointed a rival bishop to the see, he retired from the contest. Basil reproached him for his pusillanimity. Gregory could bear no more. Loving and gentle as he was, his whole soul recoiled against these repeated insults, and he thus poured forth his wounded feelings. " Wilt thou never cease to slander me, merely because I am bold enough to recognise how I have been treated? I know now the deception thou hast practised upon me, which I can no otherwise explain, than that thy elevation to the episcopal throne has suddenly lifted thee up. . . . The most charitable accuse thee of making use of me, and then casting me aside, just as the framework of an arch, as soon as the structure is completed, is struck away and counted good for nothing . . . I am not going to arm myself and learn the art of war, in order to fight the martial Anthimus. Fight him thyself; or if thou art in want of warriors, wait till he surrounds the pass and lays hold of thy mules. To what purpose is it that I should fight for sucking-pigs and chickens,

---

[1] *Verses on his own Life*, strophe 32, Opera ii. pp. 7, 8. Paris, 1630.

Per. I.
Chap. 4.

and these not my own, as if they were men's souls and Church canons ... Sweep everything into thy own lap, as the rivers do the mountain torrents, to swell thy own glory; so long as thou dost not set friendship and intimacy above right and piety ..."[1]

From this moment the confiding friendship which had subsisted between Basil and Gregory ever since their boyhood was broken. Basil, indeed, went once again to Nazianzus to visit Gregory;[2] but so far as appears, no more familiar letters passed between them. After Basil's death Gregory endeavoured to offer an apology for his friend's conduct, but the attempt only shows how incurable was the wound. In his funeral oration over him he says: " Admiring as I do, all he did more than I can express, I cannot praise his extraordinary and unfriendly conduct towards me, the pain of which time has not removed. To this I trace all the irregularity and confusion of my subsequent life. Unless, indeed, I may be suffered to make this excuse for him, that having views beyond this earth, he slighted friendship, only when it was his duty to prefer God, and to make more account of the things hoped for, than of the things that perish."[3]

---

[1] *Dict. Christ. Biog.*, ii. p. 749; Epist. 31 (22).

[2] On the occasion of Gregory's funeral oration over his father, who lived to nearly one hundred years.

[3] Newman's *Church of the Fathers*, pp. 125-127.

It is doubtful whether Gregory ever entered A.D. 371.
upon the bishopric of Sasima; but at his father's
urgent request he became his coadjutor in the see
of Nazianzus, A.D. 372. How much every call to
public service cost him may be seen by a sermon
which he preached at this time. " Between my
inward longing and the Holy Spirit, I am almost
torn asunder. The one urges me to fly to the
solitude of the mountains, to withdraw from all
sensuous things, and to retire into myself, that I
may commune with God undisturbed. But the
Spirit would lead me into active life to serve the
common weal, to spread light, and present to God
a people for his possession, a royal priesthood."[1]

It was a year or two before this happened,
namely, in 371, that Basil found himself engaged
in a personal encounter with the Arian Emperor
Valens. The Emperor had entered upon his
theological crusade against the Catholics, and was
on his march through the provinces of Asia Minor.
For awhile his progress was one of uniform victory.
"The Catholics had everywhere fallen before him.
Bithynia had resisted, and had become the scene of
horrible tragedies. The fickle Galatia had yielded
without a struggle. The fate of Cappadocia depended on Basil. His house, as the Emperor drew
near, was besieged by ladies of rank, high personages of state, even by bishops, who entreated him

---

[1] Ullmann, pp. 127-130.

to bow before the storm and appease the Emperor by a temporary submission." But Basil had no ear for such counsels; he rejected their entreaties with disdain. The arrival of Valens was preceded by a band of Arian bishops, aiming to strike awe into their opponents by their numbers, but Basil straightway refused to hold communion with them. They were followed by officers of the Imperial household, who threatened him in violent language. One of these was Demosthenes, the *chef de cuisine*, whom the Emperor carried everywhere with him, but to whom Basil paid no attention except to bid him return to his kitchen fire.[1] Another was Modestus, the prefect of the Pretorium:—

Modestus. What is the meaning of this, thou Basil (not deigning to style him bishop), that thou standest out against so great a prince?

Basil. What dost thou mean?

Modestus. Thou dost not worship after the Emperor's manner, although the rest of thy party have yielded.

Basil. Such is not my Heavenly Sovereign's will, nor can I worship any creature.

Modestus (amazed). For whom dost thou take me?

Basil. For a thing of nought while thy commands are such.

---

[1] *Dict. Christ. Biog.*, i. pp. 288, 289.

Modestus. Is it, then, nothing to have men of rank like us on your side? [A.D. 371.]

Basil. Thou art a prefect, and illustrious, I grant; but God's Majesty is greater. It would be an honour to have thee on my side, but yet no more so than to have any member of my flock; for Christianity consists not in distinction of persons, but in faith.

The prefect was enraged at this reply, and rising from his chair, abruptly asked Basil if he did not fear his power.

Basil. Fear what?

Modestus. Any one of the many penalties a prefect can inflict.

Basil. Let me know them: confiscation, exile, tortures, death? None of these can move me.

Modestus. How so?

Basil. That man is not obnoxious to confiscation who has nothing to lose, except old tattered garments and a few books. Nor does he care for exile who is not circumscribed by place, but is everywhere at home on God's earth. Nor can torture harm a frame so frail that it would break under the first blow; and death would be gain.

Modestus. No one ever yet spoke to Modestus with such freedom.

Basil. Peradventure Modestus never before met with a true bishop. O prefect, in other things we are gentle, and more humble than all men living, but when God's honour is at stake we overlook all else. Fire and the sword, beasts of prey, irons to rend the flesh, are an indulgence rather than a terror to the Christian. Therefore threaten, insult, do thy worst, make the most of thy power. Let the Emperor be informed of my purpose.[1]

Finding threats useless, Modestus tried promises and flattery, but with no better success. He had to report to his master that all his attempts to bring Basil to submission had been fruitless. Such rare intrepidity produced its natural effect on the feeble mind of Valens. He refused to sanction harsh measures against the bishop, and even condescended to present himself in the chief church of Cæsarea on the Feast of the Epiphany. The service had already commenced. When the Emperor, in the glowing words of Nazianzen, "heard the chanted psalms which rose like a peal of thunder, and beheld the sea of worshippers within and around the sanctuary, ranked in an order so comely as to resemble angels rather than men, and the bishop himself standing, like Samuel, erect before the people, body, eyes and soul, absorbed in God and the altar, and the priests on either side in reverential awe—the Emperor's spirit forsook him, and he swooned away." Gregory says Valens had never before beheld such a spectacle. This can hardly have referred to the service itself, for

---

[1] Cave, *Lives of the Fathers*; St. Basil, sect. 4; Gregory Nazianzen, *Funeral Oration on Basil*, 73-75, Opera, i. pp. 349, 350.

that would surely be as imposing in his own cathedral church at Constantinople. It was rather the oneness of purpose and spirit by which the assembly was animated, their love to Basil and their devotion to the Nicene faith. It must be remembered, too, that the Trinitarians were at that period the Nonconformists, and that persecution had weeded from their ranks the nominal and the lukewarm. Add to this the sight of the bishop himself as he stood before the altar—tall, spare, erect, with hollow cheeks and piercing eyes, and armed as he conceived with the majesty of heaven. When the time came for Valens to make his offering, and the ministers were hesitating whether they should receive an oblation from the hand of a heretic, Basil came forward, and himself accepted the gift.[1]

The next day Valens again visited the church, and was admitted by the bishop within the sacred veil. The cook, Demosthenes, rudely joining in the conversation, made a grammatical mistake. Basil smiled, and quietly observed: "We have here, it seems, a Demosthenes who cannot speak Greek; he had better attend to his sauces than meddle with theology." The retort amused the Emperor, who was so well pleased with his theological opponent, that he made him a grant of land on which to erect a poor-house.[2]

---

[1] Ibid., pp. 76, 77, Opera, i. p. 351; *Dict. Christ. Biog.*, i. p. 289.
[2] *Dict. Christ. Biog.*, ibid.

Per. I.
Chap. 4.

But the favourable impression thus made on Valens soon wore off. The Arian bishops recovered their influence, and an imperial order was issued for Basil to quit the city. He was to start at night, to avoid the risk of popular disturbance. The chariot was at his door, and his friends, Gregory amongst them, were bewailing his departure, when he was stopped by an imperial messenger sent in consequence of the sudden illness of the Emperor's only son. The Empress attributed their child's danger to the Divine displeasure at the treatment of Basil, and the Emperor sent to entreat Basil to come and pray over the sick child. On condition that he should be brought up in the orthodox faith, Basil consented. As he prayed, the child grew better.[1] But the Arians contrived that he should be baptized by one of their own bishops. The child (so the historians relate) grew immediately worse, and died the same night. Basil's enemies, however, were not even now in despair; they returned once more to the attack, and with the usual result. His exile was again determined on; but when Valens attempted to sign the order, the pens, it is declared, refused to write, and thrice split in his hand! This supposed miracle put an end to all further proceedings. "Valens left Cæsarea, and Basil remained master of the situation.[2]"

---

[1] The prefect Modestus also, who fell sick, attributed his own recovery to the prayers of Basil.   [2] *Dict. Christ. Biog.*, i. pp. 289, 290.

BASIL'S WORK IN HIS DIOCESE.   87

Thus left free to devote his energies to the A.D. 371.
internal administration of his diocese, Basil set
himself vigorously to the correction of the abuses
which had grown up within it. He was an
energetic promoter of morals, good order, and
discipline. He had, however, no thought of bringing back the worship and government of the
Church to its primitive pattern; rather were the
superstitious practices of the time strengthened,
and the authority of the bishops enhanced under
his rule. In his own province he usurped the
control of episcopal elections, and even travelled
into Armenia to appoint new bishops and infuse
fresh life into those who were already in office.
His incessant labours were performed under the
pressure of extreme bodily weakness, so that, even
when considered in health, he describes himself
as being "weaker than persons who are given
over."[1]

Basil's heaviest trial was yet to come. A
suspicion of his orthodoxy was artfully and
successfully propagated throughout the Churches.
He was unjustly accused of denying the proper
divinity of the Holy Spirit.[2] This brought great

---

[1] Id., p. 290; Basil, Epist. 136.

[2] Fear of Sabellianism restrained Basil for some time from committing himself entirely to the Homo-ousion doctrine. His usual form of doxology was "Glory be to the Father through the Son, in the Holy Spirit." On which Hooker remarks: "Till Arianism had made it a matter of great sharpness and subtilty of wit to be a sound believing Christian, men were not curious what syllables or particles of speech they used. When St. Basil began to practise the like indifferency, and to conclude public

odium upon him. In his extremity he turned first to Athanasius, whom he designates "that great and apostolic soul who from boyhood had been an athlete in the cause of religion," and then to the Western Church. The former was unable to assist him; the Western bishops sent assurances of attachment and sympathy, but nothing more. They could not move without the bishop of Rome; and the bishop of Rome was offended, because Basil did not appeal to him as supreme. This assumption of superiority was lost on Basil; he only remarked, it was in vain to send messages to "one who sat aloft, high and haughty, and would not listen to the truth from men who stood below."[1]

Even whilst he lay under the imputation of heterodoxy, Basil did not relax in the conflict he was always waging against Arianism. "Polytheism," he writes, "has got possession. A greater and a lesser God are worshipped. All ecclesiastical power, all Church ordinances, are in Arian hands. Arians baptize; Arians visit the sick; Arians administer the sacred mysteries. The pious are banished; the houses of prayer are closed; the altars forbidden;

---

prayers, glorifying sometime the Father *with* the Son and the Holy Ghost, sometime the Father *by* the Son, *in* the Spirit, . . . some (because the light of his candle too much drowned theirs) were glad to lay hold on so colourable a matter, and were exceedingly forward to traduce him as an author of suspicious innovation."—*Eccles. Polity*, V. xlii. 12: cited in *Dict. Christ. Biog.*, i. p. 293, note.

[1] *Dict. Christ. Biog.*, i. pp. 292, 293.

the orthodox meet for worship in the deserts, exposed to wind and rain and snow, or to the scorching sun."¹

A.D. 372–379.

Before his death, however, Basil was permitted to see the dawn of a brighter day. A new invasion of the Goths in 377 drew off Valens from the persecution of the orthodox; the next year his army was defeated with immense slaughter near Adrianople, and the Emperor himself perished. His successor, the youthful Gratian, belonged to the Catholic party, and one of his first acts was to recall the banished orthodox prelates. So that, before his death, Basil had the joy of seeing many of his friends restored to their sees.²

Basil died January 1, A.D. 379, at Cæsarea. Although only fifty years old, his constitution was completely worn out. His death-bed was surrounded by the citizens, "willing if so it might be," says his friend Gregory, " to give a portion of their own lives to lengthen that of their bishop." He breathed his last with the words, "Into thy hand I commend my spirit: Thou hast redeemed me, O Lord God of Truth."³ His funeral was attended by immense crowds, who almost tore the bier to pieces to secure a relic of the departed saint. "The press was so great that several persons were crushed to death; almost the object of envy, because they died with Basil."⁴

---

¹ Id., pp. 294, 295.
² Id., p. 295.   ³ Ps. xxxi. 5.   ⁴ *Dict. Christ. Biog.*, loc. cit.

Per. I.
Chap. 4.

Basil was pale, and wore a beard; through life he retained his monkish dress. In speech he was deliberate, in manner reserved and sedate. His friend Gregory especially commends his trumpet eloquence, his great and various learning, his charity, his compassion, his affability. "Who," he exclaims, "more loving than he to the well-conducted? who more severe with transgressors? his smile was praise, and his silence a reproof to the uneasy conscience. If he were not full of talk, or a jester, or a boon companion, what then? This, with men of sense, is not his blame, but his praise. Yet, that he was most agreeable in social intercourse, I who knew him so well can testify. None could relate a story with more wit; none maintain the sport of words so playfully; none convey the timely hint with greater delicacy."[1]

Basil is often called The Great, as much on account of his writings as of his character.[2] The

---

[1] Newman, *Church of the Fathers*, pp. 47, 48; *Dict. Christ. Biog.*, i. p. 295; Du Pin, ii. p. 157.

[2] He has left nearly 400 letters. Dr. Jessopp thus compares the three great letter-writers of this age, Augustine, Jerome, and Basil. "St. Augustine's can really hardly be called letters at all; they are for the most part treatises on the interpretation of sacred Scripture, or on theological or philosophical questions ... In St. Jerome's we have some valuable notices of the religious life of the time, and we get a most curious impression of the awfully high pressure at which devout people were living at the close of the fourth century. The men and women are not men and women, but creatures who are trying to be something else and who believe themselves to be something else. Jerome himself is up in a balloon, and he seems to assume that everybody else is, or ought to be, or wishes to be, or is trying to be up in a balloon too ... St. Basil's letters are very much less known, but they are far more real, genuine, human, and interesting than those of Augustine and Jerome. They have a wide range of

following passage will serve as a specimen of his style:—" The love of God cannot be taught. We did not learn from any one else to take pleasure in the light, nor to desire life. No one taught us to love our parents or our nurses. Thus, or rather far more, the learning of the love of God comes not from without, but a certain seminal power of reason is ingrafted in us, which possesses from its own store the means of that appropriation which leads to love. Which power the school of the divine commandments takes in hand, tills with care, nourishes with skill, and, by the grace of God, brings to perfection . . . We naturally love the beautiful (though to different persons different things may seem beautiful), and we delight to display all good to those who do us good. Now what more admirable than the Divine Beauty? What conception more attractive than the Majesty of God? What longing so vehement and irresist-

A.D. 379.

---

subjects, and his correspondents were people of all ranks and classes and opinions—pagan philosophers and professors, governors of provinces, ladies in distress, rogues who had tried to take him in, and, of course, a host of bishops and clergy . . . He can laugh and can be playful—witness his letter to the governor of Cappadocia, who had cured himself of an illness by dieting himself on pickled cabbage. 'My dear sir,' says Basil, 'I am delighted at the news. I never believed in cabbage before, still less in pickled cabbage; but now I shall praise it as something superior to the lotus that Homer talks of—yea, not inferior to the very ambrosia that served as the food of the gods!' The governor answered that letter very briefly, and his answer has been preserved. 'My right rev. brother,' says the governor, 'you are right, there's nothing like pickled cabbage! Twice to cabbage kills—so the saying has it. I find, many times to cabbage cures. Come and try. Dine with me to-morrow on pickled cabbage—that and nothing more!'"—Letters and Letter Writers; *Nineteenth Century*, August 1886, pp. 226, 227.

<small>Per. I. Chap. 4.</small> ible as that which is engendered of God in the soul which is purged of vice, and which cries out of unfeigned desire, 'I am sick of love?' . . . Alienation and aversion from God is worse than any torments of hell. It is as the privation of light to the eye, even if no pain be present; or as the deprivation of life to a living thing . . . Our Lord Jesus Christ, who endured a most shameful death that he might restore us to the glorious life, exacts no recompense, but is satisfied if he be only loved for what he gave. And when I think of all these things, I am in an ecstasy of fear lest ever, through inattention of mind or occupation with vanities, I should fall from the love of God and become a reproach to Christ . . . The reproach which our fall will bring on Christ, and the glorying of the enemy, seem to me worse than the punishments of hell."[1]

SECTION II. We must now go back a few years. It was only in condescension to his father's will that Gregory Nazianzen consented to become his coadjutor. On his father's death however, (which took place in 374), he continued to administer the see until a new bishop was elected. During these years some of his most brilliant discourses were delivered. He was sensible, however, of the worthlessness of mere words, and at last announced to his congregation that he had resolved not to

---

[1] Smith's *St. Basil the Great*, pp. 134-136.

preach before them again, in order that by his silence he might "check the mania for theological discussion, which was leading everybody to teach the things of the Spirit without the unction of the Spirit."[1]

Suddenly, in 375, Gregory disappeared. He had retired to a monastery in Isauria, where he remained three years in strict seclusion. He returned home before Basil's death, but was taken so dangerously ill that he could neither visit him on his dying bed nor be present at his funeral. Like Basil, he had become prematurely old. Though only fifty years of age, his bald head bent towards his bosom, and his countenance was wasted by tears and fasting, and furrowed with wrinkles. With characteristic melancholy he writes to a friend, "Thou inquirest how I am; I answer, very ill. My spiritual brother [Basil] and my natural brother [Cæsarius] are both gone. Age shows itself on my head; my cares multiply; friends prove untrue; the Church is without shepherds; good is disappearing; evil shows itself bare-faced. We are journeying in the night; there is nowhere a torch to give us light; Christ is asleep. What, then, is to be done? Alas for me! there is only one escape, and that is death!"[2]

But there was work yet for Gregory to do, and that on a higher stage than before. For fifty

---

[1] *Dict. Christ. Biog.*, ii. pp. 749, 750.

[2] Id., p. 750; Ullmann, p. 153; *De Vitâ Suâ*, Greg. Naz., Opera, ii. p. 11.

years Arianism had been dominant in Constantinople. The adherents of the Nicene faith had dwindled down to a small number, and were without church or bishop, being obliged to conceal themselves in the remote quarters of the city. The accession of Gratian restored their courage. Looking round for a pastor, they cast their eyes on Gregory, whose praise for eloquence and sanctity was in all the Churches; and they sent him an urgent appeal to take charge of their little flock. Long he remained unwilling to quit his beloved retirement, but at length he yielded to the conviction that the time for action had arrived; and he turned his face towards the great city. His opinion of the state of the Church there is conveyed in a few words: "It had passed through the death of infidelity; there was left but one last breath of life. What the people needed was solid teaching to deliver them from the spider-webs of subtleties in which they had been taken." Yet on some points the teaching of the Arians was more enlightened than that of the Catholics. Sir Isaac Newton remarks that before Gregory came to Constantinople, the city was free from that superstitious reverence for the martyrs with which it shortly after began to be inflamed.[1]

Gregory began his work in a private house; but the building quickly became too small for the

---

[1] *Dict. Christ. Biog.*, ii. p. 750; Newton's *Observations on Daniel*, pp. 218, 228.

multitudes which flocked to it, and a church was erected in its place. To this church he gave the name of Anastasia (*Resurrection, i.e.* of the true faith). Here he delivered a fresh series of those discourses which have made his name famous. The success of his preaching raised up a host of enemies, who envied whilst they affected to despise him, even ridiculing his person and attire.[1] A fierce attack was made upon his church during the hour of service. From the Arian cathedral of St. Sophia there issued a motley crowd of monks, beggars, and women more terrible than men. The assailants made free use of stones, sticks, and firebrands. The altar was profaned, the consecrated wine was mixed with blood, the house of prayer was made a scene of outrage and unbridled licentiousness. Personally Gregory cared little for the assault; stones, he said, were his delight; his care was only for his flock.[2]

In the year 380 (Nov. 26) Theodosius made his entry into Constantinople. One of his first acts was to remove the Arians from the churches and restore these to the orthodox. To Demophilus, the Arian bishop, was offered the alternative of subscribing the Nicene Creed, or of resigning his

---

[1] "I was," he says, "the very image of a beggar."—*De Vitâ Suâ*, loc. cit.

[2] *Dict. Christ. Biog.*, ii. pp. 750, 751; Ullmann, pp. 175, 176. During Gregory's abode in Constantinople, Jerome, who had just quitted Syria, became his disciple, and loved to tell how much he learned from his teacher. He calls him a "most eloquent man from whom I learned to expound the Scriptures."—*Dict. Christ. Biog.*, ii. p. 751.

office. Demophilus did not hesitate a moment. Assembling his followers in the cathedral, he said : " My brethren, it is written in the Gospel, 'If they persecute you in one city, flee ye into another.' Seeing that the Emperor excludes us from the churches, we will henceforth hold our assemblies without the city." Towards Gregory, the Emperor manifested the greatest respect. On his way to the cathedral he conversed with him for a long while, and, as though anticipating what was about to take place, concluded with these words: "This temple God delivers to thee by our hand as a reward for thy devoted labours."[1]

When the day arrived on which the orthodox were to take possession of the churches, the city was violently agitated ; cries of the most opposite kind filled the air, some shouting with joy, many more venting their grief and disappointment in tears and threats. The Emperor, in warlike state, and followed by an imposing train, proceeded to the Church of the Apostles, which he had caused to be strongly guarded. Gregory was at his side, breathing feebly from a recent fit of sickness, but full of confidence and thankfulness. The streets through which the procession marched were crowded with an innumerable multitude of either sex and of every age. The windows and roofs of the houses were thronged, and a tumultuous sound

---

[1] Socrates, *Eccles. Hist.*, b. v. c. 7.

arose, in which grief and rage predominated, so that, as Gregory himself describes it, "the city resembled a place which had been taken by storm, and was in the hands of some barbarian conqueror." The morning was gloomy; a thick fog filled the church. The Arians began to exult in this sign of heaven's displeasure, and the orthodox were dispirited, when (so Gregory relates), at the first accents of the chants, the sun broke forth and shone upon the vestments of the priests and the swords of the soldiers, reminding him of the glory which descended upon the ancient tabernacle. At the same time a cry arose from the congregation, "Gregory shall be our bishop." Unable himself to speak from bodily weakness, he desired another priest to address the people in his name: "Silence, silence; this is the time to give thanks to God; it will be time enough hereafter to settle other matters."[1]

The following year Theodosius convened a general council of Oriental bishops at Constantinople. The chief objects were to confirm the Nicene faith, and to appoint a bishop for the metropolis. Although the orthodox were especially invited, other parties, in the hope thereby of promoting union, were admitted; but when the Nicene confession was presented to the synod for its adoption, the Semi-Arian bishops, of whom

---

[1] Ullmann, pp. 222–225; *Dict. Christ. Biog.*, ii. p. 753; Gibbon, iii. p. 450.

thirty-six were present, refused to subscribe, and left the city in a body. The wish of Theodosius, that Gregory should be bishop of Constantinople, was well-known; and no opposition being made in the council, he was elected. The inaugural oration was preached by his friend Gregory Nyssen.[1]

Nazianzen's enjoyment of his lofty position was of the very briefest duration.[2] Hardly had his consecration taken place than the bishops began to repent of their choice. His homely manners and ignorance of the world offended them, and they characterised as lukewarmness the tolerance he showed to the now persecuted Arians. But this was not all. It was a time of bitter party spirit and great confusion. Meletius, bishop of Antioch, who presided over the council, held his bishopric only by a compromise between two contending parties. He died whilst the council was in session, and the question who should be his successor in the see of Antioch, rent asunder the Asiatic Church and the council itself. Gregory, by virtue of his office, now became president of the council. He was no party man, and his endeavour to preserve peace between the two parties was misinterpreted and resented; he was, indeed, of too

---

[1] *Dict. Christ. Biog.*, ii. pp. 753, 765. There remained, after the departure of the Arians, 150 bishops of the Catholics. Some additions were made to the Nicene Creed, as already detailed on p. 19, note; and the anathema at the close was omitted.—Roberts, *Church Memorials*, pp. 125, 126.

[2] He was actually bishop only a few weeks.

gentle a nature to govern the ship in such a storm. At this crisis there arrived from Egypt and Macedonia a fresh party of bishops, who objected to Gregory's appointment to the see of Constantinople, alleging that, having been formerly consecrated to the see of Sasima, he could not now (according to the 15th canon of the Council of Nicæa) fill any other.[1] In vain did Gregory and his defenders reply that this law, if not already antiquated, had been superseded by the act of the council itself. The opposition only became fiercer, and Gregory saw that there was nothing left but to resign his episcopate. He delivered an address to the council in which he sought to pour oil upon the troubled waters. Its only effect was to call forth a universal uproar, the younger ecclesiastics especially venting their ill-will towards him, "like screaming jackdaws or a swarm of angry wasps."[2] He wound up his speech with these words: "I now request permission to resign my bishopric, and to lead, if a more inglorious, yet a more peaceful life." Once again he appeared before the council, and exhorted them to occupy themselves with matters worthy of their high calling, and to cherish mutual harmony. "He was ready

A.D. 381.

---

[1] This canon forbade the translation of bishops.

[2] Elsewhere he compares them to "cranes and geese," and says it was a "disgrace to sit amongst such hucksters of the faith."—Ullmann, pp. 243-251; *Dict. Christ. Biog.*, ii. p. 754.

to be another Jonah to calm the angry waves. He owed but one debt, the debt of death, and that was in God's hands. He had but one anxiety, and that was for his beloved doctrine of the Trinity." From the council he went to the Emperor, who reluctantly consented to accept his resignation.[1]

It was hard to tear himself away from his beloved flock. They entreated him not to leave them. "Who," they asked, "will nourish thy children, if thou shouldst forsake us?" He took a public farewell of the congregation, at which the council were present; and although the cathedral was filled to every corner, not a dry eye was to be seen. "Farewell"—so he wound up this celebrated but florid oration—"farewell, my beloved church, Anastasia, by which the true faith has been raised up. And thou, too, more majestic temple, our new possession, which hast now first received thy true greatness from the true preaching of the everlasting Word . . . Farewell, O Holy Trinity, my sole thought, my only jewel; may this my people keep Thee, and mayest Thou preserve them. Cherish, O my children, the truth I have committed to you, and remember the persecutions I have endured for its sake . . . The grace of our Lord Jesus Christ be with you all! Amen."[2]

Sorrow for the loss of his church was, however,

---

[1] Newman, pp. 141-144; *Dict. Christ. Biog.*, loc. cit.

[2] Ullmann, pp. 251-258; Gregory, Oration in presence of 150 bishops, 83-95, Opera, i. pp. 527, 528.

tempered by self-gratulation on his escape from the atmosphere of the court. "Never more shall I be entertained at the tables of princes, bashful and speechless, not breathing freely, feasting like a slave. No magistrate shall again punish me with a seat either near him or below him, giving the higher place to some grovelling spirit. No more shall I clasp bloodstained hands, or take hold of beard, to gain some small favour. No more, hurrying with a crowd to some birthday, burial, or marriage feast, shall I seize on all I can, something for myself, something for my attendants, with their greedy palms, and then late in the evening drag home my ailing carcase worn out with fatigue, and panting with satiety."[1] On his way home to his native village he preached his memorial oration over the grave of Basil.

A.D. 381.

Once again in his beloved retirement, Gregory partially recovered his shattered health. There was at Arianzus a little garden with a shady walk and a fountain, which he had reserved to himself when all his other property was given to the poor. Here he soothed his irritated spirit and half forgot the turmoil and vexations of the great city. "If any of our friends," he writes, "should inquire what Gregory is doing, say that he is enjoying in perfect quiet a philosophical life, and that he troubles himself as little about his enemies as he does

---

[1] Carmina, Opera, ii. p. 17; Newman, p. 145.

about persons of whose existence he knows nothing."[1]

From his solitude he sent forth to his friends messages of sympathy, both in their joys and in their tribulations. Although he had himself renounced marriage, and had always extravagantly extolled the virgin state, yet we find him in his declining years entering into hearty sympathy with a young friend in the prospect of marriage. "Thy beloved is now thine; the moment of your union has arrived; and I who ought to have been present, and taken part in the solemn service, am obliged to remain at a distance. Several times I have made the attempt to set out, but have always been overcome by sickness. It must be for others to invoke the genius of love (for playful mirth becomes the nuptial festival), and paint the beauty of the bride and the manliness of the bridegroom. Nevertheless, I will sing you my marriage song: 'The Lord bless you out of Zion, and grant harmony upon your union. Mayst thou see thy sons (thy sons' sons, I was ready to say), still nobler than thyself.'"[2]

The next year, 382, he was invited in the Emperor's name to attend a synod at Constantinople. He thus replied: "To tell the truth, I am

---

[1] *Dict. Christ. Biog.*, ii. p. 755; Ullmann, pp. 263-268.

[2] Ullmann, pp. 279-281. In another letter on a similar occasion he writes: "The highest blessing is that Christ is present; for where He is, there is good order, and the water is changed into wine."—Ibid.

in such a temper of mind that I shun every assemblage of bishops, because I have never yet seen a good issue to any synod, have never been present at any which did not do more for the multiplication than it did for the suppression of evils. An indescribable thirst for contention and rule prevails in them; and a man who dares to lift up his voice against what is base in others, will be far more certain to bring down reproach upon himself than to succeed in removing such baseness."[1]

The spread of the Apollinarian heresy[2] alarmed the clergy and people of Nazianzus, and they entreated Gregory to return thither and help them. Very reluctantly he yielded to their importunity, and for a short time administered the affairs of the diocese. But his bodily weakness returned, and as soon as he could induce the neighbouring prelates to consecrate a new bishop, he withdrew again from public life, and spent his last six years in seclusion. He was not idle however, but continued to occupy himself with the various interests which surrounded him, political, ecclesiastical, and personal. In the mortification of the body, to which he had devoted himself from early life, he suffered no relaxation to overtake him in old age. But these austerities failed to bring him peace. To the burden of a weak and suffering body was often added a

---

[1] Id., p. 268. [2] See below, Period II. Chap. I.

spiritual agony, so great as to take from him all hope both for this world and the next. At other times, faith lifted him above his tribulations, and he could say: "I suffer and am content, not because I suffer, but because I am for others an example of patience. If I have no means to free myself from pain, I gain from it at least the power to bear it, and to be thankful, as well in sorrow as in joy; for I am convinced that, although it seems to us the contrary, there is in the eyes of the Sovereign Reason nothing opposed to reason in all which happens to us."[1]

He died A.D. 389 or 390, aged about 60 years.

In Gregory's preaching, the lessons of practical religion are never lost sight of. He often sets before his hearers the danger of empty talkativeness about divine things, and disputation on theological questions, to which they were addicted. He taught that true piety consists in doing God's will, and that the knowledge of God is attainable only in proportion as the soul is purified from the defilement of sin.[2]

In toleration of heretics Gregory was before his age. His counsel in dealing with such breathes the true Gospel spirit: "Do not rashly condemn thy brother; to condemn and to despise is nothing else than to shut out from Christ, the sole hope of sinners. It is the same as pulling up with the

---

[1] Ullmann, pp. 270-273, 279, 295, 296; *Dict. Christ. Biog.*, ii. pp. 755, 756.   [2] Ullmann, pp. 169, 170.

weeds the hidden fruit which is possibly of more value than thou art. Raise up thy brother gently and lovingly, not as an antagonist, not as a physician who administers medicine by force, or knows of no remedy but cauterising and cutting. Learn rather to know thyself in the spirit of humility, and to search out thy own infirmities. It is not one and the same thing to pull up or destroy a *plant* and a *man*. Thou art an image of God, and thou hast to do with an image of God; thou who judgest wilt thyself be judged . . . In our Father's house are many mansions, and the ways which lead to them are various." Hear how he speaks to some who denied the divinity of the Holy Spirit: "Such is the love I cherish for you, such the respect I feel for your becoming attire, your abstemiousness, your holy societies, the honour you pay to virginity, your nightly psalm-singing, your love of the poor, your brotherly kindness, your hospitality, that I could even wish myself accursed from Christ if ye were but united with us."[1] At times, however, the old bitter feeling against the Arians, so long triumphant over the Catholics, will break forth; so that if we had no other evidence than his writings, we should pronounce the whole party to be utterly base and diabolical.

Gregory's pensive spirit was especially open

---

[1] Id., pp. 172-174.

to the sweet influences of Nature. Thus he writes in spring: "How beautiful is everything that meets the eye. The meads send forth their fragrance; the plants bud; the young lambs frisk on the green plains. The bee now leaves her hive, spreads her wings, displays her sagacious instinct, and robs the flowers of their sweetness. All creation praises and glorifies God with inarticulate voice. Yes, it is now [in allusion to the Easter festival], the spring of the world, of the souls of men as well as of their bodies, the visible and the invisible spring, the same which we shall taste above if we are transformed and renewed here." Again, during a time of trial in his ministry at Constantinople, he tells his hearers: "As the day was declining I wandered alone by the sea-shore, for I was accustomed to disperse my cares by this kind of diversion; for the string will not bear to be always on the stretch, but must occasionally be loosened from the bow's end. Thus I wandered, my feet moving mechanically, whilst my eye swept over the expanse of waters. But it was not then as when the purple waves roll gently forward and break softly on the shore, for, to use the words of Scripture, 'the sea had arisen, by reason of a great wind that blew.' The billows, as they approached from a distance, increased in size, reared their crests, and discharged themselves on the beach with a thundering sound. But roar as they might, the rocks stood unmoved, regardless of the waves that broke against them. As I gazed I thought a profitable lesson was to be learnt from the sight, and how I might apply it to my own state of mind, when, as has recently happened, some untoward occurrence has burst upon me." [1]

Notwithstanding his rich Christian experience, Gregory was steeped in the superstitious spirit of the age. At Constantinople, as already remarked, he revived the practice of keeping birthday festivals, and publicly returned thanks to the martyrs for having so triumphantly assisted the true believers in their recent victory. We shall treat this subject more fully by-and-by.

The annexed passage from his *Oration on the Nativity* will convey an idea of his power to soar into the regions of abstract thought. "God ever was, and is, and will be. Or rather, He ever is; for the terms *was* and *will be* are portions of *our* fleeting duration and transient nature, but *He* always *is*; and thus He designated Himself when He appeared to Moses on the mount. For He comprehends in Himself all existence without commencement, without end, as it were a boundless and unfathomable ocean, rising above every conception both of time and nature. He is shadowed forth by the intellect alone, and that most obscurely and imperfectly, and not from the things which are inherent in Him, but from those which move around Him. Ideas collected from all parts of the

---

[1] Id., pp. 210–212, 217, 218.

Per. I.
Chap. 4.

creation combine to form a faint image of the Truth, which escapes before it is seized, and flies before it is understood, beaming for an instant on our mind, as the evanescent lightning glances on our sight; in order, as I suppose, that by the small portion which is comprehended it may allure us to itself (for that which is wholly incomprehensible is unhoped for and unattempted); and by what is unapprehended, may be admired; and being admired, may be loved the more; and being loved, may purify; and purifying, may render us divine."[1]

Another passage, less abstruse, with one of his plaintive hymns, will close this notice of Gregory.

"Christ was born indeed on the earth; but in his supernal nature He had been begotten. He was born of a woman indeed, but she was a virgin. If this was natural, that was preternatural. He was without a father in his earthly geniture, and without a mother in his heavenly generation. . . . He was oppressed with hunger, yet He fed thousands in the desert; and He is the living and celestial bread. He was parched with thirst, yet He cried aloud, 'If any man thirst, let him come unto me and drink.' He was weary, yet is He the rest of those who are weary and heavy-laden. He paid tribute, obtained miraculously from a fish, whilst He ruled over those to whom He paid the tribute . . . He wept, but He made tears to cease.

---

[1] Boyd, *Six Discourses by the Fathers*, pp. 107-109.

Because He was a man, He asked where Lazarus was laid; but He raised Lazarus from death, because He was God. He was sold for thirty pieces of silver, yet He bought the world at an inestimable price: for He bought it with his blood. He who drinks vinegar, and is fed with gall, is He who converted the water into wine, who has destroyed the bitterness of death, who is altogether sweetness, the desire of the heart. He dies, yet He gives life; and dying, He destroys death."[1]

A.D. 390.

Gregory to Himself.

Where are the winged accents? Lost in air.
    Where the fresh flower of youth and glory? Gone.
The strength of well-knit limbs? Brought low by care.
    Wealth? Plundered: nothing left but God alone.
Where those dear parents who my life first gave,
My brother, sister? Silent in the grave.

Not even my fatherland to me is left;
    The hostile billows sweep my country o'er;
And now with tottering steps, of all bereft,
    Exiled and homeless, weak and sad and poor,
No child my age to soothe with service sweet,
I wander day by day with weary feet.

What lies before me? Where shall set my day?
    Where shall these weary limbs at length repose?
What hospitable tomb receive my clay?
    What hands at last my failing eyes shall close,
Whose eyes will watch me—eyes with pity fraught,
Some friend of Christ? Or those who know Him not?

---

[1] Id., pp. 354–357. See a similar passage from Hippolytus in *Early Church History*, pp. 278, 279.

Or shall no tomb, as in a casket, lock
   This frame, when laid a weight of breathless clay,
Left without burial on the desert rock,
   Or thrown in scorn to birds and beasts a prey,
Consumed and cast in handfuls on the air,
Or sunk in some dark stream to perish there?

This as Thou wilt. The day will all unite,
   Wherever scattered, when thy word is said;
Rivers of flame, abysses without light,
   Thy great Tribunal, these alone I dread:
But Thou, O Christ, art fatherland to me,
Strength, wealth, repose, yea all I find in Thee.[1]

SECTION III. We left Basil's brother Gregory newly installed in his bishopric of Nyssa. This, it may be remembered, was in the reign of the Arian Emperor Valens. A full share of the troubles of the time fell to Gregory's lot, aggravated, it would seem, by an inaptitude on his part in dealing with men. The Imperial cook Demosthenes, whose acquaintance we have made, was appointed vicegerent of Pontus, with the understanding that he was to do all in his power to crush the adherents of the Nicene faith. Gregory was one of those who felt the weight of his tyrannical hand, and refusing to appear before a synod which was summoned to hear charges against him, he was deposed and banished, A.D. 376. In his exile he bewailed the cruel necessity which had compelled him to leave his spiritual children, and also dwells patheti-

---

[1] *The Voice of Christian Life in Song*, pp. 67, 68; slightly altered.

cally on the home of which he had been deprived —his fireside, his table, his pantry, his bed, his bench, his sackcloth, contrasting it with the stifling hole in which he was now forced to dwell, of which the only furniture was straitness, darkness, and cold. But he took comfort in the assurance that his brethren would remember him in their prayers.[1]

On the death of Valens, in 378, as already related, Gratian recalled the exiled bishops; and to the joy of the faithful, Gregory was restored to the see of Nyssa. His return was a triumphal progress. The inhabitants of the villages through which he passed poured forth to meet him, and escorted him along the road with acclamations and tears of joy. In the town the crowd was so dense as to impede his progress, and when he approached the church, a stream of flame poured into it from the multitude of lighted tapers, borne before him by the virgins who had come to welcome back their beloved bishop.[2]

The happiness of Gregory's return was, however, short-lived. Beside the severe labour and anxiety entailed upon him by the confusion consequent on the long reign of Arianism, he had to mourn the death of his brother Basil and his sister Macrina. It was many years since Gregory had seen his sister, and when at last he was able to visit her (in Pontus), he found her " hopelessly ill

---

[1] *Dict. Christ. Biog.*, art. Gregorius Nyssenus, ii. pp. 763, 764.
[2] Ibid.

Per. I.
Chap. 4.

of fever, with parched lips, and drenched with cold sweats. She was stretched on a couple of planks on the ground, one of them being sloped to support her head and shoulders, the wood barely covered with a piece of sackcloth. Her pallet faced the east. On her brother's approach she made an effort to rise and do him honour as a bishop; Gregory prevented her. With great self-command she restrained her groans, checked her asthmatic pantings, and, putting on a cheerful countenance, endeavoured to comfort her brother, who she saw was full of grief. When she spoke of Basil's death, Gregory broke down; but she rebuked him for sorrowing as those who have no hope," and in a rapturous spirit discoursed on the resurrection and the immortality of the soul. "Seeing he was weary, she sent him into the garden to rest in an arbour. The following day she employed her little remaining strength in consoling, animating, and instructing him. Then she prayed: 'Thou, O God, hast taken from me the fear of death. Thou hast granted me that the end of this life should be the beginning of true life . . . Remember me in thy kingdom; forgive whatsoever I have done amiss. Receive my soul without spot into thy hands as a burnt offering before Thee.' At last her voice failed; only her lips moved; she signed herself with the cross, gave a deep sigh, and her spirit took its flight." Round her neck was found an iron cross, and a ring containing a particle of the

"True Cross." She was buried by her brother in the grave of her parents, in the chapel of the Forty Martyrs. After her death many miracles were said to have been performed at her tomb.[1]

A.D. 378–379.

After settling some difficulties at home, Gregory undertook, by the desire of the Council of Antioch,[2] a long and toilsome journey to Babylon. He found the church in that city in a deplorable state. The people had " grown hardened in heresy, and brutish in their manners; lying was more natural to them than to speak the truth." His labour for their reformation seems to have met with but little success.[3]

During the half-century which had elapsed since the pretended discovery by the Empress Helena of the "True Cross," pilgrimages to Jerusalem had become frequent. On his way home Gregory visited the Holy City, the Emperor placing at his disposal one of the imperial carriages. Of this vehicle he made "both a monastery and a church," where he and his retinue kept up their daily fasting, psalmody, and hours of prayer. He visited

---

[1] Id., pp. 764, 765, and art. Macrina (2), iii. pp. 780, 781 ; Schaff, p. 905. Texier says that in the village Melebuhi, in Cappadocia, a few miles from Nyssa, the inhabitants, who are Greeks, still worship Saint Macrina, whose bones are supposed to lie in the neighbourhood. Possibly Gregory transported them thither: his own name is nearly forgotten.—*L'Univers Pittoresque, Asie Mineure*, p. 559. [2] A.D. 379.

[3] *Dict. Christ. Biog.*, ii. p. 765. From the time of Cyrus, Babylon rapidly declined; and at the commencement of the Christian era, the greater part of the city was in ruins. It continued to exist a few centuries longer, when it sank into the condition predicted by Isaiah, ch. xlii. 19-22.

8

Per. I.
Chap. 4.

Bethlehem, Calvary, the Mount of Olives, and the Church of the Holy Sepulchre. But although credulous and superstitious beyond many of his contemporaries, his faith received no confirmation from what he saw. His conscience was shocked by the gross immorality prevailing in the Holy City itself, which he describes as a sink of all iniquity. The evil was aggravated by Arian influences, to counteract which all his efforts were ineffectual. He returned home depressed and sorrowful. In letters written soon afterwards, he records his sense of the evil of pilgrimages. He points out that pious ladies travelling lonely roads with male attendants lay themselves open to suspicion; that the inns are notorious for dissolute conversation and loose manners; and that robbery and violence are not infrequent, even in the Holy Land itself, whose moral state he describes as infinitely below that of Cappadocia. He asks, moreover, whether a man will believe Christ's virgin-birth the more by seeing Bethlehem, or his resurrection by visiting his tomb, or his ascension by standing on the Mount of Olives. "Change of place," he wrote to a Cappadocian abbot, "brings God no nearer; God will come to thee if only the inn of thy soul is ready for Him." [1]

---

[1] Ibid.; Milman, iii. p. 192, and note; Schaff, pp. 467, 468. The pilgrims carried back with them water from the Jordan, earth from the Redeemer's sepulchre, and chips from the True Cross. Many even visited Arabia to behold Job's dunghill! But the East was not the only quarter, to which pilgrimages were made. Chrysostom lamented that want of time and

Two years later he attended the Council of Constantinople, where, as already said, he delivered the oration on the enthronement of Gregory Nazianzen. The last mention we have of him his presence at a synod held in the same city, A.D. 394, which was probably not long before the close of his life.[1]

A.D. 394.

---

health prevented him from going to Rome to kiss the chains of Peter and Paul, which "make devils tremble and angels rejoice." (*Hom.*) Jerome, however, though on his return to Bethlehem after one of his journeys, he quickened his steps that he might adore the manger and cradle of his Saviour, reminds his readers that "Britain is as near heaven as Jerusalem (Et de Ierosolymis et de Britaniâ æqualiter patet aula cœlestis), and that what is worthy of praise is not to have been at Jerusalem, but to have led a godly life there."—*Ep. lviii. ad Paulinum*, Opera, ed. Villarsii, t. i., p. 319; Schaff, p. 468. It is curious to see Britain instanced as a very *Ultima Thule*.

[1] *Dict. Christ. Biog.*, ii. p. 766. We are much indebted, both in this and other chapters, to the invaluable *Dictionary of Christian Biography*, by Dr. W. Smith and Professor Wace. We have drawn freely from the stores therein contained, signifying the same so far as was practicable by quotation marks and references in the foot-notes. A similar acknowledgment is due to some other recent works, *e.g.*, Stephens' *Life of St. Chrysostom*; Schaff's *Nicene and Post-Nicene Christianity*; Roberts' *Church Memorials*; Dr. Cutts' *St. Augustine* and *St. Jerome*; and Morison's *Life and Times of St. Bernard*.

CHAPTER V.

ULFILAS.[1]

HITHERTO we have traced the course of some of the most gifted leaders in the Christian Church within the pale of Roman civilisation. It was within the empire that Christianity was founded and established, and for a long time its organisation did not extend far beyond the frontiers. But a change was now coming over the existing civilisation. "All that is expressed by the words Christian and Teutonic is coming in; all that is expressed by the words Pagan and Roman is dying out . . . The Teuton rent away the provinces of the empire; but, in rending them away, he accepted the faith, the tongue, and, to a great extent, the law, of the empire."[2]

Of all the Teutonic nations, the Goths were the first to embrace Christianity, and their history is the most closely interwoven with that of declining

---

[1] *Chronologically*, this chapter should have preceded the last, but the historical order seems to be better consulted by following out the course of Arianism within the Empire, before referring to its fortunes beyond it.

[2] Freeman, *Methods of Historical Study*, p. 193. "This was of a truth the greatest conquest that Rome ever made; if Greece had once led captive her Roman conqueror, far more thoroughly did Rome lead captive her Teutonic conqueror."—Ibid.

Rome. "Driven like a wedge into the eastern side of Europe by the superincumbent weight of the Huns, they pass along the whole length of it, to be similarly thrust out at the west by the Franks. During this whole course they hold a place intermediate between barbarism and civilisation . . . They are not heathens, yet they are not acknowledged as Christians. Planted in an indefensible position by their Arian creed, they are crushed between the opposing masses of heathenism and Catholicism."[1]

A.D. circa 250.

The way in which Christianity was first made known to this people is related by Sozomen. "From the time of the wars under Gallus and his successors, between the Romans and the Goths, many priests were taken captive, and dwelt among those tribes. They healed the sick, purged those who were possessed, and led a holy and blameless life; and the barbarians, marvelling at their life and miracles, sought to imitate their example."[2] So also Philostorgius: "During the reigns of Valerian and Gallienus (253–268), a great body

---

[1] *Ulfilas, Apostle of the Goths,* by Charles A. Anderson Scott, pp. vii., viii. The campaign which Clovis undertook against the Visigoths, A.D. 507, was in fact a war of the Catholic priesthood against the Arians. Rich presents were sent to the shrine of St. Martin at Tours to purchase the saint's favour; and as the messengers crossed the threshold of the church, the precentor, as if by accident, chanted forth the verse: "Thou hast girded me with strength unto the battle; Thou hast subdued under me those that rose up against me" (Ps. xviii. 39). Assured by this token, Clovis pressed forward in full reliance on the protection of the saint.—*British Quarterly Review,* January 1881, p. 86.

[2] *Eccles. Hist.,* b. ii. c. 6. Gallus reigned from 251 to 253.

Per. I.
Chap. 5.

of Goths laid waste Eastern Europe, and crossing into Asia, invaded Cappadocia and Galatia, whence they returned laden with spoil, and bringing with them many captives, amongst whom were not a few ecclesiastics. These pious men induced many of their conquerors to embrace Christianity."[1]

These vague generalities are all that we know of the conversion of the Gothic tribes until we come to Ulfilas.[2] With the name of this illustrious man the Gothic Church is identified; he may almost be regarded as its founder, leader, and bishop; from his hands it received not the Scriptures only, but the very alphabet by which to read them. "He is," said Constantine the Great, "the Moses of the Goths."[3] The sources of information regarding him, though still very scanty, were augmented in 1840 by the discovery, in the library of the Louvre, of a manuscript containing a notice of him, and especially of his creed, by his friend and pupil Auxentius, Arian bishop of Dorostorus (now Silistria).[4]

Ulfilas was born about the year 311, and appears to have been the descendant of the Cappadocian captives mentioned above.[5] When still a youth

---

[1] *Eccles. Hist.*, b. ii. c. 5.

[2] It should, however, be mentioned that amongst the bishops who were present at the Council of Nicæa was a "Theophilus," before whose name stood the words "De Gothis," and after it the word "Bosphoritanus." —Scott, p. 28. See also *Early Church History*, p. 411, note.

[3] Philostorgius, b. ii. c. 5.   [4] Scott, pp. 32, 33.

[5] Philostorgius, *loc. cit.*; Article on Ulfilas by T. Hodgkin, in the *Edinburgh Review*, October 1877, pp. 365, 366.

he was sent with others of his countrymen by the ruler of the Gothic nation on an embassy to the court of Constantine, A.D. 332. From this time it is probable he resided (perhaps as a hostage) in the city of Constantinople. Here he acquired or perfected his knowledge of Greek and Latin, became a reader in the church (*lector*), commenced his translation of the Bible, and formed an acquaintance with Eusebius, the Arian or Homoi-ousion bishop of Nicomedia.[1] Sozomen says that before he went to Constantinople he held the orthodox faith, but that the theological arguments of the Arian bishops, or their promise to forward his suit with the Emperor if he would conform to their opinions, caused him to join their party. This statement is contradicted by Ulfilas himself; his Arian creed, as preserved in the manuscript of Auxentius, commencing with the words, "I, Ulfilas, bishop and confessor, have always thus believed."[2]

At the age of thirty, A.D. 341, Ulfilas was consecrated bishop of the Goths by Eusebius, and sent beyond the Danube to preach the Gospel to his countrymen. Here he laboured until the success of his efforts alarmed the Gothic sovereign, and gave rise to a persecution in which "many servants and handmaids of Christ yielded up their

---

[1] Philostorgius, *loc. cit.*; Scott, pp. 51, 52. Auxentius speaks of him as preaching constantly in Greek, Latin, and Gothic.—Id.

[2] Sozomen, b. vi. c. 37; Scott, pp. 36, 37.

lives." At the end of seven years Ulfilas himself, with a great body of his converts, was expelled, and crossing the Danube took refuge within the empire, where he was honourably received by the Emperor Constantius. They settled in Mœsia, at the foot of the Balkan Mountains,[1] " possessors," says Jordanes,[2] " of cattle, pastures, forest, and a modicum of wheat, but otherwise poor and unwarlike." Here Ulfilas continued to govern and instruct them, and they in return yielded to him the most confiding obedience, being firmly convinced that he could neither utter nor do anything evil.[3]

From this time we hear no more of Ulfilas for twenty years, except that in 360 he attended a synod of Arian bishops at Constantinople, at which the creed of Ariminum was adopted, and was subscribed by Ulfilas.[4]

In 370 the Gothic ruler Athanaric renewed the persecution in Dacia, and many Christians were put to death or driven to take refuge on Roman soil. In this instance it was not only Arians who were thus harassed, but also Catholics and Audians. These last were the followers of Audius, a zealous man of pure life, who in Syria made himself obnoxious by censuring the vices of the

---

[1] Around Nicopolis, near the site of the modern Tirnova.
[2] Sometimes written Jornandes.
[3] Sozomen, loc. cit.; Scott, pp. 54-58.
[4] Socrates, b. ii. c. 41; Sozomen, b iv. c. 24.

clergy. Being banished to Scythia,[1] he made his A.D. 370. way into the interior of Gothia, and himself and his successors gathered congregations and founded convents for men and women. The names of some of the martyrs in this persecution have been preserved. One was Saba, respecting whom the afflicted Church, after the manner of the Church at Smyrna,[2] when it testified to the victorious faith of Polycarp, issued an encyclical letter: "The Church of God which is in Gothia to the Church of God which is in Cappadocia, and to all Christians of the Catholic Church wheresoever in the world they dwell:—Mercy, peace and love, from God the Father, and Jesus Christ our Lord, be fulfilled."[3]

From this letter it appears that the Gothic princes and magistrates insisted on the Christians eating meat which had been sacrificed to idols. Some of the heathens, touched with compassion, secretly substituted instead of the offerings meat which had not been thus polluted; but Saba, who had known the faith from a child, scorned the subterfuge, declaring that no true Christian could accept escape on such terms. The persecution cooled for a season, but broke out again in a general inquisition, from which Saba's would-be friends again sought to shield him by swearing that there were no Christians in the village. But Saba burst into the assembly, exclaiming, "Let no one

---

[1] Scythia parva, now the Dobrudscha.
[2] See *Early Church History*, pp. 74–80.   [3] Scott, pp. 71–84.

swear for me, for I am a Christian." Summoned before the chief persecutor, he was, on the discovery of his poverty, contemptuously dismissed, as one who could do neither good nor harm. Some time afterwards it became known that Saba was keeping Easter with a presbyter. The king's son came into the village by night with a band of armed men, and carried off both Saba and the presbyter naked and bound. Neither torture nor promises could induce Saba to touch the polluted meat. Left for the night made fast to a log, he was released by a compassionate woman, but nevertheless refused to escape. A beam being fastened to his neck, he was thrown into the river Musæus and drowned, confessing with his last breath his faith in God, and glorifying the Saviour's name. His body was recovered and taken away by Julius Soranus, the *dux*, or Roman governor, of Scythia, himself a Christian, who, to use the words of the Church Letter, "has by permission of the presbytery sent the same to Cappadocia to your Church, a precious gift, and glorious fruit of the faith." The foregoing particulars derived from the *Acts of the Saints* [1] are confirmed by some letters of Basil. Writing to Julius Soranus, Basil says : "In all the good thou doest thou layest up treasure for thyself; and thou wilt do well, if thou shouldst also send to

---

[1] *Acta Sanctorum*, the great collection of saintly biographies by the Bollandists and their successors.

thy fatherland relics of the martyrs, since, as thou hast reported, the persecution is even now creating martyrs for the Lord." And in a letter to another correspondent, Basil, groaning under "the state of his own Church, the coldness of the love, the strife of parties, the zeal which caused bitterness, but neither roused nor could support persecution," tells how his heart had been warmed by receiving the relics of a martyr from the barbarians beyond the Danube.[1]

A.D. 370.

Eating polluted meat was not the only test by which the Christians were tried; Sozomen describes how a wooden idol placed upon a waggon was drawn through the villages, and the Christians were summoned to come forth from their houses to worship and offer sacrifice to it. On their refusal the heathens burnt their dwellings to the ground, and their occupants within them. On one occasion, some men, with their wives and children, who had been driven by fear or force to offer sacrifice, fled "to the tent of the church," to which the pagans set fire, and consumed it with all who were therein.[2]

The bulk of the Gothic nation still remained pagan. In 375 the shock of the Huns, that "terrible 'riding folk,' who had just passed the Gate of Nations and entered Europe," shattered the empire of the Ostrogoths on the Volga. Pur-

---

[1] Scott, pp. 71-84.   [2] Sozomen, b. vi. c. 37 ; Scott, pp. 84-88.

suing their wild victorious march, they came upon the Visigoths in Dacia, and drove them forward as far as the waters of the Danube. The Romans from the southern shore of the great river beheld the opposite bank crowded with a countless multitude—men, women, and children, "looking behind them with terror for the approach of the dreaded foe, and stretching out their hands to the land of plenty and of safety which lay before them. Their chief Frithigern sent envoys to the Emperor Valens, begging him to receive his flying people and give them leave to settle on Roman soil. Valens, after long debate with his advisers, consented, and almost before the negotiations were complete, the impatient people, 200,000 armed men with their families, began to cross. Some attempting to swim over were drowned, others crossed on rafts and canoes; while the main body were transported in boats. The passage lasted through several days and nights."[1]

With their change of country the Visigoths exchanged also their national religion. The Catholic historian Jordanes relates that when the envoys besought the Emperor to grant them shelter, they promised, if he would give them teachers in their own tongue, to become Christians; and that the Emperor, who was smitten with the perverted faith of the Arians, and had suppressed all the orthodox Churches, sent them for preachers

---

[1] Id., pp. 62, 63; Ammianus Marcellinus, b. xxxi. c. 4.

supporters of his own creed. "The Goths," continues Jordanes, "having come thither ignorant and unlearned, were thus imbued with the poison of this perverted faith; and afterwards in their turn, sending forth preachers to carry the Gospel in the same guise to the Ostrogoths and Gepidæ, all the nations of this speech were drawn into the same sect."[1]

A.D. 378.

Through the greed and folly of the imperial officers, the conditions of the treaty were, in the absence of the Emperor, shamefully violated, and the Goths were turned from subjects into enemies. They flew to arms and invaded Thrace, and in 378 a great battle was fought between them and the imperial forces, near Adrianople, which was so disastrous to the Roman arms, as to be called a second Cannæ. Valens himself was slain. He was carried wounded to a cottage, to which the barbarians, ignorant of the prize it contained, set fire, and thus destroyed at once the enemy of their nation and the champion of their faith. This manner of death, Jordanes, with the other orthodox historians who relate it, regards as a judgment from God, "who," say they, "inflicted upon Valens the same torture of burning which, by perverting their faith, the Emperor had secured for the Goths in the world to come."[2]

---

[1] Scott, pp. 93, 94.
[2] Gibbon, iii. pp. 403, 405; Ammianus Marcellinus, b. xxxi. c. 13; Scott, p. 92.

On the form of Christianity which the Goths received, Mr. Scott observes: "In this dim twilight of Arianism the figure of the Christ appeared familiar to them, and comprehensible by its resemblance to their own old deities who stood between man and the absolute divine—the All-Father. It did not cost them much to exchange these demigods, who were just one step removed from heroes, for one heroic figure, in whom all the powers and qualities of the rest should combine. But the All-Father remained as far removed as ever from reach and contact of human needs. Christ was not God come down from Heaven to reveal the God-head in the flesh, to deliver man from sin; He was a creature like man, exalted above man by the design and will of the Father, not by virtue of his own divine essence . . . It was thus that the Arian Christ found responsive acceptance in the Teutonic mind. They pictured Him as a king upon earth, moving about the highways of Palestine, attended by troops of loyal followers, from among whom He had chosen the Twelve as captains. When He 'went up into a mountain,' and took his seat, his captains stood in obedient readiness before Him, and all below and around, the faithful host was waiting to hear his commands. Or if at any time the Teutonic mind took a deeper and more spiritual view of the Saviour's work, it was as the Healer that they loved to behold Him, moving about amongst suffering humanity, touching for the evil, restoring sight and power and hearing. Nevertheless," he continues, " Teutonic Arianism is to be carefully distinguished from Hellenic Arianism. Even if the two could be shown to occupy the same platform of belief, the moral value of the same faith was very different in and for the two parties who had approached it from different directions. For the Goth it was an upward step in faith when he confessed a belief in an historic revelation, and submitted himself to the teaching of the Gospel through which Jesus was manifested as the Son of God. For the Hellenic Christian the acceptance of an Arian creed, or of any of the Post-Nicene compromises, was a step backwards and downwards. He left the high-level of conception of the nature of God, to which, after a great struggle and, as it were, by a supreme effort, the Nicene Council had sprung ; and he fell back upon a philosophical heathenism, which began by denying the God-head of Christ, and afterwards sought to bring about a compromise of faith with reason at the cost of logic, by proclaiming Christ to be God, but God in the ' second degree.' " [1]

Ulfilas' own creed is preserved and expanded by Auxentius. The diversity between its language and that of Nicæa is of the most subtle kind, but amounts when pursued to its logical

---

[1] *Ulfilas*, pp. 104–106.

Per. I.
Chap. 5.

issue to this, that whilst the Son is held to be the Creator and Maker of all things, King, Redeemer, Saviour, and Judge, he is yet only a "Second God," subject and obedient in all things to the Father; and that the Holy Spirit is neither God nor Lord, but the minister of Christ, subject and in all things obedient to the Son. But whilst Ulfilas thus rejected the Homo-ousion faith, he professed in after-life but little more affinity with the Homoi-ousion party, with whom he had at first been associated. "Not only," says Auxentius, "did he spurn and trample on the detestable and abominable confession of the Homo-ousions as an invention of the devil; but being himself most carefully instructed out of the Holy Scriptures he also deplored and shunned the error and impiety of the Homoi-ousions."[1]

Ulfilas' translation of the Bible marks an era in the history of the Church. It was the earliest version of the Scriptures into an unlettered tongue; it was, moreover, the first translation into one of the dialects of that great family of nations "in whose hands was the future of the world." Philostorgius tells us that Ulfilas translated all the books of both the Old and New Testaments, with the exception of Samuel and the Kings, which he omitted because of the wars that are related in them, judging that his people, who

---

[1] Id., pp. 108-116.

were passionately fond of war, were more in need of a bit than of a spur.¹ The translation was lost to sight for many centuries; but about the year 1500 the four Gospels² were discovered in the monastery of Werden in Westphalia, near Düsseldorf, arranged in the order of Matthew, John, Luke, and Mark. This is the famous *Codex Argenteus* (or Silver Book), now in the library of Upsala University. At the end of the sixteenth century it found its way to Prague, whence it was carried off by the Swedes after the siege in 1648, and presented by the victorious Königsmark to Queen Christina.³

A.D. 332-381.

The manuscript is referred to the close of the fifth century, a hundred years after the death of Ulfilas, and is believed to have been written in Italy, probably at Ravenna. It is on purple vellum, in letters of silver, "a few words at the beginning of each section being blazoned in gold. At the bottom of each page a sort of gallery of four arches resting on Corinthian columns, suggests the influence of the architecture of Ravenna on the mind of the amanuensis, and serves the useful purpose of enclosing the numbers which under the well-known name of the *Eusebian*

---

[1] *Eccles. Hist.*, b. ii. c. 5; Scott, p. 53. Socrates (b. iv. c. 33) and Sozomen (b. vi. c. 37) also say that Ulfilas invented the Gothic letters. He formed them chiefly from the Greek.

[2] Or rather portions of them, for nearly half the leaves were missing.

[3] Scott, pp. 125-127.

Per. I.
Chap. 5.

Canons enabled the student, before the introduction of chapters and verses, readily to compare the text of one gospel with the parallel passages in the other three."[1]

We naturally ask whether any trace of Arian doctrine is to be discovered in Ulfilas' translation. Little evidence of this kind has been detected; but in Philippians ii. 6, " Who being in the form of God thought it not robbery to be equal with God," the Greek ἴσα (equal) is rendered by the Gothic *galeiko* (German *gleich*, English *like*), a word everywhere else used for the Greek ὅμοιος (like). " The substitution of *likeness* for *equality* in the relation of the Son to the Father is the point most characteristic of the party to which Ulfilas belonged."[2]

Another inquiry, interesting equally to the missionary and the scholar, is, how did Ulfilas, in this first essay to clothe the Gospel in the language of an uncivilized tribe, render the Greek terms relating to Sin and Redemption? Mr.

---

[1] T. Hodgkin, *Edinburgh Review*, pp. 368, 369; Scrivener, *Plain Introduction to the Criticism of the New Testament*, 1883, pp. 405, 406. In 1736 a Gothic manuscript came to light at Wolfenbüttel, which was found to contain large portions of the Epistle to the Romans; and in 1817 Cardinal Mai deciphered several other manuscripts, apparently of the sixth century, from the monastic library at Bobbio in Lombardy. By means of these a considerable part of Paul's Epistles and of the missing Gospels has been supplied, together with some verses from Nehemiah and Esdras, a quotation from the Psalms, and allusions to passages in Genesis and Numbers. With these small exceptions, the whole of the Old Testament, together with the Acts of the Apostles, the Catholic Epistles and the Apocalypse, are still wanting.—Scott, pp. 128, 129.   [2] Scott, pp. 133, 134.

Scott thus answers the question: "The word for Law is not command, but *Vitoth*, from *vitan*, to know, and thus signifies self-knowledge, conscience, corresponding exactly with the Apostle's description, 'a law unto themselves.' Sin is *Fra-waurhts* (compare our *froward*). As to condemnation: Amongst tribes where every stranger was a foe, the simplest and worst punishment an injured community could inflict was to drive the offender from their midst. He became a wanderer on the face of the earth, or in Teutonic phrase, a *vearges*, or wolf; and Ulfilas making use of *gavarjan* and its derivatives, pictured the sinner after judgment as the outcast and the wanderer." In his treatment of the words ᾅδης and γέεννα, Ulfilas manifested a more critical mind than the translators of our Authorised Version, who rendered both alike by the word Hell. In the Gothic it is the former only which is thus represented, namely, by "Halja (the hollow place), in accordance with the old Teutonic mythology in which Hel was known as the goddess of the place of darkness and of the newly-departed." The word γέεννα, the valley of Hinnom, he left untranslated, writing it *gaiainna*. "Parallel with the notion of sin as a crime, and redemption as the payment of the penalty it had entailed, was the conviction, deep-rooted in Teutonic thought and language, that Sin is a disease, and the Redeemer a healer. The Greek σώζειν (to save) is represented by the Gothic *nasjan.* Salvation was regarded as 'healing;' the Saviour was the Nasjands, the 'Healer.'"[1]

But the importance and interest which the Gothic translation possesses for the Christian and the scholar is doubled in the case of those nations which, like ourselves, belong to the Teutonic stock. The language of Ulfilas is the eldest branch of the Teutonic tree, and in its grammar and vocabulary it is easy to trace a close affinity with the English of the present day. More than this, to the student of comparative philology these fragments of the Gothic Scriptures are invaluable, as supplying a link in the chain between the various forms of the Teutonic tongue and the ancient Sanskrit with which they are radically connected.

The translation thus made was a priceless treasure to the northern tribes for many ages. "Goths and Vandals alike carried it with them on their wanderings through Europe. Whether as a religious observance, or in the superstitious hope of reading the future on the chance-appointed page, it was consulted on the battle-fields of Gaul before the fight began. In Italy it was diligently compared with the Latin authorities, and notes were made of the discrepancies. The Vandals took it into Spain and Africa, and with their leader Genseric it came round again to Rome."[2]

---

[1] Id., pp. 134-136. [2] Id., pp. 136, 137.

Besides the Bible, Ulfilas made other transla- A.D. 381.
tions, and composed treatises in Gothic for the use of his people. In 381, the year of the great Orthodox Council, Theodosius summoned Ulfilas to Constantinople. Although the Emperor was bent on crushing the Arians, it was yet his policy to flatter the Goths, whose stalwart warriors were the support of his throne. A schism had taken place in the Arian ranks, and it is no slight tribute to Ulfilas that he appears to have been chosen as the only man who could reconcile the disputants. He was aged and infirm; and he had no sooner reached the city than he was seized with a mortal sickness. The matter on which he had been called had weighed much on his mind, but before he had begun to put his hand to it, he was, in the words of his admiring biographer, "taken up to heaven after the manner of Elijah the prophet."[1]

Great as was the work of Ulfilas, and mighty as was his influence in his own age, that influence had little of lasting effect. The changes of events in the West were rapid, and they destroyed any abiding traces of his labours. Moreover, "the professor of an Arian or Semi-Arian creed could not become the apostle of Teutonic Christendom, and the Goth, foremost and noblest branch of the great family, was too soon cut off by the sword of

---

[1] Id., pp. 137-139; T. Hodgkin, *op cit.*, pp. 392, 393

134 SPECIMEN OF THE *CODEX ARGENTEUS.*

Per. I.
Chap. 5.

the East-Roman or trampled under the horsehoofs of the Saracen."[1]

The annexed chromo-lithograph is a fac-simile of a page from the *Codex Argenteus,* reduced to rather less than one-half the size of the original.[2] The Gothic in Roman characters with the English translation are subjoined. The *th* in Gothic is a single character.

MARK vii. 3-7.

thairh *Marku.*

3. iudaieis niba ufta thwahand handuns ni matjand. habandans anafilh thize sinistane.
4. jah af mathla niba daupjand ni matjand. 'jah anthar ist manag thatei andnemun du haban daupeinins stikle jah aurkje jah katile jah ligre:
5. thathro than frehun ina thai fareisaieis jah thai bokarjos. du hwe thai siponjos theinai ni gaggand bi thammei ana fulhun thai sinistans. ak unthwahanaim handum matjand hlaif.
6. ith is andhafjands q'ath du im. thathei waila praufetida esaïas bi izwis thans liutans. swe gamelith ist. so managei wairilom mik sweraith. ith hairto ize fairra habaith sik mis.
7. ith sware mik blotand. laisjandans . . .

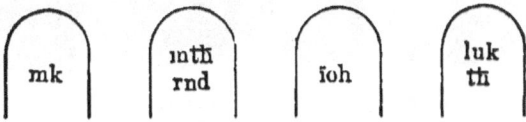

---

[1] Freeman, *op. cit.,* p. 194.

[2] It is copied by permission of the publishers from Dahn's *Urgeschichte der Germanischen und Romanischen Völker,* in Oncken's *Allgemeine Geschichte,* pt. 33 (Berlin, 1881); assisted by a photograph, kindly sent to us by Dr. Claes Annerstedt, librarian of Upsala University.

Facsimile of a page from the *Codex Argenteus* (Gospels in Gothic); reduced. End of the fifth century.

SPECIMEN OF THE *CODEX ARGENTEUS.* 135

By *Mark* (understood).[1]

A.D. 332-381.

3. . . . the Jews, except they wash their hands oft, eat not, holding the tradition of the elders.
4. And *when they come* from the market-place except they wash (baptize) they eat not: and many other things there be which they have received to hold, washings (baptizings) of cups and pots, and brazen vessels and couches.
5. And the Pharisees and the Scribes asked Him, Why walk not thy disciples according to the tradition of the elders, but eat bread with unwashen hands?
6. But he answered and said unto them, Well did Esaias prophesy of you hypocrites, as it is written, This people honoureth Me with their lips, but their heart is far from Me,
7. but in vain do they worship Me, teaching . . .

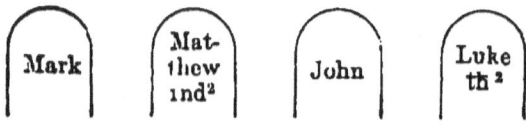

[1] The *name* of the Evangelist is on the *opposite* page in the *Codex.*

[2] These are in the original the Gothic characters for the Greek letters of the *Eusebian Canons*, a system adopted by Eusebius the historian for finding the parallel passages of the four Gospels.

CHAPTER VI.

MARTIN OF TOURS.

Per. I. Chap. 6.

HITHERTO the scene of our history has been in the East; we now turn for a while to France and Italy.

Martin, born about A.D. 316, was the child of heathen parents, and a native of Pannonia; but his infancy was passed at Pavia in Italy, where his father was stationed as a military tribune. When only ten years of age, he felt the need of something which heathenism could not supply, and making his way to the church demanded to be received as a catechumen. His ambition was to be a hermit, but his father compelled him, at the age of fifteen, to enter the army. It is to this period of his life, between his fifteenth and eighteenth year, that the well-known incident of the beggar and the cloak, so familiar to us in the picture galleries of Europe, belongs. Being with his regiment at Amiens during a winter of unusual severity, he met at one of the city gates a poor man naked and shivering. Martin's purse was empty, but with his sword he divided his military cloak, and gave one-half of it to the beggar. That night he had a dream. He saw Christ Himself clad in that half cloak, and heard him say to the angels who stood around, "Martin, though only a catechumen, has clothed me with his garment."[1]

The barbarians having made an irruption into the Gallic provinces, a donative was to be distributed to the soldiers of the army, then stationed at Worms on the Rhine. Martin, who had always chafed under the military service, embraced the occasion to solicit his discharge. When it was his turn to receive the gift he said to the general: "Hitherto I have been *thy* soldier; let me now be *God's*. I am the soldier of Christ; it is not lawful for me to fight." The general tauntingly replied that it was not for the sake of religion Martin wished to quit the service, but for fear of the battle which was to be fought the next day. Martin answered with firmness: "If my conduct is attributed to cowardice, and not to faith, to-morrow I will stand unarmed in front of the line, and in the name of the Lord Jesus, protected by the cross, instead of shield or helmet, will penetrate secure into the thickest ranks of the enemy." He was placed under arrest, to be taken at his word. The next day, however, the enemy sued for peace.[2]

At length obtaining his discharge Martin was taken into the household of Hilary,[3] bishop of Poictiers. The condition of his parents, who still remained pagans, lay heavy on his heart, and he

---

[1] *Life of St. Martin*, by Sulpicius Severus, c. i., in Ruffner's *Fathers of the Desert*, ii. p. 68 et seqq.   [2] Ibid.   [3] See *ante*, p. 25, note.

felt himself impelled by filial duty to visit them. On his way, while crossing the Alps, he fell in with a band of robbers. One of them raised an axe and aimed a blow at his head, but another intercepted the stroke. However, his hands were bound behind him, and he was delivered to one of the party to be stripped of what he had. The man took him aside, and asked who he was. He answered, "A Christian." He then asked him whether he felt afraid? Martin calmly replied that he never felt more secure, being confident that the Lord's mercy is especially with his servants in times of trial; but that he grieved for those who, living by robbery, had forfeited the favour of Christ. The robber was convicted in his conscience, released Martin, and set him on his way, begging his prayers.[1]

Martin's mother received the faith, but his father remained a heathen. In that part of the empire Arianism was in the ascendant, and Martin, whose repugnance to heresy was almost as strong as his zeal against idolatry, became so offensive to the inhabitants by his teaching that he was publicly scourged and compelled to depart. On his way back he tarried at Milan, but the Arian bishop Auxentius could not tolerate his presence, and he withdrew to the little island of Gallinaria.[2]

In 360 he returned to Hilary, and settling him-

---

[1] *Life of St. Martin*, c. ii.
[2] Ibid.: Gallinaria lies off the Riviera, near Albenga.

self five miles from Poictiers, on land which that bishop gave him, planted what is believed to have been the earliest monastery in Gaul. His reputation soon spread, and in 371 he was called, by the popular voice, to the bishopric of Tours. "It required 'a pious fraud' to entice him from his monastery. A leading citizen of Tours, pretending that his wife was ill, begged Martin to come and visit her. A crowd, not only of the people of the city, but collected also from neighbouring towns, had been gathered, and the all but unanimous desire was for the election of Martin. A few objected that his personal appearance was mean, his garments sordid, and his hair unkempt (the outward signs of a monk). One of the objectors was a bishop named *Defensor*. At the service that day the reader whose turn it was to officiate failed, through pressure of the crowd, to arrive in time." A priest who stood by took up the Psalter, and, opening at hazard, read from the 8th Psalm. The second verse, "Out of the mouths of babes and sucklings hast Thou established strength, because of thine adversaries," ended in the Latin translation then in use, "*ut destruas inimicum et defensorem*" (that Thou mightest destroy the enemy and the defender, *defensor*).[1] On hearing this last word, Martin's friends raised a shout of triumph. The Reader's choice of the psalm was

---

[1] Jerome, in the Vulgate, substituted the word *avenger*, as we have it in the Authorised Version.

regarded as a Divine inspiration, and the opponents were confounded.[1]

Martin, although he faithfully discharged his episcopal duties, still longed for his monkish manner of life. He was impatient of the frequent interruptions to his devotions. Leaving the city, therefore, he founded a monastery at the foot of a precipitous rock on the Loire. Some of the cells, his own amongst them, were built of logs rudely joined together, but most of the eighty brethren whom he gathered round him, dwelt in grottoes or cavities hollowed out of the rock. Unlike Basil's monks, they practised no industry except the art of writing, which was assigned to the younger members; the elder gave themselves incessantly to prayer and devotional exercises. Their austerities were of the severest kind. Sulpicius Severus, Martin's biographer, saw one of them balancing himself in a most painful position. His eyes were fixed on a cross, and his left hand rested on a skull, whilst he continually lacerated his naked breast with a flint, his lips moving, but without sound, to the form of the words, "Mea culpa, mea culpa, mea maxima culpa."[2] Some of the monks were men of noble birth, but whether gentle or simple, they had all things in common, retaining no property, no earthly interests, no will of their own. Obedience was the pivot on which

---

[1] *Life of St. Martin*, c. iii.; *Dict. Christ. Biog.*, iii. p. 840.
[2] "My sin, my sin, my heinous sin."

their life turned. Not a word was spoken at their meals, which consisted of bread, vegetables, and olives. Everything in the way of recreation was banished; the only emulation was who should fast the longest, practise the most painful postures, wear the roughest hair-cloth to irritate the skin, relate the most extravagant visions, and come nearest to Martin in preternatural deeds.[1]

Martin's reputation for miraculous powers equalled the fame of his sanctity. Sulpicius saw groups of people carrying the sick and infirm to his cell to be healed. "If we can but receive his blessing," said they, "these will be made whole; or if we can only get within his shadow or touch his garment; or if this be denied us, we will kiss the place where he has sat, or the path he has trod." Peasants, pointing to their sheep and cattle, said, "We have to thank the holy Martin for expelling the rot from our flocks, and the murrain from our herds." Even the Roman prefects were kept in awe by the dread of incurring the displeasure of a man whose word could "paralyze their limbs, or fix them to the ground upon which they stood"![2]

Many of the miracles, indeed, which Martin is

---

[1] *Life of St. Martin*, c. iii.; Gilly's *Vigilantius and his Times*, pp. 149, 150. "The lives of the monks," observes Ruffner, "were so monotonous and insipid; they had so little of nature, reason, or learning in or about them, and such dreamy notions of spiritual things, that miracles became a necessary stimulant to them."—*Fathers of the Desert*, i. p. 287, note.

[2] *Life of St. Martin*, c. iv.

said to have performed were of the magical type so common in the stories of the *Arabian Nights*. Meeting a procession of peasants, whom he supposed to be carrying round the images of their gods, he lifted up his crucifix, and at his bidding they became immovable as so many rocks. But when he discovered that it was a funeral train, he raised his hand again and set them free. Another time his long black cloak alarmed the horses of a treasure-waggon and threw them into confusion. The impatient soldiers vented their anger on Martin, and beat him unmercifully. But when they returned to their horses, they found them fixed to the spot like brazen statues; and it was not until they threw themselves at the saint's feet and implored his forgiveness, that the animals recovered their power of motion.

One more legend may be given as typical of many. After he had destroyed an ancient village temple, he proceeded to cut down a pine-tree close by. The priest and the pagan populace had held their peace while their idol-house was being pulled down, but began to resist when the sacred tree was threatened. When Martin reasoned with them, one of them answered, "If thou hast any faith in thy God, let us cut this tree down, and do thou catch it when it is falling; if the Lord is with thee, thou wilt not be harmed." Martin accepted the condition, and so did all the pagans, deeming that the loss of their tree would be well compensated by the death of their sacrilegious enemy. They bound him therefore and set him in the spot where it was evident the tree must fall. Then they began exultingly to hew it down. The crowd of wondering spectators stood at a respectful distance. Presently the pine began to nod and bend over the place where Martin stood. The monks grew pale; their terror augmented as the danger increased; they lost all hope, looking only for his death. But he awaited the falling tree with quiet confidence, and when it cracked, and came rushing down towards him, he raised his hands and held up against it the "sign of salvation" (the cross). Suddenly arrested in its downward course, the tree whirled round like a top and fell in another direction, nearly crushing the rustics who thought themselves out of danger. A cry of wonder and dismay from the pagans rent the sky; the monks wept for joy. There was scarcely one of all the heathen multitude who did not that day offer himself as a catechumen.[1]

Martin's work as a bishop was especially to do battle with paganism. Although the law forbade heathen sacrifices, the country people throughout a great part of Gaul still practised idolatry, and

---

[1] Id., c. iv.; *Dialogues* of Sulpicius Severus, ii. § 4, in Ruffner, ii. pp. 150, 151; Gilly, p. 144. Martin was worshipped by his own people. At a certain village he lodged in the vestry of the church. "On his departure all the virgins rushed into the room, licked every spot where he had sat or stood, and divided among themselves the straw on which he had lain."—*Dialogues*, ii. § 8.

Martin, at the head of his monks, made regular campaigns through his extensive diocese, destroying the ancient temples and consecrated trees, and replacing them by churches and monasteries. "To his excited imagination Satan often assumed the visible forms of Jupiter, Mercury, Venus, or Minerva, in the fruitless endeavour to protect the tottering fanes."[1]

When the usurper Maximus kept his court at Trèves, A.D. 385, Martin was the only prelate who slighted his favours. He declared it was impossible to sit down to meat with a prince who had dethroned one emperor and slain another.[2] At length, however, the arguments or the solicitations of Maximus overcame his scruples, and he accepted an invitation to the imperial table. The banquet was attended by guests of the highest distinction, and the place of honour, on a couch close beside the Emperor, was assigned to Martin. In the midst of the feast a goblet of wine was, according to custom, brought to the sovereign. Maximus, who had set his mind on receiving the cup from the hands of the bishop, ordered that it should first be taken to Martin, who, he did not doubt, would think it an honour to pass it on to his prince. But Martin's notions of the priestly dignity did not fall below those of Cyprian and Basil, and, on the ground that a presbyter ranks

---

[1] Milman, *History of Christianity*, iii. p. 78.
[2] Valentinian II. and his brother Gratian.

higher than an emperor, when he had drunk he handed the goblet to his own chaplain.[1]

Martin's name is honourably associated with the unhappy fate of the Priscillianists. Priscillian was a Spaniard of birth and fortune, highly esteemed for his piety, his austerities and his eloquence. His opinions, which seem to have partaken both of the Gnostic and Manichean errors, excited the alarm of the bishops, and in the year 380 he was excommunicated, and the churches of his followers confiscated. The leaders of his party appealed to Damasus, bishop of Rome, and Ambrose of Milan, from neither of whom, however, could they obtain a hearing. They succeeded better by bribing the imperial master of offices, and by order of the Emperor Gratian their churches were restored to them. But when Maximus, after the murder of Gratian, came to Trèves, Ithacius, the chief of the Anti-Priscillianist party, brought the matter before him. Maximus referred it to a synod which was held at Bordeaux; and Instantius, a bishop who was first examined, was condemned. Upon this, Priscillian, distrustful of the tribunal, appealed to the Emperor, who by an arbitrary act, until then unheard-of, removed the cause to the Imperial Court. The bishops, from weakness and hatred to the Priscillianists, offered no resistance; but this usurpation of spiritual authority by a secular tribunal excited general indignation in

---

[1] *Life*, c. 6.

the Church. Ambrose of Milan, Siricius, who had succeeded Damasus in the see of Rome, and Martin protested against it, the last entreating that the matter might be disposed of in the customary way, namely, by the removal of the heretical bishops from their sees. Compassion for his fellow-men whose lives were thus jeopardised doubtless stimulated Martin's zeal for the honour of the Church. He presented himself at court, and implored the Emperor not to proceed with the trial. Maximus yielded to his entreaties, ordered the proceedings to be stayed, and promised that no blood should be shed. But as soon as Martin had left the city, the trial was resumed, Priscillian's property, which, if sentence of death should be passed upon him, would be confiscated, offering, it is said, a temptation too strong for the imperial virtue. The accused persons were put to the torture, until a confession of impure doctrines and practices was wrung from them. Ithacius, who had indecently urged on the trial, now handed over the matter to an inhuman magistrate, professing that his own episcopal character forbade him to proceed further in a case of life and death. Priscillian, with six of his adherents, amongst whom was Euchrotia, the widow of a distinguished poet and orator, were beheaded. Instantius was banished to the Scilly Islands, and others of the party were variously punished.[1]

---

[1] Neander, iv. pp. 491-495; Robertson, i. pp. 284-288.

Soon afterwards Martin came again to Trèves to A.D. 385. solicit the Emperor's clemency on behalf of some political offenders of Gratian's party. The bishops, hearing of his approach, entreated Maximus not to let him enter the city, unless he would promise to keep peace with them. Martin answered, that he would come with the peace of Christ. He was admitted, and the Emperor did all in his power to reconcile him to the bishops. Finding his efforts useless, he dismissed him in anger, and not only ordered that Gratian's adherents should be put to death, but sent a military commission into Spain for the summary trial of the rest of the Priscillianists. As soon as Martin, who had laboured assiduously to avert these measures, heard that the orders were signed, although it was night, he hastened to the palace, and offered to partake of the bread and wine with the bishops, if the Emperor would recall the military commission and spare the political prisoners. The Emperor consented; the orders were countermanded; and Martin went to the altar with the men whose hands, in his view, were stained with the blood of Priscillian and his fellow-sufferers.[1]

But no sooner was the Communion over than his conscience began to upbraid him. Unable to bear himself in the city, he set out for home the next day, perplexed and disconsolate. About ten

---

[1] Neander, iv. pp. 495, 496.

miles on the road there was a lonely wood. Sending forward his companions, he remained awhile by himself, anxiously pondering what had occurred, and by turns condemning and excusing his conduct. "Whilst thus occupied," writes his biographer, "he was favoured with a supernatural vision. An angel appeared to him and said, 'Martin, it is with good reason thou art pricked in thy heart. Retrieve thy virtue; resume thy firmness; lest thou risk not thy reputation only, but thy salvation.'" "Ever after," continues Sulpicius, "when Martin was engaged with the demoniacs, he used to confess, with tears, that the mischief of that Communion in which he joined for a moment, not in heart but by constraint, had sensibly diminished his supernatural gift." Sulpicius adds that for the remainder of his life he avoided all councils and assemblages of bishops.[1]

Martin attained to a good old age. With the weight of eighty years upon him, he betook himself to a place at the extremity of his diocese to settle a quarrel amongst the clergy. When he set out to return home, his strength suddenly failed, and he felt his end approaching. His disciples broke out into passionate laments at the loss they were about to sustain. He quieted them with words of prayer: "Lord, if I be yet necessary to thy people, I decline not the labour; thy will be

---

[1] Newman, *Church of the Fathers*, pp. 345, 346; *Dict. Christ. Biog.*, iii. pp. 842, 843.

done." In his sickness he continued his usual devotions, "compelling his failing limbs to serve his spirit in prayers and vigils, as he lay on his couch of sackcloth and ashes;" and on his attendants asking to be allowed to place straw under him, he made answer, "Sons, it becomes a Christian to die in ashes; were I to set any other example I should commit sin." They wished to turn him on his side to ease his position, but he replied that he desired to look up towards Heaven rather than upon the earth, that his spirit might, as it were, be setting out on its journey. The Satanic appearances which troubled him during his life are said to have been repeated even in his last moments. Seeing the evil spirit at his side, he rebuked him with the words: " Why standest thou here? Deadly one! thou shalt find nothing in me; Abraham's bosom is receiving me."[1]

The date of Martin's death is assigned to A.D. 397; it took place on the 11th of November, named from him Martinmas Day. His funeral was attended by 2,000 monks.[2]

His life, as related by his friend Sulpicius, who styles him his patron saint, is full of incredible stories. These stories were a little too marvellous for the educated classes even in that credulous

---

[1] Epistles of Sulpicius Severus, 3; Newman, pp. 347, 348.

[2] *Dict. Christ. Biog.*, iii. p. 843. Ninyas, who preached the Gospel to the Southern Picts, heard of Martin's death while he was labouring in Galloway, and dedicated to him the first stone church in the country.—Ibid.

age, so that Sulpicius is obliged to confess that there were some which the monks of Martin's own cloister could not receive.[1] The biography was the most popular work of the day. In his *Dialogues*, Sulpicius introduces Postumian the pilgrim, who has just related his travels, as requesting Sulpicius to repay him with some anecdotes of Martin. Sulpicius answers, "Is not the book which I have written on his life and miracles sufficient for thee?" "That book," replies Postumian, "I am well acquainted with; it never leaves my right hand. "Here," pulling it out of his bosom, "here it is, well-worn; it has been my constant associate and comforter by land and sea. The book has penetrated through the world, and supplies matter for agreeable reading to the whole population. Paulinus first carried it to Rome. Soon there was an eager scramble for it, to the great profit of the booksellers, who found the sale quicker than for any other book. It went far ahead of me in my travels. When I went to Africa, I found them reading it, through all the country of Carthage. The Cyrenian priest with whom I tarried on my way to Egypt was the only man without it, and he got permission to copy mine. At Alexandria nearly all the people have it by heart. It has gone through Egypt, Nitria, Thebaïd, and the region about Memphis.

---

[1] *Dialogues*, i. § 18: ii. § 14: iii. § 5.

In the desert I found it in the hands of an old man, who, as soon as he heard that I was an intimate friend of thine, charged me, as did all the brethren, that I should tell thee, if ever I reached home, by all means to complete the book, by putting in the miracles thou hadst omitted."[1]

The heathenism, which was supposed to have been destroyed by Martin's preaching and miracles, was not really dead, it had only changed its name. The saint's tomb became the resort of the afflicted, whether in mind or body, and innumerable wonders were believed to be wrought even by the very dust which covered it and the ends of the tapers which were burnt before it. Gregory of Tours, Martin's successor in the bishopric towards the end of the sixth century, observing that one of his own vineyards was every year injured by hailstorms, took a morsel of wax from one of the tapers at Martin's shrine, and fixed it to the top of a tall tree. The charm was effectual; from that time, we are told, the vines were spared. The very same irreverent language in which the people had been accustomed to address their divinities, they used towards Martin: "If thou dost not do what I request, we will burn for thee no more lamps nor pay thee any more honours."[2]

---

[1] *Dialogues*, i. § 15, 16: iii. § 16. Not a little of this popularity was due to the attraction of the style. "The *Dialogues*," observes Du Pin, "are so skilfully composed that one can never weary of reading them" (iii. p. 112).

[2] Neander, v. p. 183. Paulinus, an intimate friend of Sulpicius, in one

Per. I.
Chap. 6.

Cardinal Newman concludes his biography of Martin by relating one of his interviews with the Evil One. "One day, while Martin was praying in his cell, the Evil Spirit stood before him, environed in a glittering radiance; by such pretence more easily to deceive him; clad also in royal robes, crowned with a golden and jewelled diadem, with shoes covered with gold, with serene face and bright looks, so as to seem nothing so little as he was. Martin at first was dazzled at the sight; and for a long while both parties kept silence. At length the Evil One began: 'Acknowledge, O Martin, whom thou seest. I am Christ, I am now descending upon earth, and I wished first to manifest myself to thee.' Martin still kept silent, and returned no answer. The devil ventured to repeat his bold pretence; 'Martin, why hesitate believing, when thou seest I am Christ?' Then he, understanding by revelation of the Spirit, that it was the Evil One, and not God, answered, 'Jesus, the Lord, announced not that He should come in glittering clothing, and radiant with a diadem. I will not believe that

---

of his poems, relates a story of his patron saint Felix. "A man who was robbed of two favourite bullocks prayed vigorously to the saint, blamed his carelessness, and, declining the trouble of searching for his cattle, insisted that they should be restored to him on the spot. The saint being deaf to his prayers and reproaches, the man accused him as a party to the theft, and as a last resource threatened to die on the threshold of the church, and thus deprive him of the opportunity of restoring the bullocks. In the night a knocking was heard at the man's door; he rose in alarm, but was speedily comforted by seeing the horns of the beloved animals in the doorway."—Maitland's *Church in the Catacombs*, pp. 296, 297.

Christ is come, save in that state and form in which He suffered, *save with the show of the wounds of the Cross.*' At these words the other vanished forthwith as smoke, and filled the cell with so horrible an odour as to leave indubitable proof who he was. The application of this vision," observes the cardinal, " to Martin's age, is obvious. I suppose it means in this day, that Christ comes not in pride of intellect, or reputation for ability. These are the glittering robes in which Satan is now arrayed. Many spirits are abroad; more are issuing from the pit : the credentials which they display are the precious gifts of mind, beauty, riches, depth, originality. Christian, look hard at them with Martin in silence, and then ask for the print of the nails." [1]

A.D. 397.

---

[1] *Church of the Fathers*, pp. 352, 353; *Life*, by Sulpicius, c. 6.

CHAPTER VII.

AMBROSE.

Per. I. Chap. 7.   THE other Catholic Witnesses whom we have selected, all of whom were bishops except Jerome, rose to ecclesiastical rank through the regular

Episcopal Chair of Ambrose, of white marble, in the church of St. Ambrose, Milan.
(*From a photograph.*)

gradations of the priesthood, and most of them also by the way of the monastic cell. It was quite otherwise with Ambrose. From the ivory chair of the Roman magistrate (*sella curulis*) he stepped at once to the marble chair (*cathedra*) of the bishop, which he filled to so much purpose as to leave it at his death superior in authority to the imperial throne. The scene of his sovereignty was Milan, the usual residence of the Western Emperors from the reign of Diocletian till the invasion of the Goths under Alaric.

A.D. 340-374.

The father of Ambrose was a Roman of rank, and prefect of that division of the empire to which Gaul, Spain, and Britain belonged. His son was born about A.D. 340. After receiving a liberal education, the young man devoted himself to the profession of the law, which was the customary road to promotion in the State. He made rapid advances, and was appointed to the high dignity of "Consular" magistrate at Milan, in which post he gained the good opinion of all parties. Whilst he held this office, the Arian bishop of the city died, and the Catholics determined to elect one of their own party in his place. The Arians resisted, and a vehement strife arose; the public peace was in danger. The Consular hastened down to the church and made a speech to the people, exhorting them to peace and mutual concord. Whilst he was speaking, a cry was heard "Ambrose for bishop." The voice was said afterwards to have been that of a child. However this may have been, the name met with an instant and enthusiastic response, the whole multitude, with one voice, shouting out, "We will have Ambrose for our bishop." Ambrose, who had not even been baptized, made all the resistance he could to this popular nomination, even resorting to very doubtful means to divert the people from their object. All was of no avail, and when he tried to escape the citizens took him into friendly custody, and sent a letter to the Emperor Valentinian I., praying for his approval of their election. As soon as the imperial confirmation was received, the bishop-elect was baptized, passed summarily through the intermediate ecclesiastical stages, and on the eighth day received episcopal consecration. This was in 374, a year after the death of Athanasius, and two years after Basil had compelled the two Gregorys to accept the same honour. Ambrose was thirty-four years of age.[1]

On his ordination he at once divested himself of his private property, bestowing part on the poor and the Church, reserving a portion for his sister's maintenance, and placing the rest under the management of his brother Satyrus. To this voluntary poverty he joined the rigid asceticism of the times. He attended no banquets, dined only on Sundays, Saturdays, and festivals, and devoted the greater part of the night to prayer. It was one of his first cares to make up by study for his want of education in Christian doctrine.

---

[1] *Dict. Christ. Biog.*, art. Ambrosius, i. pp. 91, 92.

PRAISE OF VIRGINITY. 157

"Hurried as I was from the judicial bench to the priesthood, I began to teach what I had not myself learned, so that I had to learn and teach at the same time, because I had not had time to learn before."[1]   A.D. 374.

In Ambrose the stern rule of the Roman magistrate,[2] was united to the zeal of the ambitious churchman; he was, as Milman expresses it, "the spiritual ancestor of the Hildebrands and the Innocents." Of such a man it was not to be expected that he would oppose the growing superstitions of the age. On the contrary, he promoted some of them to the utmost of his influence. He was never weary of extolling the merits of virginity, on which he discoursed with such eloquence that the mothers of Milan locked up their daughters lest they should come under his spell. Nevertheless, troops of virgins flocked to him for consecration, some of them even so far as from Mauritania. Still his success fell short of his desires, and he even commended those who took the veil in spite of their parents.[3]

No less did he foster the growing veneration for relics. A splendid basilica[4] had just been erected. As a check to the Arians, the orthodox

---

[1] Cave, *Life of St. Ambrose*, § i. (6); *St. Ambrose*, by Dr. Thornton, p. 28.

[2] He was several times employed in political negotiations; his statesmanship was second only to his churchmanship.

[3] Milman's *History of Christianity*, iii. pp. 151-153; Robertson, i. p. 319; Du Pin, ii. p. 210.

[4] On the site of the present cathedral.

wished it dedicated with the same pomp as had been used in the case of another new church near the Roman Gate. To this Ambrose consented, on condition that some new relics should be found to consecrate it. These were discovered in the church of St. Felix and St. Nabor. Let us hear his own account of the matter. " Since," he writes to his sister, " I never conceal from thy Sanctity anything which takes place, thou must know that we have actually discovered some holy martyrs. I felt an ardent presentiment of what was to happen. Notwithstanding the diffidence of the clergy, I commanded the earth to be removed from the space before the rails. I recognised the appropriate tokens; and some persons being presented for the imposition of hands, the holy martyrs began so to bestir themselves, that before I had spoken, an urn was snatched up, and thrown down on the place of the holy sepulture. We found two men of extraordinary size,[1] such as a former age has produced; all the bones entire, and plenty of blood. There was a great concourse of people during two days. We transferred the remains to the church, which they call the Ambrosian; and while we were removing them a blind man was cured." " The miracles of old time," he adds in a sermon preached on the occasion, " are now

---

[1] Afterwards identified as Gervasius and Protasius, two brothers supposed to have been martyred under Nero at Ravenna, and thence removed to Milan.

revived; for you see many healed by the mere shadow of the saints' bodies. How many kerchiefs are displayed in triumph! How many coverlets are sought for, as having by mere contact with these most holy relics become capable of curing disease!" [1]

Under Ambrose the ceremonial of Divine service was invested with increased solemnity and magnificence. During the anxious vigils of the congregation, when his basilica was beset by the soldiers of Valentinian II., Ambrose introduced from the East the practice of antiphonal singing, in which, instead of leaving the psalmody to the choristers, the whole congregation, divided into two choirs, bore an alternate part.[2] So affecting did Augustine find the solemn music, that, not without reason, he took alarm lest he should be yielding to the luxury of sweet sounds instead of imbibing the devotional spirit of the hymn.[3]

Profound, however, as was his veneration for the externals of religion, Ambrose knew how to disregard them when weighed against the lives and liberty of men. The Gothic invasion brought with

---

[1] Isaac Taylor's *Ancient Christianity*, ii. pp. 242-244. The Arians derided the whole affair as a trick. An annual procession used to take place at Milan in honour of these saints, but it was forbidden by the authorities, because the people of Piacenza threatened, if it occurred again, to produce *their* relic, the third leg of St. Protasius!—Hare's *Cities of Italy*, i. p. 134, note.

[2] Ambrose's care in this matter has been perpetuated in the name of the Ambrosian Chant, but the connection of this latter with Ambrose is uncertain.

[3] Robertson, i. p. 270; Milman, iii. p. 405; *Dict. Christ. Biog.*, i. p. 95.

it unutterable calamities. From Thrace and Illyricum, especially, an immense number of captives were carried off; and these the Church, as in the days of Cyprian, hastened to redeem. When the common chest of the Milanese Church had been emptied, and the rich offerings of piety exhausted, Ambrose caused the sacramental vessels to be melted down and sold, to supply money for the ransom. "The Church," he wrote, "possesses gold, not to treasure up, but to distribute for the welfare and happiness of men. It is not merely the lives of men and the honour of the women which are endangered in captivity, but the faith of their children. The blood of redemption which has gleamed in those golden cups has sanctified them, not for the service alone, but for the ransom of man."[1]

In one instance, too, we find him forbidding a superstitious custom which had been much abused. When Monnica, Augustine's mother, followed her son to Milan, she took to the oratories of the martyrs, baskets of cakes, bread, and wine, as she had been accustomed to do at Carthage. But the doorkeeper would not permit her to make the offering, telling her that such practices were forbidden by the bishop, both for the avoidance of excess in drinking, and because such feasts in honour of the dead resembled the superstition of the Gentiles.[2]

---

[1] *Dict. Christ. Biog.*, i. p. 94; Milman, iii. p. 154.
[2] Augustine's *Confessions*, b. vi. c. 2.

In 382 an attempt was made to prop up declining paganism. In Rome the ancient families still generally adhered to the old religion, and nearly one half of the senate were worshippers of the heathen gods. In the hall where the senate met stood an altar dedicated to Victory, at which oaths were taken and oblations and incense offered. This altar, which had been removed by Constantius, was replaced by Julian, and had been suffered to remain. Gratian caused it to be again removed, and at the same time he confiscated the temple property, and revoked all State support of idolatry. The pagan senators chafed under these measures: they chose Symmachus, a man distinguished alike for his personal character and his eloquence, to plead their cause before the Emperor. The Christians made Ambrose their spokesman. Gratian, without even condescending to grant Symmachus an audience, confirmed the decrees he had already made. Two years afterwards, when the youthful Valentinian II. had succeeded his brother, the pagans renewed their suit, and Symmachus, now become prefect, was allowed to plead their cause in the presence of the Emperor. Ambrose stood forth again as the advocate of the Church. He told the Emperor that compliance on his part would be a sanction of paganism, and a tacit denial of his own Christian convictions. "We bishops," he said, "would not tolerate it. Thou might come to the church, but thou would find no priest there, or a priest who would forbid thy approach. The altar of Christ would disdain the offerings of one who had erected an altar to idols, for thy word, thy hand, thy signature, are thy works. The Lord has said, 'Ye cannot serve two masters.'" These arguments prevailed, and Valentinian rejected the heathen petition.[1]

Ambrose had not long taken possession of his office when he was brought into sharp collision with the Imperial authority. The see of Sirmium was vacant. Disregarding the limits of his own diocese, he went thither to prevent the election of an Arian and to secure the appointment of an orthodox bishop. By this act he incurred the displeasure of Justina, the Empress-mother, who was a zealous Arian, and had her residence at Sirmium. Some years afterwards she demanded the basilica in Porta Romana at Milan, which was outside the walls of the city, for the Arian worship.[2] The answer of Ambrose was: "A bishop cannot alienate that which is dedicated to God." A second demand for the possession of a new church within the walls met with the same repulse. The Imperial officers were ordered to take possession of the church; a tumult arose, and an Arian priest was severely handled, and only rescued by the interference of Ambrose. Many wealthy citizens were

---

[1] Neander, iii. pp. 100-103.

[2] Mr. Scott thinks the church was wanted for the Gothic auxiliaries, at that time with the Court at Milan.—*Ulfilas*, pp. 162, 163.

thrown into prison, and heavy fines imposed. But the bishop was inflexible; and when the Empress commanded him to tranquillize the populace, he answered, "It is in my power to refrain from exciting their violence, but it is for God to appease it when excited." The soldiers surrounded the church. The bishop who was performing the religious rites was apprised of their arrival, but went on as if nothing was happening. The doors were burst open; the affrighted women began to fly; but when the soldiers saw the dignified and undisturbed countenance of the bishop, as of one whose whole soul was absorbed in his office, they fell on their knees and assured him that they came to pray, and not to fight.[1]

In 386 an edict was passed permitting free worship to the Arians, and rendering liable to capital punishment all who should obstruct them. Under this edict the basilica of Porta Romana was again demanded, but Ambrose again refused: "God forbid that I should yield the heritage of Jesus Christ. Naboth would not part with the vineyard of his fathers to Ahab, and should I surrender the house of God—the heritage of all the faithful bishops who have been before me?" An order of banishment was served upon him, but in terms very unusual in the imperial chancery: "Depart from the city, and go whither thou

---

[1] Milman, iii. pp. 154-156; Thornton's *St. Ambrose*, p. 50.

pleasest." Ambrose, however, did not please to depart, but remained in the city preaching with the utmost fearlessness, and even attacking the Empress-mother in a style which cannot be defended. He took his text from the book of Job, and compared the Empress to the patriarch's wife, who bade her husband blaspheme God. He went on to liken her to Eve, to Jezebel, and to Herodias. Upon this the youthful Emperor Valentinian II. sent his private secretary, not to expel the refractory prelate, but to deprecate his tyranny. "If I am a tyrant," replied Ambrose, "why not strike me down? So far from being a tyrant, my only defence is the power to expose my life for the honour of God." He added, with sacerdotal pride, "Under the ancient law, priests *bestowed* empire, they did not condescend to assume it; kings desired the priesthood, not priests the sovereignty." When the Emperor himself was urged to confront Ambrose in the church, he replied: "His eloquence would compel you yourselves to lay me bound hand and foot before his throne."[1]

But it was not boys[2] and dowagers only that Ambrose brought to his feet. The great Theodosius I., Emperor of the East, was in his turn compelled to give way before the commanding genius and spiritual assumption of the bishop. A

---

[1] Stephens, *Life of St. Chrysostom*, pp. 188, 189; Milman, iii. pp. 155-158.
[2] Valentinian was not more than fourteen when these events took place.

synagogue of the Jews in Mesopotamia[1] had been burnt by the Christians, at the instigation, it was said, of the bishop of the place. At the same time the church of the Gnostics had been destroyed and plundered by the furious zeal of some monks. Theodosius commanded that the local bishop should rebuild the synagogue at his own expense, and that the Gnostics should be indemnified and the rioters be punished by the governor. The party spirit of the Christian world was affronted, and the "pious" indignation of Ambrose aroused, by this equitable decree. He stood forward as the champion of the faith, and in a letter to the Emperor vindicated the conduct of the bishop: "I protest that I would myself have burnt the synagogue, certainly that I would have given orders for it, that no place might be found where Christ is denied." "If," he continues, "the bishop shall comply with the mandate he will be an apostate, and the Emperor will be answerable for his apostasy. What has been done is but a trifling retaliation for the acts of plunder and destruction perpetrated by the Jews and heretics against the Catholics."[2]

No answer being returned to this letter, Ambrose had recourse to the pulpit. In a sermon delivered in the presence of the Emperor, he compared the Christian priest to the prophets of the Old Testament whose duty it was to pro-

---

[1] At Callinicum, in Osrhoëne.
[2] Milman, iii. pp. 163, 164, and note (y).

claim God's message to the king himself; and he admonished Theodosius that he owed everything to God's mercy, and that therefore it was his duty to wash and kiss the feet of the Church, the body of Christ, to honour all the disciples, even the least, and to pardon their faults. As he was leaving the pulpit the Emperor stopped him, asking, "Is it I whom thou hast made the subject of thy discourse?" "I have said that which I deemed useful for thee," was the reply. "I own," rejoined Theodosius, "that my commands have been a little severe, but I have already relaxed them, and these monks commit many crimes." This concession did not satisfy Ambrose. "I am going," he said, "to offer for thee the sacrifice; enable me to do so with a clear conscience." The Emperor sat down and nodded assent, but the pertinacious prelate remained standing. "Suppress the whole matter," he said, "swear it to me, and on thy sworn promise I will proceed to offer the sacrifice." The Emperor swore. Ambrose celebrated the Eucharist. "But," as he wrote the day after to his sister, "I would not have done it unless he had given me his solemn promise; and never did I experience such sensible marks of the presence of God in prayer."[1]

Two years later, A.D. 390, Theodosius was again compelled to humble himself before Ambrose, and

---

[1] Stephens, *Life of St. Chrysostom*, pp. 192, 193; *Dict. Christ. Biog.*, i. p. 96.

this time for worthy cause. "With all his wisdom and virtue the Emperor was liable to paroxysms of ungovernable fury." A tumult had arisen in Thessalonica about a favourite charioteer of the circus. The riot was quelled with difficulty. The imperial officers were treated with the utmost indignity, and some of them brutally murdered. When the news was brought to the Emperor, who was then at Milan, his rage was unbounded. But Ambrose was at his side, and succeeded for the time in calming his excitement, and in obtaining from him a promise that the affair should be judicially dealt with. Unhappily the bishop was called away to preside at a synod, and during his absence other counsellors, particularly Rufinus, the master of the household, obtained the Emperor's ear, and in an evil moment he sent secret orders to Thessalonica for a general massacre. A fresh exhibition of games was announced, and, in order to make the number of victims as large as possible, the whole population were invited to them in the Emperor's name. Eager to propitiate their offended sovereign, the citizens crowded into the circus. The troops were ready; instead of the games the signal for the massacre was given, and before sunset seven thousand, at the lowest computation, men, women, and children, had been "mown down like ears of corn at harvest time."[1]

A.D. 390.

---

[1] Milman, iii. p. 166; Gibbon, iii. pp. 483, 484; Thornton, pp. 84, 85.

On hearing of this atrocity, Ambrose withdrew into the country and wrote to the Emperor. The letter set forth the horror which he and his brother bishops felt at this inhuman deed, in which he should consider himself an accomplice if he did not avow his detestation of its guilt, and refuse to celebrate the Eucharist in the presence of one so stained with blood. He exhorted Theodosius to penitence, and promised to offer up prayers on his behalf. When the Emperor presented himself with his royal retinue at the door of the church, to join as usual in the public worship, he was confronted by the indignant prelate in his episcopal robes: "How wilt thou dare, O Emperor, to set foot in the sanctuary, and with hands dripping with the blood of men unjustly slain, to receive the body of the all-holy Lord, or dare to raise his precious blood to lips from which words of so great wrath and destruction have proceeded. Retire, and add not a fresh crime to those with which thou art already burdened."[1]

This incident is perhaps scarcely paralleled in Church history. Whilst we see in the conduct of the ecclesiastic much of that assumption which was leading the Church into a false and mundane position, we cannot but admire the courage which overcame all fear of the highest earthly potentate,

---

[1] Milman, iii. p. 166; Stephens, p. 196.

in protesting against the evil of his deeds. Not so have Church rulers behaved in other ages:

A.D. 390.

Doors of the basilica of St. Ambrose, Milan, containing (at the top of each) a small panel of cypress wood, believed to be part of the gates which Ambrose closed against the Emperor Theodosius. *From a photograph.*—See pp. 168, 173, note; and Hare *Cities of Italy*, i. p. 131.

too often the blood-stained hands of kings have

been welcomed in the temples of the Prince of Peace.

The Emperor returned to his palace conscience-stricken and weeping. For eight months he endured his ignominious exclusion. The festival of Christmas came, and found him utterly disconsolate. Rufinus inquired the cause of his grief. He replied, "I am lamenting my unhappy lot; the church of God is open to slaves and beggars, but is closed to me. Heaven, too, is closed; for our Lord said, 'Whatsoever ye shall bind on earth, shall be bound in heaven.'" "I will go to Ambrose," answered Rufinus, "and compel him to release thee from this bond." "It is in vain," replied the Emperor, "thou wilt not persuade Ambrose to violate the Divine law from any fear of Imperial power." Rufinus, however, sought an interview with the bishop, who spurned him as the chief counsellor of the massacre. And when Rufinus said the Emperor was approaching: "If he comes," replied Ambrose, "I will repel him from the vestibule of the church."[1]

The minister returned to the Emperor, and advised him to remain in his palace. But the Imperial will was now thoroughly subdued. "I will go," he answered, "and receive the chastisement I deserve." Proceeding to the consecrated precincts, he found the bishop sitting in his par-

---

[1] Stephens, pp. 196, 197.

lour; and humbly begged for absolution. The bishop sternly asked, "What penitence hast thou shown for thy great fault? What remedy hast thou applied to the incurable wound thou hast inflicted?" "It is *thy* duty," answered the penitent, "to prescribe the remedies; *mine* to obey." Ambrose imposed two conditions, that the law of the Emperor Gratian should be re-enacted, which required on every sentence of death or confiscation the lapse of thirty days before execution, and that Theodosius should perform public penance in the church. The conditions were accepted; the enactment was signed; and "the sovereign of the Roman Empire—the victor in so many battles, the legislator of the world—entered the sacred enclosure as an abject penitent. Laying aside every ornament that marked his rank, prostrate on the pavement, smiting his breast, tearing his hair, watering the stones with his tears, he cried aloud, 'My soul cleaveth to the dust, quicken Thou me, according to thy word.'" In this posture he remained during the first portion of the Liturgy. When the offertory began, he rose, advanced within the choir to present his offering, and was about to take the seat usually accorded to the Emperor in the midst of the clergy. But Ambrose took advantage of his humiliation to put an end to this practice. A deacon stepped up to Theodosius and informed him that no layman might remain in the choir during the celebration.

A.D. 390.

Per. I.
Chap. 7.

The submissive Emperor withdrew outside the rails.[1]

In 395 Theodosius died. Calling for Ambrose on his death-bed, he entreated him to be a father to his youthful sons Arcadius and Honorius,[2] as he had been twenty years before to Gratian and Valentinian.[3] But only two more years were allotted to Ambrose. They were years of activity and busy work. Clouds were gathering on the northern horizon, but the high-souled Churchman did not live to share the troubles which beset the sons of Theodosius. He passed away whilst Alaric was even now planning the invasion of Italy, which ended in the sack of Rome.[4]

The great Stilicho, who ruled the West in the name of Honorius, held Ambrose in the same esteem as Theodosius had done. When he heard that the bishop was dying, he summoned the clergy, and, with mingled entreaties and commands, persuaded them to go to his bedside, and bid him pray to be permitted to live. The dying prelate calmly replied, " I have not so lived among you as to be ashamed to live on ; but I do not

---

[1] Id., pp. 197, 198 ; Milman, iii. p. 167. When Theodosius returned to Constantinople he was invited by the bishop Nectarius to occupy his accustomed chair in the choir. "No," replied Theodosius with a sigh ; " I have learned at Milan the insignificance of an Emperor in the church, and the difference between him and a bishop. But no one here tells me the truth. I know not any bishop save Ambrose who deserves the name."—Stephens, p. 198.

[2] Arcadius was twelve, Honorius eleven years old.

[3] Thornton, p. 105. [4] See *ante*, p. 22.

fear to die, for our Lord is good." As the end drew near, the question arose who should succeed him. Four deacons, standing at the farther end of the gallery in which his couch was placed, were conversing in a low tone on this subject. The dying man overheard them, and when they mentioned the name of Simplician, they were startled to hear him say three times, "Old, but good."[1] Ambrose died A.D. 397, in his fifty-eighth year. His body was laid in state in the cathedral until Easter Eve, and buried in the church which now bears his name,[2] in presence of an immense crowd, Jews and pagans joining with his flock to pay him honour.[3]

A.D. 397

Ambrose left a multitude of works, which, "though deficient in originality," have acquired for him a distinguished place as a teacher in the Western Church. He is esteemed also by many Protestant writers, especially by Luther. "Amongst the Fathers," says the great Reformer, " St. Augustine holds unquestionably the first place, Ambrose the second, Bernard the third. Ambrose is admirable when he treats upon that most essential article, the forgiveness of sins."[4]

---

[1] Simplician was elected his successor.

[2] The basilica of St. Ambrose; see pp. 158, 169. The present building is of Lombard style, and dates from the latter part of the ninth century. Its chief feature is the rich facing of the altar in gold and silver work, richly set with precious stones. The twelve bas-reliefs on the back represent scenes in the life of Ambrose: they appear to have been executed about 835.—Murray, *Handbook for Northern Italy*.

[3] Thornton, pp. 114, 115.

[4] *Dict. Christ. Biog.*, i. p. 98; Luther's *Table Talk*.

HYMN BY AMBROSE.

Per. I. Chap. 7.

Amongst the best known of Ambrose's writings are the hymns which bear his name. With one of these Augustine consoled himself the day after his mother's death. "I slept," he writes, "and awoke again, and found my grief not a little assuaged; and as I lay alone on my bed, I called to mind those verses of thy Ambrose."

Hymn at the Cock-crowing.

Eternal Maker of the world,
   Who rulest both the night and day,
With order'd times dividing Time,
   Our toil and sorrow to allay.

The watchful herald of the dawn
   Announces day with trumpet shrill;
Lamp to the wayfarer at night,
   Night from itself dividing still.

The morning star arising bright
   Dissolves the darkness from the sky;
And, startled from their baleful schemes,
   The armèd powers of darkness fly.

The mariner reknits his strength;
   The stormy sea is lull'd to sleep;
And Peter, called the Church's Rock,
   Hearing this sound, his sin doth weep.

      *   *

Jesus! upon the falling look,
   And looking, heal us, Lord, we pray;
For at thy look the fallen rise,
   And guilt in tears dissolves away.

Do Thou, our Light, illume our sense,
   Do Thou our minds from slumber free;
For Thee our voices first proclaim,
   And with our lips we sing to Thee.[1]

---

[1] *The Voice of Christian Life in Song*, pp. 91, 92. See Augustine, *Confessions*, b. ix. c. 12, § 32.

CHAPTER VIII.

CHRYSOSTOM.

SECTION I. We return now to the East. John, surnamed for his eloquence Chrysostom, or the golden-mouthed,[1] was a native of Antioch and was born A.D. 345 or 347. His father was a military officer of rank; his mother Anthusa, who was left a widow at the age of twenty, refused to marry again, that she might devote herself to the education of her infant son and the care of his property. When his pagan tutor Libanius, who, we may remember, was also the great Basil's instructor, and who had returned to his native city of Antioch, heard that Anthusa remained unmarried, he exclaimed, " Good heavens, what women these Christians have!" And when on his death-bed, many years afterwards, Libanius was asked by his friends which of his pupils he thought most worthy to succeed him in his professorship, he replied, "John, if the Christians had not stolen him from us."[2]

A.D. circa 345.

---

[1] This epithet was not in common use until the fifth century; in his lifetime he was always called John.—*Dict. Christ. Biog.*, art. Chrysostom, i. p. 518.

[2] *Saint John Chrysostom, his Life and Times*, by W. R. W. Stephens, p. 13.

Per. I.
Chap. 8.

On the completion of his education Chrysostom commenced life as an advocate, a calling for which his brilliant powers of oratory especially qualified him; but the pious instructions of his mother were beginning to bear fruit, and he recoiled from the practices in use in the legal profession. His disinclination to the law and to the worldly life by which he was surrounded was strengthened by the influence of Basilius,[1] "the companion of his studies and the sharer of all his thoughts and plans." Like most of the earnest spirits in that age, Basilius had adopted the monastic life, and Chrysostom prepared to follow his example. It was, as he afterwards said, a sense of the glaring contrast between the Christianity of the Gospel and the Christianity of ordinary life which drove him to this resolution. The world seemed to him "to wage an implacable warfare against the commands of Christ, and he determined therefore to seek in seclusion that kind of life which he saw exhibited in the gospels, but nowhere else."[2] He does not seem to have asked himself, What is to become of the community of men if the salt is taken away?

Up to this time he had not been baptized. Of all the eminent men whose lives we are passing under review not one can be shown to have received

---

[1] This name and Basil are the same; the Latin form is here used to distinguish Chrysostom's friend from Basil the Great (Chaps. 3, 4).

[2] *Dict. Christ. Biog.*, i. p. 519; Stephens, pp. 14, 72.

baptism in infancy, and of most it can be said with certainty that they were not baptized until they were of full age; yet all, except two, were the sons of Christian parents, and Augustine's mother was a Christian.[1] Chrysostom was about twenty-three years old when he received the rite, and the public profession of his faith thus made was very helpful to his character. "From the hour of his baptism," says his biographer Palladius, "he neither swore, nor defamed any one, nor spoke falsely, nor cursed, nor even tolerated facetious jokes."[2]

A.D. circa 370.

When Chrysostom's mother heard of his intention to become a monk her affectionate heart sank within her. Taking him by the hand she led him into her chamber, and making him sit beside her on the bed, burst into tears, and "with words more moving than tears" thus poured out her heart. "Not long, my child, was I permitted the enjoyment of thy father's virtues, whose premature death brought orphanhood on thee, and on me the miseries of untimely widowhood. Words cannot describe the troubled sea into which a young woman who has just left her father's roof, and is unused to the world, is suddenly plunged by this insufferable calamity; what idleness and misconduct of servants she has to put up with, against what cabals of kinsfolk she has to defend herself; what

---
[1] See *Early Church History*, p. 132.
[2] *Dict. Christ. Biog.*, ubi suprà.

insolence of assessors and tax-gatherers she has to submit to. By none of these difficulties, however, was I prevailed upon to contract a second marriage, but endured the tempest without shrinking, being supported in the first place from above, and next by thy features, on which I gazed incessantly as on the living image of my departed husband. I have not suffered thy patrimony to diminish, but, whilst I have denied thee nothing which thy condition required, the expense has been defrayed from my own purse and my father's dowry. Do not think however that I speak this to reproach thee. In return for all I have but one favour to entreat; make me not a second time a widow, awaken not again my slumbering sorrows. Wait for my death, which cannot be very long; and when thou hast laid me in the dust and mingled my bones with those of thy father, then travel whither thou wilt, even beyond the sea. Only so long as I live be contented to dwell with me, and do not rashly provoke God by afflicting thy mother."

Chrysostom could not withstand so tender an appeal. He did not, however, entirely relinquish his purpose. Like Gregory Nazianzen, prevented from entering a monastery he made a monastery of his home, and withdrew from all worldly occupations and amusements. He ate little and seldom,

---

[1] Chrysostom, *On the Priesthood*, b. i.

slept on the bare ground, and rose frequently for prayer; he rarely left the house, and lest he should fall back into the habit of evil speaking he maintained almost unbroken silence. In this recluse manner of life he was joined by several youthful companions. One of these was Theodore, afterwards bishop of Mopsuestia, famous for his advocacy of the rational as opposed to the allegorical method of scripture interpretation. Unable to bear the strain of so severe a discipline, Theodore drew back, and plighted himself for marriage with a young lady named Hermione. To Chrysostom this relapse of his friend seemed to be nothing less than a profound and disgraceful fall, and he wrote him two long letters of expostulation and warning: "Oh that my head were waters and mine eyes a fountain of tears! If the prophet uttered such a lamentation over a ruined city, surely I may express a like passionate sorrow over the fallen soul of a brother." His remonstrances prevailed, Theodore abandoned the world once more, and his matrimonial intentions, and again joined himself to the brotherhood. What became of Hermione we are not told.[1]

We have more than once had to deplore the low standard of truthfulness which prevailed at this period, even amongst the most devoted Christians.[2] Chrysostom shared this failing. Several sees

---

[1] Stephens, pp. 27-39; *Dict. Christ. Biog.*, ubi suprà.
[2] See *ante*, pp. 66, 68, 71.

Per. I. Chap. 8.

became vacant in Syria which it was desirable to fill without delay. A body of bishops met at Antioch for this purpose. Amongst those deemed eligible Chrysostom and Basilius were named, although they were not yet even deacons. Basilius proposed that they should act in concert, and either both accept or both refuse the office, and to this Chrysostom pretended to agree; but, terrified at the bare idea of ordination, he secretly resolved to elude the appointment and let his friend be chosen alone. When the time arrived, and Basilius was seized and carried before the bishops, Chrysostom was not to be found. To his inquiries for him Basilius received the evasive answer, "that it would be strange indeed, if, when the self-willed Chrysostom had yielded submissively to the decision of the fathers, Basilius, his superior in understanding and experience, should show any reluctance." On the faith of this, Basilius allowed the ordaining hands to be laid upon his own head. Discovering too late the trick which had been played upon him, he upbraided Chrysostom with his breach of their friendly compact. So deeply were his feelings touched that words choked his utterance. But Chrysostom, unmoved by his reproaches, answered only with a burst of laughter, and forcibly seizing his hand and kissing it, gave thanks to God for the success of the plot. He went further and defended the fraud, on the oft-asserted but rotten principle that deceit is praiseworthy when practised in a good cause.¹ A century and a quarter before, Julius Africanus had penned this honourable maxim, "May the opinion never prevail in the Church of Christ that any false thing can be fabricated for Christ's glory."² Unhappily the Church has too often glossed over this golden rule.³

A.D. 374.

Just at this period paganism was rigorously proscribed. An imperial decree, issued by Valentinian and Valens against such as practised magical arts, was being enforced at Rome and Antioch. The mere possession of a book of divination might lead to torture, banishment, or even death.⁴ It

---

¹ *On the Priesthood*, b. i.; *Dict. Christ. Biog.*, i. p. 520.
² Letter to Aristides, c. i., *Early Church History*, p. 299.
³ "Jerome not unfrequently violated the sanctity of truth. He defends himself by the examples of Plato, Xenophon, Aristotle, and still more by the practice of Christian controversialists, as Origen, Methodius, Eusebius, Apollinaris, who often allowed themselves to advance what they knew to be untrue, in order to strengthen their argument. This laxity concerning truth passed under the name of οἰκονομία in Greek, and *dispensatio* in Latin [both signifying management], or sometimes *officiosum mendacium* [serviceable falsehood]. It had chiefly footing in the Greek Church."— Roberts, *Church Memorials*, p. 232. These loose principles were not shared by Augustine, who stands almost alone amongst the Fathers of this age in his steadfast adherence to truth. "Every lie is a sin. Speech was given to man, not to deceive another, but to make known his thoughts; and to use it for deception, and not for its appointed end, is a sin. Nor are we to suppose that there can be a lie which is not sinful, because it is sometimes possible by telling a lie to serve another. It cannot be denied that those have reached a high standard of goodness who never lie except to save a man from injury, but it is not the deceit, but the good intention that is praiseworthy. It is quite enough that the deception should be pardoned without being made the subject of laudation, especially among the heirs of the New Covenant, to whom it is said, 'Let your communication be yea, yea, and nay, nay, for whatsoever is more than these cometh of evil.'" —*Enchiridion*, c. xxii.

⁴ Of the dominion which magic exerted over the ancient world we have

Per. I. Chap. 8. happened that Chrysostom, walking with a friend through the public gardens by the banks of the Orontes, fished out of the river some leaves of a book. "A playful contest for the prize ensued, but was changed into horror on finding it to be a book of magic. Their dismay was increased by seeing a soldier approach. What was to be done? To keep the leaves or to throw them away seemed

at this day little conception. The stringent and frequent repetition in the Old Testament of the law against enchantments, necromancy, familiar spirits, and other forms of divination, proves the prevalence of this superstition in the early ages of the world; nor was its hold less powerful on the nations, classic or barbarian, over which the Roman Empire extended. In the Acts (xix. 19) we read of the converts at Ephesus (one of the chief centres of the magical art) burning the books they were accustomed to use, to the value of nearly £2000.

It was a piece of treasonable practice which provoked the inquisition at Antioch. Many plots were in agitation against the life of the Emperor Valens, and in one of these the conspirators fixed upon Theodorus, an Imperial Secretary, to be Emperor in his stead. To confirm this choice, the magical art was invoked. According to the evidence of one of the actors given under torture, a tripod of laurel twigs was constructed in imitation of that of the famous oracle at Delphi, and, after being consecrated with mysterious incantations, was placed in the middle of a room which had been purified by Arabian incense. On the tripod was set a metal dish with the twenty-four letters of the Greek alphabet engraved round the edge. Then a priest, clothed in linen, and holding a sprig of vervain, called upon the divinity who presides over foreknowledge, and extending his hand above the tripod, let fall a ring suspended by a flaxen thread of extreme fineness. As the ring, gently set in motion by his fingers, touched and bounded off from the successive letters, the priest following the order in which the letters were touched gave forth metrical replies to the questions put by the bystanders. And when one of them inquired who should succeed the present Emperor? the ring touched successively the four letters ΘΕΟΔ (THEOD), on which some one exclaimed: "This is the decree of fate; Theodorus is to be our Emperor." On the discovery of the plot Theodorus was put to death in a barbarous manner, and with him a multitude of persons of various ranks, some of whom, it would seem, were guilty of no other crime than owning in their names the fatal syllables. The actual successor of Valens was Theodosius. —Ammianus Marcellinus, *Roman History*, b. xxix. c. 1.

equally dangerous. At last they flung them back into the water. The soldier's suspicions had not been aroused, and the two friends passed on unchallenged." "Chrysostom always gratefully looked back to this escape as a signal instance of providential deliverance."[1]

Shortly after this occurrence (his mother probably being then deceased), Chrysostom left his home to join a monastic community on the mountains to the south of Antioch. Here he spent four years, "a hallowed and peaceful time," to which he loved to recur in after-life. He paints the daily round of the cloister in warm colours. "Before the first rays of sunlight the abbot went round, and with his foot woke up those who were still sleeping. When all had risen, and before they broke their fast, they united in a hymn of praise and in prayer. At sunrise each went to his allotted task—some to read or write, others to manual labour. Four hours during the day—the third, sixth, ninth, and at even—were appointed for prayer and psalmody. When the day's work was over, reclining on strewn grass, they partook of a common meal of bread and water, with occasionally vegetables and oil for the sick. After this they again sang a hymn, and then betook themselves to their straw couches, and slept, Chrysostom says, free from those anxieties which

---

[1] Stephens, p. 58; *Dict. Christ. Biog.*, i. p. 520.

beset men in the world. No need was there of bolts and bars, for the monk had nothing to lose except his life, the loss of which he counted an advantage, since he could say, 'to me to live is Christ, and to die is gain.' When death entered the monastery no sound of lamentation was heard. It was not said such a one is dead, but, 'he has been perfected;' and his body was carried forth to burial with hymns of thanksgiving, and the prayers of his companions, that they, too, might soon see the end of their labours, and be permitted to behold Jesus Christ."[1]

But being still unable to attain the object he had in view, namely, "the utter extirpation of his human instincts, he proceeded to abandon altogether the society of man, and taking up his abode in one of those solitary caves with which the mountains abound, he braved the intense cold of that elevated region, and limited himself to the smallest portion of food and sleep on which life could be sustained. At the end of two years his

---

[1] Stephens, pp. 66, 67. In his homilies he speaks of the ascetic life with still more enthusiasm. "Visit the Egyptian deserts, and you will find there what is better than any paradise, innumerable choirs of angels in human form, tribes of martyrs, bevies of nuns; the tyrannous empire of Satan brought to nothing and the kingdom of Christ shining forth."— I. Taylor, *Ancient Christianity*, vol. i. p. 200. There is, he says in another place, a great difference between a good king and a holy monk who hath bestowed all his time and care upon praising God. The monk, when he dies, goes in splendour to meet Christ, and enters at once into Heaven; whereas a king, however just, is less glorious and happy, there being a great difference in point of holiness.—Du Pin, iii. p. 30. Chrysostom must have found it hard to reconcile these opinions with his own experience of the fraternity in his later days.

health so completely broke down that he was forced to quit his cave, and forsaking 'the life of angels' for that of men, he returned with a shattered constitution to his home in Antioch."[1]

After teaching as a deacon for five years, Chrysostom was ordained presbyter in 386, and for ten years diligently occupied himself with the duties of his office, sometimes preaching five days in the week. Bishop Flavian opened the pulpit of the cathedral to him, and whenever it was his turn to preach, the building was sure to be thronged. In the great cities the congregations were of a very motley character; and there also the most popular preachers were to be found. An unseemly and reprehensible practice had crept in of signifying approbation by applause. It is a notable evidence of the decay of the Church that the manners of the theatre should thus have been imported into divine service. So inveterate had this habit become, that when Chrysostom rebuked his auditory for their irreverent behaviour, they applauded the very rebuke. Such, too, was the charm of his eloquence that, in these crowded audiences hanging in rapt admiration on the preacher's lips, pickpockets found a profitable occasion for plying their trade, and Chrysostom had to warn his hearers to leave their purses at home.[2]

---

[1] *Dict. Christ. Biog.*, ubi suprà.
[2] *Dict. Christ. Biog.*, i. pp. 520, 521.

Per. I.
Chap. 8.

Here it may be well to pause a moment and inquire whether the Church has not been mistaken in offering so high a premium for pulpit oratory. The popular admiration of this gift and the prizes offered to those who excel, lead to a contempt of simple Gospel ministry when unaccompanied by learning and eloquence. When, in the still earlier period of the Church, the free exercise of prophecy and teaching in the congregation was exchanged for the ministry of one man only, grievous loss was incurred; and this loss was yet more enhanced when it came to be held of first importance that the minister should be both scholar and orator. No warranty for such a change is to be found in the New Testament, where a sound knowledge of scriptural truth, with faith and love, and the anointing of the Holy Spirit, are set forth as the only and sufficient qualifications of the Gospel herald. This departure from the original Christian institutes brought with it a train of evil consequences. Not only were those gifts stifled which the Apostle so fully recognizes as the spiritual possession of the many, but the congregation no longer came together to realise the presence of Christ in their midst, and to wait for the manifestation of his spirit. They came to see, to hear, and to be entertained. "The preachers," as Gregory Nazianzen observes, "too often seek to adorn the artless piety of our religion by introducing into the sanctuary a new sort of secular oratory, borrowed from the forum and the theatre." "The multitude seek not priests, but rhetoricians; and I must say something in their defence. We have thus brought them up, by our desire to become all things to all men,—I know not whether for the *perdition* or *salvation* of all."[1]

A.D. circa 387.

Chrysostom himself whilst at Antioch suffered from this perversion of Gospel order. "Most men," he says, "listen, not for improvement, but to be pleased, and to criticise, just as though a player or musician were before them. They require eloquence more peremptorily from preachers than from professed rhetoricians ... The most eloquent preacher, unless his discourses come up to the measure of their expectations, is exposed to innumerable sneers and censures from his audience, none considering that a temporary depression of spirits, some anxiety, perhaps a fit of ill-humour, may dim the brightness of his intellect, and hinder the development of his thoughts;"[2] and, in a homily delivered some years afterwards at Constantinople, he brings out the bitterness of a more extensive experience. "Many take infinite pains to prepare a long sermon, and if they win applause, it is as though they had gained the kingdom of Heaven itself, but if silence follows their discourse the dejection which covers their spirits is worse than hell. This has turned the churches upside

---

[1] *Life*, by Ullmann, p. 158; *The Friend Journal*, 1844, p. 248, note.
[2] *On the Priesthood*, b. v.

down; because both *you* are impatient of those discourses which might produce compunction, and will endure only such as tickle your ears by their composition and euphony; and *we* act a pitiful part in suffering ourselves to pander to your appetites, when we ought to be combating them. ... When, as I discourse, I hear myself applauded, at the moment as a man (why should I not confess the truth?) I am delighted, and indulge in the pleasurable feeling; but when I get home, and bethink me that those who have applauded have derived no benefit from my sermon, but that the good they ought to have received was dissipated by their plaudits, I am in pain, I groan and weep, and feel as though I had spoken all in vain." [1]

Perhaps the most notable display of Chrysostom's brilliant eloquence belongs to his ministry at Antioch. A disgraceful riot had taken place in the city, the statues of the Imperial family were thrown down, mutilated, and dragged through the streets, and one of the public buildings was set on fire. The aged bishop Flavian had hastened to Constantinople to appease the wrath of the Emperor Theodosius I., and the inhabitants were

---

[1] Homilies. Compare the Apostle's experience: "To preach the Gospel, not in wisdom of words, lest the cross of Christ should be made void." "My speech and my preaching were not in persuasive words of wisdom, but in demonstration of the Spirit and of power; that your faith should not stand in the wisdom of men, but in the power of God."—1 Cor. i. 17: ii. 4 and 5.

waiting in an agony of suspense the result of his mission. During his three weeks' absence Chrysostom devoted day after day all the powers of his soul and intellect to allay their fears, revive their hopes, awaken repentance, and enforce amendment of life. Day after day his small figure was to be seen either sitting in the ambo,[1] from which he sometimes preached on account of his diminutive stature, or standing on the steps of the altar. The market-places were deserted, the theatres and circuses were empty, but the church was always thronged, and it is noted as a very unusual circumstance that the people came to hear even after dinner.[2]

A.D. 387.

Before Flavian's arrival at Constantinople, the Emperor had already sent down two commissioners to execute condign punishment upon the rebellious city. It was to be degraded from its rank as the capital of Syria, all places of public recreation were to be closed, and the guilty were to be rigorously punished. But there were powerful intercessors at hand. A band of hermits from the mountains came down into the city, and confronting the commissioners in the public streets commanded them in God's name to stay their hands. The commissioners consented to suspend the exe-

---

[1] Or reading desk, from which he could be better heard than from the pulpit. The most common practice was for the preacher to sit, the people to stand.—Stephens, p. 154, note.

[2] *Dict. Christ. Biog.*, i. p. 521; Stephens, pp. 151-154.

cution of the sentence; and one of them even went to Constantinople with an intercessory letter from the hermits; but the most powerful mediator was the aged bishop, who by this time had presented himself before the Emperor and appealed to his Christian clemency and forbearance. This he did in so moving a manner that the Emperor was deeply affected and granted to the city a free pardon.[1]

In 397 Chrysostom's connection with Antioch was suddenly dissolved. Nectarius, bishop[2] of Constantinople, an amiable and indolent prelate, died. The appointment to the vacant place virtually rested with the eunuch Eutropius, the chief minister of the feeble Emperor Arcadius. He cast his eyes upon Chrysostom, but fearing lest the people of Antioch should refuse to part with their favourite preacher, he had recourse to a stratagem. On a

---

[1] Stephens, pp. 165-174; where the episode in all its details is related with the author's accustomed lucidity. Theodosius, though subject to outbursts of violent temper, was remarkably open to the influence of Christian men. We have already seen how completely he was subjugated by the lofty dignity of Ambrose.

[2] Church historians are accustomed to give the titles of Archbishop and Patriarch to the occupants of the great sees during the fourth century; this is somewhat anticipatory. Alexandria appears to be the only see whose bishop was so styled before the fifth century, and there the title was not officially conferred until A.D. 431. The first mention of the designation of Patriarch is found in Socrates Scholasticus, who wrote his history about A.D. 440; its earliest official use was at the Council of Chalcedon, A.D. 451, where it is applied especially to Pope Leo I. The term Metropolitan is earlier; it is found in the canons of the Council of Nicæa. An Archbishop presided over both Patriarch and Metropolitan.—Bingham, *Antiquities of the Church*, b. ii. cc. 16, 17.

false pretext, Chrysostom was induced to visit a martyr's chapel outside the city walls. Here he was apprehended by one of the Imperial officers, conveyed to the first post-station on the road to Constantinople, and being placed in a public chariot and guarded by a military escort, he was whirled along from stage to stage over the 800 miles which intervened.[1]

A.D. 397, 398.

Whether the dignity of bishop of the Imperial city, thus thrust upon him, was welcome or otherwise, Chrysostom submitted to it with a good grace. The probability is that, although it was a wrench to be snatched from his native city in the midst of his loving labours, the extended field now opened before him for pastoral work and for the exercise of his unrivalled powers as a preacher fully reconciled him to the change. He was consecrated, A.D. 398, by Theophilus, bishop of Alexandria, who had been summoned to Constantinople for the purpose. But Theophilus had set his mind on another candidate, and performed the ceremony with the utmost reluctance: he would even have entirely refused to act, if it had not been for the threats of Eutropius.[2]

SECTION II. The citizens were not long in perceiving the difference between the new bishop and his predecessor. Nectarius had lived in a style

---

[1] *Dict. Christ. Biog.*, p. 522. From Antioch to Constantinople was reckoned a week's journey travelling day and night.   [2] Ibid.

of luxury and magnificence, which to Chrysostom's severe character seemed to be utterly inconsistent with the profession of a Christian bishop. He accordingly disfurnished the episcopal residence, sold the costly plate and rich carpets, and with the proceeds erected hospitals for the sick and strangers, and provided for the support of virgins and widows. He even disposed of some of the marbles and other ornaments of the churches. Instead of interchanging grand dinners with the wealthy, he ate the simplest fare in his solitary chamber. He avoided the Court and the company of the great, and even seems to have regarded social intercourse with his fellow-men as waste of time. The bishops who visited Constantinople no longer found the episcopal palace open to them, Chrysostom alleging that there were houses of the faithful in abundance where they would meet with a welcome. One, a Syrian bishop named Acacius, was so provoked by the meanness of the table and lodging which had been provided, that he exclaimed, "I'll season his pot for him."[1]

Besides carrying into the episcopal palace the habits he had acquired in the cloister, thus ignoring some of the duties of his exalted station, Chrysostom provoked hostility by his ecclesiastical reforms. The moral tone of the clerical order had sunk to a low ebb—worldliness, avarice, flattery of

---

[1] Palladius, *Dialogus De Vitâ S. Chrysost.*, c. vi.; Robertson, *History of the Church*, i. pp. 381, 382.

the great, and yet graver faults were common. A thorough reform was needed, and Chrysostom set himself to the arduous task with unsparing severity. His measures were rendered the more unpalatable by his unbending manner and irritable temper. From the reform of the clergy he passed to that of the Court. The dissolute manners and frivolous lives of the nobles and Court ladies furnished a frequent theme for his discourses, and the fulminations he uttered from the pulpit, whilst they drew immense crowds to the cathedral and daily increased his popularity with the multitude, continually raised up new enemies against him.[1]

Before, however, we enter on the memorable contest with vice and folly in high places, which in the end caused Chrysostom's downfall, we must introduce two episodes—his work of evangelisation amongst the Goths, and his connection with the fate of the minister Eutropius.

Many thousand Goths dwelt in Constantinople and the neighbouring provinces, and Chrysostom, zealous for the recovery of this people from the Arian doctrine, set apart one of the churches in the city for divine service in their native tongue. One Sunday, about the year 398, he himself attended. The Bible was read in the translation of Ulfilas, and a discourse delivered in Gothic by a Gothic preacher. A number of Chrysostom's own

---

[1] *Dict. Christ. Biog.*, i. pp. 522, 523.

congregation seem to have been present, and he took advantage of the scene before him to deliver an eloquent discourse (interpreted into Gothic) on the transforming power of Christianity. Quoting Isaiah (lxv. 25), " the wolf and the lamb shall feed together, and the lion shall eat straw like the ox," he said: "The prophet is not speaking here of lions and lambs, but predicting that, subdued by the power of the divine doctrine, the brutal sense of rude men should be transformed into gentleness, and they should unite in the same community with the meek. And this you have witnessed to-day, the most savage race of mankind standing side by side with the lambs of the Church —one pasture, one fold for all, one table set before all." Besides his care for the Goths in and around the city, he also sent forth missionaries to those tribes which had remained on the banks of the Danube, consecrating a native to be their bishop; and he showed a like interest in the Syrian nomads. Up to the end of his life, he did not cease, in sickness and exile, to further these cherished aims.[1]

Between Chrysostom and the minister Eutropius, by whom he had been raised to the primacy, there was nothing in common. The latter was cruel and rapacious, and instead of finding in the new bishop a subservient tool, he found a man of lofty

---

[1] Neander, iii. pp. 181, 182; *Dict. Christ. Biog.*, i. p. 523.

spirit who vigilantly guarded the ecclesiastical prerogative. When the victims of Eutropius' extortions fled to the churches to claim the right of asylum, they found in Chrysostom a powerful and resolute protector. In an evil hour for himself the minister had procured from the feeble Emperor a law abolishing the privilege of sanctuary. By a change of affairs at Court, Eutropius suddenly fell from his lofty station. Deprived of his rank, his property confiscated, driven from the palace, and exposed to the insults of the populace, he found himself homeless and friendless. Whither should he flee? No asylum remained but through the very door which he had done his best to close. He might still find that door open. The law which he had made was hateful to the clergy, it might be that the bishop would connive at its violation, even by the very man who had framed it. "In the guise of a suppliant, tears streaming down his cheeks, his scant grey hairs smeared with dust, he crept into the cathedral, pushed aside the curtain which divided the chancel or sanctuary from the nave, and, clinging closely to the 'holy table,' awaited the approach of the bishop or any of the clergy. The enemy was on his track. As he lay quaking with terror, he could hear on the other side of the thin partition the trampling of feet, mingled with the clattering of arms and voices raised in threatening tones by soldiers on the search. At this crisis he was found by the bishop

A.D. 399.

Per. I.
Chap. 8.

in a state of pitiable and abject terror, his cheek blanched with a death-like pallor, his teeth chattering, his whole frame quivering, as with faltering lips he craved the asylum of the Church. . . . Chrysostom led the unhappy fugitive to the sacristy, and, having concealed him there, confronted his pursuers, asserted the inviolability of the sacred precincts, and refused to surrender the refugee. 'None shall penetrate the sanctuary save over my body; the Church is the bride of Jesus Christ, who has entrusted her honour to me, and I will never betray it!' The soldiers threatened to lay violent hands on the bishop; but he freely presented himself to them, and only desired to be conducted to the Emperor, that the whole affair might be submitted to his judgment. He was accordingly placed between two rows of spearmen, and marched like a prisoner from the cathedral to the palace." In the presence of Arcadius he maintained the same lofty tone: "What were human laws when weighed against divine?" The Emperor was unable to resist the authority with which he spoke, and promised to respect the asylum. But when the soldiers heard this, they were furious at the loss of their victim, and it was only by a passionate harangue, ending with a flood of tears, that Arcadius succeeded in restraining them from breaking into the chancel and dragging forth the suppliant.[1]

---

[1] Stephens, pp. 248-251.

"The next day was Sunday. The places of public amusement were deserted, and the cathedral was filled with a vast concourse of men and women. All were in a flutter of expectation to hear what the Golden Mouth would utter in defence of the Church's privilege, and in defiance of the law. The bishop took his seat in the ambo; all faces were upturned; but, before the preacher uttered a word, the curtain which separated the nave from the chancel, was partially drawn aside, and disclosed the cowering form of the unhappy Eutropius clinging to one of the columns which supported the holy table. Presently the bishop burst forth: 'Vanity of vanities! Where is now the pomp of yonder man's consulship? Where his torch-light festivities? Where the applause which once greeted him? Where his banquets and garlands? They are gone, all gone; one rude blast has shattered all the leaves, and shows us the tree stripped quite bare, and shaken to its very roots. . . . Vanity of Vanities; all is vanity. These words should be inscribed on our walls and on our garments, in the market-place, and by the wayside, but above all on our consciences.' Then, turning towards the pitiable figure by the holy table: 'Did I not continually warn thee that wealth is a runaway slave, a thankless servant? but thou wouldst not heed. Lo, now experience has proved to thee that it is not only fugitive and thankless, but

A.D. 399

murderous also; for this it is which causes thee now to tremble. Did I not tell thee, when thou rebuked me for speaking the truth, that I loved thee better than thy flatterers? If thou hadst endured my wounds, the kisses of thy enemies would not have wrought thee this destruction. . . . The Church which thou treated as an enemy has opened her bosom to receive thee; the theatre which thou favoured has betrayed thee, and whetted the sword against thee.'" . . . Then, turning back again to the audience, he declared the trembling suppliant whom they beheld to be "the ornament of the altar." "'What,' you will say, 'this iniquitous rapacious creature an ornament to the altar!' Hush! the sinful woman was permitted to touch the feet of Jesus Christ Himself." . . . Then, addressing himself especially to the rich, he said: "Such a spectacle as this, of one lately at the pinnacle of power, now crouching with fear like a hare or a frog, chained to yonder pillar, not by fetters, but by fright, is sufficient to subdue arrogance, and teach the truth of the Scripture precept, 'All flesh is grass, and all the glory of man as the flower of grass.'"

After remaining several days in the sanctuary, perhaps finding his asylum no longer safe, Eutropius quitted it, and escaped in disguise from the city. He was taken, tried on sundry charges of treason, and beheaded.[1]

---

[1] Id., pp. 251-256.

CHAPTER IX.

Chrysostom (*continued*).

SECTION I. The beautiful Eudoxia, the haughty A.D. 398. and intriguing wife of Arcadius, was the real sovereign of the East. For a short while Chrysostom enjoyed her favour. Soon after his arrival she was seized with "a fit of religious excitement," which found vent in the translation of some martyrs' relics to the great church of St. Thomas in Drypia, nine miles from the city. The august ceremonial took place at night; "the Empress in her royal diadem and purple, attended by nobles and ladies of distinction, walked by the side of the bishop in the rear of the chest enclosing the sacred bones," and so vast was the number of torches that Chrysostom compares the procession to a river of fire. It was dawn before they reached the church. The bishop ascended the pulpit and preached a sermon full of "extravagant laudations of Eudoxia, and of ecstatic expressions of joy" at this auspicious event.[1]

But Eudoxia's devotion soon "burnt itself out," and the public censures of her own conduct, as well

---

[1] *Dict. Christ. Biog.*, i. p. 523; see also Stephens, pp. 222, 223.

as of her court, which the bishop now began to introduce into his discourses, turned her imperial favour into implacable enmity.[1]

Chrysostom's zeal for the maintenance of Church discipline carried him beyond the bounds of discretion. Not content with setting his own diocese in order, he quitted the capital for Asia Minor, A.D. 401, to correct some flagrant abuses in Ephesus and the neighbouring sees. He left Constantinople in charge of a bishop named Severian. The harshness with which Chrysostom exercised his usurped authority at Ephesus increased the number of his enemies; and the length of his absence from the capital gave them opportunity to conspire against him.[2]

On his return he found that through the treachery of Severian the affairs of the Church at Constantinople had fallen into confusion. Instead, however, of adopting the measures which prudence would have dictated, he was excited to a vehement display of his feelings. In his very first sermon he attacked Severian. A few days later he aimed his shafts higher, and held up to public odium the whole cabal of bishops who played the part of court flatterers, and even Eudoxia herself. Like Ambrose,[3] he compared the Empress to Jezebel. "Gather together to me,"

---

[1] *Dict. Christ. Biog.,* i. p. 524.
[2] Ibid.; Schaff, p. 278. He deposed twenty bishops in the course of his visitation.—Roberts, p. 143.   [3] See *ante,* p. 164.

he exclaimed, " those base priests that eat at Jezebel's table, that I may say to them, as Elijah of old, ' How long halt ye between two opinions?' . . . If Jezebel's table be the table of the Lord, eat at it; eat at it till you vomit." The allusion was too patent to be mistaken. From that moment his fate was sealed.[1]

The conduct of Chrysostom on this occasion has been much praised. No one will deny that it manifested daring courage: but courage is not everything in a Christian minister. This outburst of indignation was indeed far nobler than his previous flattery, but it was not wise or defensible. To speak of the faults of others behind their back is contrary to Gospel rule, and it does not mend the matter if the defamation is public, and in the presence of thousands. Moreover, the respect and honour which are due to all men, are doubly due to kings and those in authority. When Paul administered a richly deserved rebuke to the high-priest Ananias, he apologised, because of the commandment, " Thou shalt not speak evil of the ruler of thy people." Again, the object of reproof is reclamation, but the offender is hardly likely to give heed to the reproof when it is wrapped in words of fire, and published through a trumpet. Evil, too, must have been the effect of Chrysostom's philippics on the people of Constan-

---

[1] *Dict. Christ. Biog.*, i. p. 525.

tinople. Denunciations of rulers and public characters from his golden lips could not fail to render the Church more attractive than the theatre. What flattery is sweeter to the populace than to be told of the vices of their superiors? And when the ear is filled with such words, no room is left for the great purpose for which men come together in the church, the worship of God.

Chrysostom was not without personal friends in high station. Besides several men of influence, some eminent women were devoted to him and his cause. The most celebrated of these was the deaconess Olympias. She was early left an orphan, and came under the oversight of Gregory Nazianzen, whom she addressed as "father," and who loved to call her his " own Olympias." Her husband, the prefect of Constantinople, died about two years after their marriage, and Olympias regarded this event as an intimation that she should consecrate the rest of her days to the Lord. After she was made deaconess she seldom departed from the church night or day. She gave her time and scattered her wealth with profuse liberality, assisting the clergy of Greece, Asia, and Syria in their charitable works. Between her and Chrysostom there was a strong bond of mutual affection; "she repaid his spiritual care by many little feminine attentions, especially by seeing that he was supplied with wholesome food, and did not overstrain his feeble constitution by a too rigid abstinence."[1]   A.D. 401.

The time was not yet ripe for the enemies of Chrysostom openly to show themselves. The Empress even found it expedient to maintain for a while the semblance of friendship with the popular preacher. When, on a charge being preferred against Severian, Chrysostom, without inquiry, excommunicated that bishop and commanded him to leave the city, Eudoxia presented herself before him in the church of the Apostles, placed her infant son on his knees, and conjured him to reverse the sentence. But Severian, though restored, was not reconciled, and the number of Chrysostom's enemies from the ranks of the Court ladies and the offended ecclesiastics increased daily. They were joined by the bishop Antiochus of Ptolemais, and by Acacius mentioned above, who was not at all displeased at the prospect of fulfilling his coarse threat.[2]

Courtiers and offended bishops were not the only foes against whom Chrysostom had to contend. The Arians who had been deprived of their churches by Theodosius[3] were determined, if possible, to recover their influence in the city. They assembled at night in the public piazzas to sing responsive hymns, and at break of day marched in procession through the midst of the city, passing

---

[1] Stephens, pp. 280-282; Roberts, p. 147, note.
[2] *Dict. Christ. Biog.*, i. p. 525.
[3] See *ante*, pp. 19, 95.

out at the gates to their places of worship. To make these demonstrations more defiant they interspersed with the hymns insulting questions or expressions. Chrysostom, to counteract their influence, organised similar processions of the Orthodox, and as these were the more numerous party, and the Empress placed her purse at their disposal, they presently surpassed the others in pomp, carrying crosses of silver illuminated by wax tapers. This display provoked the Arians to attack their rivals. Blood was shed on both sides, and the Imperial eunuch who was leading the Homo-ousion choir was wounded. On this the Emperor forcibly put a stop to the Arian processions. The historian who relates this occurrence refers to it as the origin of such public demonstrations: "The Orthodox party," he says, "having thus commenced the practice of singing hymns in procession, did not discontinue it, but have retained it to the present day." [1]

The Court party only wanted a leader to open the campaign against Chrysostom. One was found in Theophilus, the bishop of Alexandria, who had so unwillingly consecrated him to the episcopal

---

[1] Sozomen, b. viii. c. 8; see also Socrates, b. vi. c. 8. "Chrysostom in Constantinople sealed the victory of the Catholic party. He achieved what all the edicts of Theodosius failed to do; detached the populace of the city from their persistent and often tumultuous support of Arianism, and before the end of his brief opportunity made them devoted adherents of himself, and through himself of the Catholic Church."—Scott's *Ulfilas*, p. 151.

chair. He was "a man who knew better how to manage a court intrigue than to resolve a question of divinity, and the only rule of whose opinions was interest or ambition."[1] In a former chapter[2] mention was made of Isidore and the four monks of the Nitrian desert, known as the Tall Brethren. These men, who had now reached an advanced age, had with their fellow-recluses the misfortune to incur the ill-will of Theophilus. They had withstood his attempt to divert money given for the poor to the building of churches, and had protested against his avarice and other failings. The bishop determined to be revenged: an occasion was not long in presenting itself.[3]

The controversy on the theological opinions of Origen, which had slumbered during the long Arian war, had lately revived. Many of the monks were offended at Origen's spiritual conception of God, whom they were accustomed to represent to themselves as having the form and passions of a man, whence they were called Anthropo-morphites.[4] But the more studious, like Isidore and the Tall

---

[1] Du Pin, iii. p. 63. [2] See *ante*, p. 26.
[3] *Dict. Christ. Biog.*, i. p. 525; Stephens, pp. 293-295.
[4] I.e., *Representers of God under a human form*. Augustine tells us that the great impediment in his way from Manicheism to the true faith, was the difficulty of conceiving of God as a Spirit without corporeal extension. He describes the Anthropo-morphites as "the carnal and weak of our faith, who when they hear the members of the body used figuratively, as when God's eyes or ears are spoken of, are accustomed to picture Him to themselves in a human form."—*Against the Epistle of Manichæus, called Fundamental*, c. xxiii.

Brethren, followed the teaching of their illustrious countryman, and were determined adversaries of the Anthropo-morphite school. Hitherto Theophilus also had professed himself an admirer of Origen, and had written so decidedly against the more sensuous conception of the Deity, that an aged monk cried out: "They have robbed me of my God, and I know not whom to worship." It now suited Theophilus' purpose to change his position, and he all at once declared himself an opponent of Origen. He encouraged the more coarse and ignorant of the Anthropo-morphites to make tumultuous assaults on the monastic retreat of Nitria, and when some of the injured monks repaired to Alexandria to remonstrate, he flew into a rage, struck one of them, named Ammonius, violently on the face till the blood trickled down, and threw another into prison. He then announced, with shameless effrontery, that "he had himself at one time been in the fiery furnace of the Origen error, but, like the Three Children, had now come out unscathed, not a hair of his head, or his garments, being singed."[1]

Theophilus' thirst for revenge was insatiable. He convoked a synod, excommunicated three of the most eminent of the Nitrian monks as heretics and magicians, and, by means of false complaints and charges, induced the governor of Egypt to

---

[1] Stephens, p. 295; Robertson, pp. 384, 385.

order a night attack upon the monastery. The cells were pillaged and burned, and the valuable libraries destroyed. "The terrified monks, wrapping themselves in their sheepskins, their only remaining property, fled from their beloved solitude. Three hundred, with the Tall Brethren at their head, took their journey towards Palestine; only eighty reached Jerusalem." But they were not suffered to rest even here; commissioners were despatched to hunt them up in their hiding-places. The remnant of the exodus, consisting of the Tall Brethren and about fifty companions, arrived at length at Constantinople.[1]

They repaired at once to Chrysostom, who received them with great respect, and shed tears of compassion when he heard the tale of their sufferings and wanderings. But he acted with caution. He lodged them in the precincts of the church of Anastasia, but refused to admit them to the Eucharist until their cause was examined and their excommunication revoked. Finding themselves still pursued in the capital by the emissaries of Theophilus, they resolved to make an appeal to the Empress. One day, as she was riding to church, a party of them presented themselves before her, in their "white sheepskins and bare arms and knees." She stopped her litter, bowed graciously to them, and implored their prayers on

A.D. circa 401.

---

[1] Stephens, pp. 295-297.

Per. I.
Chap. 9.

behalf of the Emperor, herself, and her children; and when they besought her protection, she promised that a council should be convened, and Theophilus summoned to attend.[1]

On hearing these tidings Theophilus was furious. Epiphanius, bishop of Cyprus,[2] a restless controversialist, was foremost amongst the opponents of Origen, whom he designated the "ancestor of the Arian heresy." This man, then verging towards 90 years old, Theophilus sent to Constantinople, at once to extinguish Origenism, and to bring Chrysostom to account for sheltering the Tall Brethren. On Epiphanius' arrival, Chrysostom received him courteously, and invited him to take up his abode in the episcopal palace; but Epiphanius, rejecting his overtures, called together the bishops who were then in the city, and laying before them the decree of his own provincial council against the writings of Origen, required them to put their hands to it. Some complied; others refused. Amongst the latter was a Goth who had adopted the name of Theotimus, and had been appointed metropolitan of Lesser Scythia. He was not only bishop; he was also physician and commercial agent to the nomadic tribes. Only half a convert to Greek habits, he still allowed his

---

[1] Id., pp. 297-301.

[2] The same we met with in the *Early Church History* as a Puritan in matters of church decoration, and also as condemning, in his *Great Work against Heresies*, the reformer Aërius, pp. 478, 552.

long hair to float over his episcopal robe. Educated in Greece, he had carried back with him some precious books; and when not galloping across the plains, or baptizing some barbarian, he would unrol his parchments, and drink at the flowing spring of knowledge which the earlier writers, especially Origen, had opened. The anathemas uttered against his favourite author by Epiphanius and those who sided with him, astonished and shocked him. He made no reply at the moment, but when the company met again, the Gothic bishop drew from the folds of his garment a roll which he began to read in a loud voice. It contained passages from Origen of unimpeachable doctrine, glowing with elevated thoughts and ardent faith. Passage succeeded passage; and when at length Theotimus paused, it was only to give vent to his pent-up indignation. "I cannot comprehend, my brethren, how any one should dare to asperse a man who has written a thousand passages as excellent as these, and to pronounce him a child of Satan and an arch-heretic. If you find in his books anything less admirable than what I have read, or even something which you cannot approve, lay it on one side; leave the bad and choose the good."[1]

Epiphanius had not been long at Constantinople

---

[1] *Dict. Christ. Biog.*, art. Epiphanius of Salamis, ii. p. 152; *Chrysostome et Eudoxie*, by Thierry, in the *Revue des Deux Mondes*, 1 Sept. 1867, pp. 99, 100; Sozomen, b. vii. c. 26; b. viii. c. 14.

before he discovered that he had come upon a fool's errand, and growing weary of the miserable business he returned to Cyprus. He bade farewell to the bishops who accompanied him to the ship, with these words: "I leave you your city, and your Imperial palace, and all this stage-acting."[1]

In accordance with the promise given by Eudoxia to the monks, Theophilus was summoned to Constantinople. He hailed the occasion as the wished-for opportunity of accomplishing the ruin of Chrysostom. He was attended by a strong body-guard of sailors, and took with him costly presents for the disaffected clergy and persons of rank. He did not even scruple to give out, whilst on his journey, that he was going to depose Chrysostom for grave offences. Many bishops accompanied him from Egypt and Asia, some of the latter being those whom Chrysostom had deposed. So far from conducting himself as one accused, he made his entry into Constantinople "surrounded by the pomp and dignity of a judge."[2]

Chrysostom did not fail to offer to Theophilus the hospitality due to a brother bishop, but it was disdainfully rejected. Theophilus took up his lodging in one of the Emperor's palaces in the suburb of Pera. During the three weeks he resided there he refused all communication with Chrysostom. "His house was the resort of the

---

[1] Sozomen, b. viii. c. 15.
[2] *Dict. Christ. Biog.*, i. p. 526; Stephens, pp. 306, 307.

disaffected clergy, and the affronted ladies and gentlemen, who were drawn thither, not only by a common hatred to Chrysostom, but also by the handsome gifts, the dainty repasts, and the winning flattery of Theophilus."[1]

A.D. 403.

SECTION II. Chrysostom was directed by the court to repair to Pera and open an inquiry into the offences of which Theophilus was accused. Either from scruples as to his ecclesiastical jurisdiction, or from the love of peace, he declined. It was now Theophilus' turn to bring his rival to account. Not daring to institute proceedings in the city, he assembled a synod in the Asiatic suburb of Chalcedon,[2] which, however, was attended by only thirty-six bishops. Two deacons who had been degraded by Chrysostom for misconduct were suborned to prefer charges against him, and he was summoned to defend himself before the council.[3]

The scene which took place when Chrysostom received the summons is thus described by his biographer, Palladius. We give it as translated by Mr. Stephens. "We were sitting, to the number of forty bishops, in the dining-hall of the palace, marvelling at the audacity with which one, who had been commanded to appear as a culprit

---

[1] Stephens, pp. 307, 308.

[2] The assembly met in a mansion close to a celebrated oak, whence it was called the *Synod of the Oak*.—Roberts, p. 143.

[3] Stephens, pp. 308, 309.

Per. I.
Chap. 9.

at Constantinople, had arrived with a train of bishops, had altered the sentiments of nobles and magistrates, and perverted the majority even of the clergy. Whilst we were wondering, John [Chrysostom], inspired by the Spirit of God, addressed to us the following words: 'Pray for me, my brethren, and if ye love Christ, let no one for my sake desert his see, for I am now ready to be offered, and the time of my departure is at hand. I know the intrigues of Satan, that he will not endure any longer the burden of my words delivered against him.' Seized with inexpressible sorrow, some of us began to weep, and others to leave the assembly, after kissing, amid tears and sobs, his sacred head and eyes and eloquent mouth. He, however, exhorted them to return, and as they hovered near like bees humming round their hive, 'Sit down, my brethren,' he said, 'and do not weep, unnerving me by your tears, for to me to live is Christ, to die is gain. Recall the words which I have so frequently spoken to you: our present life is a journey; both its good and painful things pass away; present time is like a fair: we buy, we sell, and the assembly is dissolved. Are we better than the patriarchs, the prophets, the apostles, that this life should remain to us for ever?' Here one of the company, uttering a cry, exclaimed, 'Nay, but what we lament is our bereavement, and the widowhood of the Church; the derangement of sacred laws; the ambition of those who fear not the Lord and violently seize the highest positions; the destitution of the poor, and the loss of sound teaching.' But John replied, striking (as was his custom) the palm of his left hand with the forefinger of his right, 'Enough, my brother—no more; only, as I was saying, do not abandon your churches; for neither did the office of teaching begin with me, nor in me has it ended. Did not Moses die, and was not Joshua found to succeed him? Did not Samuel die? but was not David anointed? Jeremiah departed this life, but Baruch was left. Elijah was taken up, but Elisha prophesied in his place. Paul was beheaded, but did he not leave Timothy, Titus, Apollos, and a host of others to work after him?'"[1]

At this point it was announced that two deputies had arrived from the Synod of the Oak. Chrysostom inquired of what rank they were, and on hearing they were bishops, begged them to be seated, and to declare the purpose of their coming. "We are," said they, "the bearers of a document which we request thou wilt command to be read." It was a citation, and as though Chrysostom had already been degraded, he was addressed only by his name. "The Holy Synod assembled at the Oak to John. We have received," so ran the paper, "an infinite number of charges against

---

[1] Id., pp. 309–311; Palladius, *Dialogus de Vitâ S. Johann.*, c. viii.

Per. I.
Chap. 9.

thee: present thyself therefore before us, bringing with thee the priests Serapion and Tigrius, for their presence is necessary." Chrysostom's friends were indignant at the insolence of the message, and drew up a reply addressed to Theophilus, of which three bishops and two priests were the bearers. It was in these words: "Subvert not nor rend the Church for which God became incarnate; but if, in contempt of the canons framed by 318 bishops at Nicæa, thou wilt judge a cause outside thy jurisdiction, cross over into our city, which is at least governed by law, and do not, after the example of Cain, call Abel out into the open field. For we on our side possess charges of palpable crimes against *thee*, drawn up under seventy heads; and we by the grace of God are assembled after a peaceful manner, not for the disruption of the Church, and are besides more numerous than you, for with thee there are but thirty-six, but we are forty, seven of whom are metropolitans."[1]

Chrysostom approved of this answer, but sent also a separate letter on his own behalf, addressed not to Theophilus, but to the synod. "If you wish me to appear before you, eject from your assembly my declared enemies, Theophilus whom I could convict of having said, 'I am setting out for the capital to depose John,' Acacius, Severian, and

---

[1] Palladius, ibid.; Stephens, pp. 311, 312.

Antiochus. If these are removed, I am ready to appear, not before you only, but before a council of all Christendom. But know that, unless this is complied with, I will still refuse to present myself, though you should summon me ten thousand times over."[1]

The charges against Chrysostom were presented under twenty-nine heads; some of them were contemptibly frivolous, and some utterly false. "He had struck people on the face; had calumniated and even imprisoned his clergy; had illegally deposed bishops in Asia, and ordained others without sufficient inquiry; had alienated the property and sold the ornaments of the church; had held private interviews with women; had dined gluttonously by himself as a cyclops; had robed and unrobed himself on his episcopal throne; had eaten a lozenge after holy Communion; and had administered both sacraments after he himself or the recipients had broken their fast." The culminating offence was that of uttering treasonable words against the Empress (in comparing her to Jezebel), which was construed into exciting the people to rebellion. To the citation four times repeated, to appear before this packed tribunal, Chrysostom's reply was always the same, refusal to attend, and an appeal to a general council. Thus baffled, "the cabal expended their

---

[1] Palladius, ibid.; Stephens, pp. 312, 313.

fury on his messengers; they beat one bishop, tore the clothes of another, and placed on the neck of a third the chains they had designed for Chrysostom himself; their intention having been to put him secretly on board ship and send him off to some remote part of the empire." Sentence was pronounced against him: he was "condemned as contumacious, and deposed from his bishopric. The charge of treason his judges left to be dealt with by the civil power, secretly hoping that a capital sentence would be the issue. To their mortification, however, the Imperial rescript, which confirmed the sentence of deposition, condemned the bishop only to banishment for life."[1]

But if the disappointment of his enemies at the lenity of the sentence was great, "the wrath of the populace at the condemnation of their favourite preacher knew no bounds. As evening wore on, the news flew from mouth to mouth, and a crowd collected at the doors of his residence and of the great church, to keep watch lest he should be forcibly carried off. This voluntary guard protected him for three days and nights, during which he continually passed from one building to the other. His power over the popular mind was never greater." He had the wisdom not to abuse it. "The sermons he addressed to the vast crowds which filled the cathedral[2] inculcated patience and

---

[1] Palladius, ibid.; Stephens, pp. 312-316; *Dict. Christ. Biog.*, i. p. 526.
[2] The Church of St. Sophia.

resignation to the Divine will." He himself determined to bow to the storm. On the third day he took advantage of the hour of the noontide meal to slip out unperceived by a side door, and quietly surrendered himself to the Imperial officers, by whom he was conducted after dark to the harbour, and put on board a vessel which conveyed him to the Bithynian coast.[1]

A.D. 403.

"The victory of his enemies seemed complete. Theophilus entered the city in triumphal state, and wreaked his vengeance on the bishop's partisans. The people, who had crowded to the churches to pour forth their lamentations, were forcibly dislodged, not without bloodshed. Furious at the loss of their revered teacher, they thronged the approaches to the Imperial palace, clamouring for his restoration, and demanding that his cause should be heard before a general council. Constantinople was almost in revolt."[2]

The following night the city was convulsed by an earthquake. The shock was felt with peculiar violence in the Empress's bed-chamber. Eudoxia, as superstitious as she was implacable, fell at Arcadius' feet, and entreated him to avert the wrath of Heaven by revoking the sentence against Chrysostom. The flexile Emperor complied. Messengers were despatched in pursuit of the banished prelate, bearing letters from Eudoxia,

---

[1] Stephens, pp. 317-320; *Dict. Christ. Biog.*, i. pp. 526, 527.
[2] *Dict. Christ. Biog.*, ibid.

couched in terms of abject humiliation. "Let not thy holiness imagine that I was cognizant of what has been done. Wicked men have contrived this plot. I remember the baptism of my children by thy hands. God whom I serve is witness of my tears."[1]

"The news of Chrysostom's recall caused a universal jubilee. Late in the day as it was, his friends took shipping, and a fleet of barks put forth to meet him. The Bosphorus blazed with torches and resounded with psalms of welcome. Chrysostom at first halted outside the city, claiming to be acquitted by a general council before resuming his see. The people suspected treachery, and loudly denounced the Emperor and Empress. Apprehensive of a serious outbreak, Arcadius sent a secretary to desire Chrysostom to enter the walls without delay. As a loyal subject he obeyed. On passing the gates he was borne aloft by the crowd, carried into the church, placed on his episcopal seat, and forced to deliver an extemporaneous oration. His triumph was now as complete as that of his enemies had been a few days before." The leaders of the cabal could scarcely show themselves in public; and after a short delay, Theophilus, on the plea that his diocese could no longer dispense with his presence, left the city by night, and sailed for Alexandria.

---

[1] Id., i. p. 527; Stephens, p. 321.

His flight was speedily followed by the assembling of about sixty bishops friendly to Chrysostom, who annulled the proceedings of the Oak, and declared him to be still the legitimate bishop of Constantinople.[1]

For a while the Empress yielded to the tide, and professed to be completely reconciled to Chrysostom. Strange to say, he responded to her overtures, and they vied with each other in compliments and eulogistic phrases. It is not easy to account for such weakness on the part of a man of Chrysostom's high character. The servile adulation paid to Oriental monarchs might perhaps be advanced as an excuse, if Chrysostom had not shown how easily he could break through such trammels. A more probable cause is to be found in the fatal maxim he had adopted, that the end sanctifies the means. He doubtless persuaded himself that to propitiate the Empress was essential to the interests of the Church, even at the expense of truth. But this delusive calm was presently succeeded by another storm.[2]

SECTION III. Lofty as was her position, Eudoxia aspired to still higher honours. Not content with the virtual rule of the East, she panted for that half-divine homage which by ancient custom was still paid to the Emperor himself.[3] She caused her

---

[1] *Dict. Christ. Biog.*, ibid.   [2] Id.
[3] "When on rare occasions, Arcadius condescended to show himself in public, he was preceded by a vast multitude of attendants glittering in

Per. I.
Chap. 9.

statue to be cast in silver, and set up on a lofty column of porphyry in the centre of the market-place, in front of the church of St. Sophia. Its dedication was accompanied by the boisterous revelry of the old pagan rites, which the Christian Emperors, in their short-sighted and faithless policy, had retained as a means of preserving the loyalty of the people. The sound of the music and dancing was heard in the church, and disturbed the service. "Chrysostom's holy indignation took fire, and with ill-timed zeal he mounted the reading-desk, and thundered forth a homily, embracing in its fierce invective all who had any share in these profanities: the prefect who ordered them, the people who joined in them; and, above all, the arrogant woman whose ambition was the cause of them. 'Herodias,' he is reported to have exclaimed, 'is once more maddening; Herodias is once more dancing; once more Herodias demands

---

gold. The streets were cleared before the Emperor's approach, who stood or reclined in a gorgeous chariot adorned with precious stones, and drawn by white mules in gilded trappings. The cushions were snow-white; the carpets of silk, embroidered with dragons in the richest colours. Gilt fans, waved by the motion of the chariot, cooled the air. The Emperor himself was laden with jewels, ears, arms, and brow; whilst his robes of imperial purple, to which colour none else might aspire, were embroidered in all their seams with precious stones. He was attended by a bodyguard carrying shields with golden bosses set round with golden eyes. Ships were employed for the express purpose of bringing gold dust to strew the pavement, that the Emperor's foot might touch nothing but gold."—Milman, *Hist. Christ.*, iii. pp. 243, 244. The household of his predecessor Constantius numbered no fewer than a thousand barbers, a thousand cup-bearers, a thousand cooks, and so many eunuchs that they could be compared only to the insects of a summer day.—Schaff's *Nicene Christianity*, p. 129.

the head of John on a charger.'¹ These scathing words were reported to Eudoxia. Can we wonder that all her former fury revived, and that she demanded of the Emperor signal redress for such treasonable insolence? Compromise was no longer possible; the bishop or the Empress must yield."²

The hostile bishops who had returned to their dioceses now flocked again to the metropolis, ready with the fashionable ladies and the worldly clergy of the city, to contrive new plots for Chrysostom's ruin. He had demanded a general council; let such a council be called, and let his treasonable language against the Empress be laid before it, and the result could not be doubtful. But to make matters still more secure, Theophilus put forward a canon of the Council of Antioch, A.D. 341,³ pronouncing the *ipso facto* deprivation of any bishop who after deposition should appeal to the secular power for restoration. The general council met towards the end of the year (403), and seems, without passing any formal sentence, to have considered this canon as decisive.⁴

---

¹ These words are now extant only as the exordium of a homily, ascribed to Chrysostom, but pronounced by some of the best critics to be spurious.—Stephens, p. 328, note. That they nearly represent what was uttered is probable, both from Chrysostom's language on the former occasion, and because they could not have been laid hold of for his ruin unless they had been in the highest degree offensive.

² *Dict. Christ. Biog.*, *loc. cit.*; Stephens, p. 327.

³ For the character of this council and the estimation in which its canons were held, see *ante*, p. 9, and note.

⁴ *Dict. Christ. Biog.*, i. pp. 527, 528.

The Emperor accepted this conclusion, and accordingly, on Christmas day, refused to attend divine Service in the cathedral. But this token of imperial displeasure was lost on Chrysostom. Supported by forty-two bishops, he continued to administer his episcopate, and to preach to the people as before. Matters went on in this way until near Easter, when it was resolved that Chrysostom must be removed at all hazards. Arcadius sent him an order forbidding him to enter the church during Easter. Chrysostom's dignified reply was, "I received this Church from God my Saviour, and am charged with the salvation of this flock, which I am not at liberty to abandon. Expel me if thou wilt, since the city belongs to thee, that I may have thy authority as an excuse for deserting my post."

Fearing to use force, lest he should again provoke the vengeance of Heaven, Arcadius, on the advice of Acacius and Antiochus, commanded the bishop to remain a prisoner in the episcopal palace, not leaving it even for the church without permission. The Emperor could scarcely have looked for obedience to this command, least of all on Easter Eve (the great season of baptism), when three thousand catechumens were expected to present themselves. The bishop again answered that he would not desist from officiating, unless compelled by actual force. "When the time arrived, he calmly left his residence and proceeded to the cathedral. The Imperial guards, forbidden to use A.D. 404. violence, dared not interfere. The perplexed Emperor summoned Acacius and Antiochus to his presence, and reproached them with the failure of their counsel. They replied that Chrysostom being no longer a bishop was acting illegally in administering the sacraments, and that they would take on themselves the responsibility of his ejection."[1]

On this, the Emperor at once ordered the guards to act. "The church was thronged with worshippers keeping" the vigil of the Resurrection. Baptism was being administered to the long files of catechumens, male and female, whom the deacons and deaconesses had prepared for the rite by the removal of their outer garments. Suddenly the din of arms broke the solemn stillness. A body of soldiers, sword in hand, burst in, and rushed, some to the baptisteries, some up the nave to the altar. The catechumens were driven from the fonts at the point of the sword; women as well as men, half-dressed and shrieking, rushed into the streets. Many were wounded, and the baptismal water was red with blood. Others of the troop, some of whom were pagans, forced open the inner doors, and not only gazed on the sacred vessels, but handled the Eucharistic elements, and spilt the wine on their garments. The clergy in their liturgical robes were forcibly ejected from the church, and with the mingled crowd of men,

---

[1] Id., p. 528; Stephens, pp. 329-332.

women and children, chased along the dark streets. Taking refuge in the baths of Constantine, and hastily "blessing" the profane building, to serve as a baptistery, they began to collect the terrified catechumens and proceed with the ceremonial. But they were again interrupted by the soldiery, who drove them out as before; and the same scene was enacted wherever the scattered congregations endeavoured to re-unite. "The horrors of that night remained indelibly imprinted on the minds of those who witnessed them, and were spoken of long afterwards with shuddering." For the greater part of the week Constantinople wore the aspect of a city which had been taken by storm. The partisans of Chrysostom, now called "Joannites," were hunted out, thrown into prison and scourged, the sound of the scourge and the oaths of the soldiers being heard even in the churches.[1]

For two months, however, the timid Arcadius could not summon resolution to sign the decree for Chrysostom's banishment. At length it was signed. The bishop received it with submission, and entering the cathedral, said to those who accompanied him, "Come and let us pray. At my own fate I can rejoice: I only grieve for the sorrow of my people." Then entering the baptistery, he sent for Olympias and three other of the deaconesses, to whom he said, "Come hither,

---

[1] *Dict. Christ. Biog.*, i. pp. 528, 529; Stephens, pp. 332-334; Milman, iii. p. 145. The pursuit was continued the next day to a place outside the walls, whither the fugitives had betaken themselves.—Sozomen, b. viii. c. 21.

my daughters, and hearken to me. I have finished my course; perchance you will see my face no more. Submit to the authority of my successor. Remember me in your prayers." Overwhelmed with grief, they threw themselves at his feet; he made a sign to one of the priests to remove them, lest their wailing should be heard outside. Being informed that the troops were in readiness to compel his removal, and advised by one of his friends to take his departure in secret, he directed that his mule should be saddled, and led, according to custom, to the western gate of the cathedral. Whilst the people's attention was diverted by this feint, he passed out unobserved at a postern, and surrendered himself to some of the soldiers. Two faithful bishops accompanied him, and a vessel bore them under cover of night across to the Asiatic shore.[1]

When the people discovered that the bishop was gone, they became violently agitated. Some rushed to the harbour, others made an attack upon the cathedral, and battered the doors, which had been locked by the soldiery. Suddenly flames burst forth from the building; all attempts to extinguish them were in vain, and this magnificent structure, the erection of Constantine the Great, was in three hours reduced to a heap of cinders.[2]

---

[1] Stephens, pp. 338–340; *Dict. Christ. Biog.*, i. p. 529.

[2] It was again destroyed in 532, and was rebuilt with yet greater skill and splendour, by Justinian, A.D. 544. In 1453, at the capture of the city

The flames spread to the senate-house, which was also destroyed. Suspicion, real or affected, fell on Chrysostom and his flock; and a fresh chapter of persecution followed, worthy of the pagan rule. In fact, the government of the city was at the time in the hands of a pagan prefect, who hunted down the followers of the bishop with relentless cruelty. To the pretended crime of incendiarism was added that of refusal to recognise Chrysostom's successor, Arsacius, a very old man, described by Palladius as "more dumb than a fish and more incapable than a frog," and who appears to have been appointed by the sole fiat of the Emperor. Clergy and laymen, and even women, were subjected to intimidation, imprisonment, insult, and torture. Eutropius, a reader, a young man of a delicate frame, refusing (probably unable) to name the persons who had set fire to the church, was scourged, and brutally tortured, after the most approved model of the Decian or Diocletian persecutions. When it was found that nothing could be extorted from him, he was thrown into a dungeon, and there expired. Tigrius, a priest, was stripped and scourged, and then stretched on the rack till he too died under his tortures; and Serapion, who like Tigrius had been summoned, with Chrysostom, to "the Oak," was barbarously scourged and banished.[1]

by Mohammed II., Justinian's church was converted into a mosque which still bears the name of St. Sophia.

[1] Stephens, pp. 341-345; *Dict. Christ. Biog.*, i. p. 520.

Those ladies who were most distinguished for their friendship with the deposed bishop were taken before the prefect, and admonished to acknowledge Arsacius. Some from timidity complied, but others met the arbitrary command with a dauntless spirit. Amongst these was the deaconess Olympias. Being asked why she had set fire to the great church, " My manner of life," she answered, " is a sufficient refutation of such a charge. One who has expended large sums of money to restore and embellish the churches of God is not likely to burn them." " I know thy past course of life well," cried the prefect. " If thou knowest aught against it," was the intrepid reply, " descend from thy place as judge, and come forward as my accuser." Unable to fix any charge upon her, the prefect changed his tone, and advised her and the other accused ladies to save themselves further trouble by "communicating" with Arsacius. Her companions yielded, but Olympias boldly replied: " It is an injustice, that, after being publicly calumniated, I should be called upon to clear myself of charges utterly foreign to the issue. Not even on compulsion will I hold communion with those from whom it is my duty to secede." She was mulcted in a heavy fine, which she paid, and then withdrew to the other side of the Straits.[1]

Chrysostom and his friends sent four bishops of

---

[1] Sozomen, b. viii. c. 24; Stephens, pp. 345, 346; *Dict. Christ. Biog.*, loc. cit.

their party to the bishop of Rome and the Western Churches to inform them of the ordeal through which the faithful in Constantinople were passing. Innocent expressed his sympathy with the sufferers; and at the request of the Italian bishops, the Emperor Honorius wrote letters to his brother Arcadius. But the sympathy and the letters were alike fruitless. The bearers were insulted and ill-treated, and compelled to return to Italy; and the four Eastern bishops were banished to distant quarters of the empire, and harried on their way with brutal insults and indignities.[1]

Arsacius survived his elevation to the patriarchate less than a year. His successor Atticus was equally determined to stamp out the Joannites. The wealthier clergy of the party mostly made their peace by concession, the poorer sought refuge in flight, either to Rome or the monasteries; some obtained a precarious livelihood by manual labour, farming or fishing : laymen were degraded, fined, and banished. On the other hand, the delinquent bishops whom Chrysostom had expelled were restored; and ordinations were conducted with feasting, drunkenness, and bribery. "The spirit of lawlessness and selfishness which was let loose during this period of misrule, dealt a blow to morality and discipline from which the Church at Constantinople never recovered."[2]

---

[1] Stephens, pp. 348-356.   [2] Id., 356-359.

CHAPTER X.

CHRYSOSTOM (concluded).

SECTION I. Landing on the Asiatic coast, Chrysostom was conveyed to Nicæa. Not until he reached that city was he informed of his destination, the mountain village of Cucusus[1] on the borders of Cilicia and Armenia, in a lonely valley of the Taurus range. The climate was inclement; the country was exposed to perpetual inroads from the Isaurian marauders: it was the hottest season of the year (July), and the journey was long and toilsome. His heart sank within him. His guards had received instructions to push on with all speed; and although they compassionated the sufferings of their prisoner, they dared not disobey. The squalid villages, where the convoy halted, furnished no food but black bread, which had to be steeped before Chrysostom could masticate it. The water was unwholesome, exciting rather than allaying thirst. Chrysostom was seized with ague, yet he was not permitted to halt, but was hurried forward to Cæsarea in Cappadocia, some 600 miles from the capital.[2]

A.D. 404.

---

[1] Now Gogison. Smith and Dwight, *Missionary Researches in Armenia*, p. 46, note.   [2] *Dict. Christ. Biog.*, i. pp. 529, 530.

Per. I.
Chap. 10.

"I entered Cæsarea," he writes to Olympias, "worn down and exhausted, and in the crisis of a tertian fever. There was at first no one to nurse me, no physician to be had, no alleviations necessary for my state. Soon, however, the clergy, the people, monks, and medical men flowed in upon me, proffering their services: only Pharetrius (the bishop) came not.[1] After a time the disorder abated, and I began to think of setting forward, when news was brought that the Isaurians were laying waste the country, and that the tribune had marched out to oppose them. Whilst things were in this posture, a cohort of monks, set on by Pharetrius, came to the house where I lodged, and threatened to set it on fire if I did not immediately leave the city. So furious was their behaviour that the soldiers who came to protect me were overawed, for these brutes boasted that they had on former occasions shamefully handled the city guard. Even the prefect lost courage and sent to Pharetrius, imploring him not to expose me to the Isaurian bands, but to allow me a few days' delay. But all was of no avail; the next day the monks renewed their attack; and about noon, throwing myself into my litter, I quitted the city, all the people bewailing my departure, and devoting to perdition the man who had occasioned it.

---

[1] He was secretly in league with the enemies of Chrysostom, and had many of the monks on his side; but his clergy were Joannites almost to a man.—*Dict. Christ. Biog.*, i. p. 530.

"Hearing what had taken place, the excellent lady, Seleucia, besought me to take up my abode at her villa, some five miles distant, where there was a strong tower, proof against any attack which could be made upon it. At the same time she ordered her steward, if the monks should pursue me, to summon the peasants from her other villas, to contend with them hand to hand. But in the middle of the night Pharetrius came to the villa, and with vehement threats insisted upon my being ejected. The lady was unable to withstand his importunity, and the presbyter Evetheus, coming into my chamber, and supposing the alarm to be caused by the Isaurians, waked me, crying out, 'Rise, I pray thee, the barbarians are upon us!' The night was moonless and gloomy; we had no guide, nor any to help us. Expecting death at any moment, and almost sinking under my trials, I rose and ordered torches to be lighted; these, however, the presbyter extinguished, lest the barbarians, attracted by the light, should rush upon us. The way being stony, the mule which carried my litter fell, and I was thrown to the ground. Raising myself, I crawled along, Evetheus, who had leaped from his horse, holding my hands. From the roughness of the way and the darkness of the night I was unable to use my feet."[1]

It was the end of August before Chrysostom

---

[1] Roberts' *Church Memorials*, pp. 148-151.

reached Cucusus. His reception almost made him forget the sufferings of the journey. Every comfort was provided for him; friends from Constantinople and Antioch came to visit him, some even to share his exile. Far removed as he now was, he did not settle down in inaction. "The three years spent at Cucusus were the most glorious of his life."[1] Hitherto, in the perilous position of a popular preacher, his infirmities of temper and character had marred his work. Now exiled, shorn of outward honour, and chastened by suffering, he yet laboured unremittingly as ever for the weal of his fellow-men. His letters are very numerous, and bear witness to his care, not alone for his flock in the Imperial city, but for the interests of the Churches far and near. "Never did he exert a wider and more powerful influence. His advice was sought from all quarters; no important ecclesiastical measure was undertaken without consulting him. The East was almost governed from a mountain village of Armenia."[2]

His chief hardships were occasioned by the forays of the brigands, and the extremes of the climate. With difficulty could he endure the severity of the winter. "I am just recalled," he says, in another letter to Olympias, "from the gates of death, having passed two months in a state of suffering more grievous even than the agonies of

---

[1] Gibbon, iv. p. 186.   [2] *Dict. Christ. Biog.*, i. p. 530.

death itself. All that I seemed to live for was to be sensible of the ills with which I was encompassed. Whether it was morning or noon, it mattered not; all was night to me. I passed whole days without rising from my bed; and although I kept a good fire, enduring the smoke, and was covered with a pile of blankets, and never ventured to the door, I suffered extreme torture; each sleepless night was like a long sea voyage. As soon, however, as spring appeared all my ailments left me."[1]

In the winter of 405, an alarm was raised that the marauders were coming. Nearly the whole of the inhabitants fled. Chrysostom and a few faithful companions wandered hither and thither, sometimes even passing the night without shelter, until they reached a mountain-fort, sixty miles from Cucusus. Here, cut off from his friends by the snow and by the brigands, who one night had nearly captured the castle, unable to procure his usual medicines, and the place crowded like a prison, he struggled through the winter. With the return of spring the Isaurians retired, and Chrysostom went back to Cucusus. After the hill-fort "this desolate little town seemed to him a paradise. His wonderful preservation from danger, and the manner in which his feeble health, instead of sinking under the accumulated trials

---

[1] Roberts, pp. 152, 153.

of his banishment, became invigorated, awoke sanguine anticipations, and in his letters written at this time he confidently foretold his return to Constantinople." But this was not to be.[1]

"The unhappy Eudoxia had preceded the victim of her hatred to the grave to which she had destined him, but she left other not less relentless enemies behind. Stung with disappointment that the climate of Cucusus had failed to do the work they intended, they obtained a rescript from Arcadius, transferring the exile to Pityus,[2] a frontier fortress on the eastern shore of the Euxine, where the roots of the Caucasus come down to the sea. This was the most inhospitable spot they could choose, and therefore the most certain to rid them of their victim, even if the long and toilsome journey should fail to quench the feeble spark of life."[3]

"Two prætorian guards of ferocious temper were selected to attend him, with instructions to push forward with merciless haste, the hint being privately given that they might expect promotion if he died on the road. One of the two furtively showed some little kindness to the sufferer, but the other followed literally his instructions. The journey was to be made on foot; towns where Chrysostom might enjoy any approach to

---

[1] *Dict. Christ. Biog.*, i. pp. 530, 531.
[2] Now Soukoum-Kaleh (?). Pitsunda, according to Smith and Dwight.
[3] *Dict. Christ. Biog.*, i. p. 531.

comfort, or have the refreshment of a warm bath, were to be avoided; all letters were forbidden, and the least communication with passers-by was punished with blows." So slow was the progress that in three months they had travelled no further than Comana, in Pontus.[1] Here it was evident that the bishop's strength was exhausted: "his body was almost calcined by the sun. Nevertheless his guards hurried him through the town 'as if its streets were no more than a bridge.'"[2]

"Five or six miles beyond Comana stood a chapel erected over the tomb of a martyred bishop. Here they halted for the night. It is said that in his sleep Chrysostom saw the martyr standing by his side, and bidding him be of good cheer, for on the morrow they should be together; and that the priest in charge of the chapel saw in a vision the same martyr, bidding him 'prepare a place for our brother John.' In the morning Chrysostom

---

[1] This does not appear to lie in the direct route from Cucusus to Pityus, which would surely be up the Euphrates valley. No doubt the *détour* was purposely made. Armenian tradition places the site of Comana at some ruins on the banks of the Iris, situated two hours' journey east of the large manufacturing town of Tokát. Here Henry Martyn, in 1812, a few months after completing the translation of the New Testament into Persian, closed his brief devoted life, and lies buried in the Armenian cemetery. There is something of similarity in the closing scene with that of the elder brother, who had gone before. Like Chrysostom, he was on a long journey across Asia Minor; he was worn by fever, and harassed by hardships, far from friends and loved ones, and with none near him but "merciless" and alien attendants. "O, when shall time give place to eternity," is the last entry in his journal.—See Smith and Dwight, *op. cit.*, pp. 42, 44; *Memoir of Rev. H. Martyn*, 6th ed., pp. 412, 473, etc.

[2] *Dict. Christ. Biog.*, ibid.

earnestly begged for a brief respite, but in vain; he was hurried off, but had scarcely gone three miles when a paroxysm of fever compelled his guards to carry him back to the chapel. On reaching the place he was supported to the altar, and having asked for the white robes of baptism he put them on, distributing his own clothes to the bystanders. He then partook of the bread and wine, prayed a last prayer, uttered his accustomed doxology, 'Glory be to God for all things,' and yielded up his spirit." He died A.D. 407, in the sixtieth year of his age, and was buried by the side of the martyr in the presence of a large concourse of monks and nuns.[1]

Thirty-one years afterwards, when Theodosius II. was Emperor, Chrysostom's body was exhumed and translated with great pomp to Constantinople. "As once in his lifetime to greet him on his return from exile, so now, but in still greater numbers, the city poured itself forth to receive all that remained of their beloved bishop. The corpse was deposited near the altar in the church of the Apostles, along with the dust of Emperors and bishops, the youthful sovereign and his sister Pulcheria assisting at the ceremony, and asking pardon of Heaven for the wrong inflicted by their parents on the sainted bishop."[2]

---

[1] So Palladius relates, who adds that they came out of Syria, Cilicia and Armenia. "How," asks Stephens, "could this be, if it took three months to convey Chrysostom from Cucusus to Comana?" p. 387, note.

[2] *Dict. Christ. Biog.*, i. p. 531; Stephens, pp. 388, 389.

SECTION II. Chrysostom, as already mentioned, was "small of stature: his limbs were long, and so emaciated that he compared himself to a spider. His forehead was lofty, expanding at the summit, and furrowed with wrinkles; his head bald; his eyes deep-set, but keen and piercing; his cheeks pallid and withered; his chin pointed and covered with a short beard."[1]

Chrysostom's genius was comprehensive and his industry unwearied. In eloquence he was without a rival. "His virtues were those of the monk rather than of the Christian citizen." Himself of dauntless courage and inflexible purpose, he was unable to make allowance for the more pliable temperament of others; and he was wanting in discernment of character, and tact in the management of men. His naturally irritable temper was aggravated by feebleness of digestion, " the excessive austerities of his youth having rendered him incapable of taking food, except in very small quantities and of the plainest kind." In spite, however, of his infirmities, he was, as we have seen, greatly beloved by those who were most intimate with him.[2]

His writings are very voluminous and highly esteemed, especially his commentaries on Scripture.[3] He was, however, no reformer. The state

---

[1] *Dict. Christ. Biog.*, i. pp. 531, 532.
[2] Ibid.; Stephens, p. 217.
[3] The Benedictine edition of his works is contained in thirteen large

of the Church cried aloud for teachers of clear vision and honest heart, to bring back the golden days ere men began to teach for doctrines their own inventions and commandments. Chrysostom answered to no such call. Spiritually-minded as he was, we yet find him giving his countenance to the worst superstitions of the times, and urging them forward with all the force of his eloquence. We have seen how profound was his reverence for the ascetic life. In a future chapter we shall notice his extravagant views on celibacy, fasting, and almsgiving, as well as the support he gave to the worship of saints and their relics. Let us here consider what he has to say on the priesthood and the Eucharist. Surely no man ever carried sacerdotal pretensions to a greater height, or ever set them forth in more rhapsodical language.

"Although the priesthood is discharged upon earth," so he writes in his celebrated treatise, "it is ranked among heavenly ordinances; for it was established by the Comforter Himself, who has entrusted men yet dwelling in the flesh with a ministry like that of angels. For if the institutions of the law were awful and most impressive,

---

folios, one-half however being a translation into Latin. In the Greek Church he ranks above all other Church writers. The Czar Alexis, father of Peter the Great, was accustomed to rise at four o'clock, and go into the oratory, where, after a quarter of an hour in prayer, the deacon of the palace read to him books of devotion, most frequently the writings of Chrysostom.—Schuyler's *Life of Peter the Great*, vol. i. p. 21.

the bells, the pomegranates, the stones worn on the breast and shoulders, the mitre, the crown, the robe reaching down to the feet, the golden fringe, the holy of holies, the great stillness of all in the Temple; . . . yet that which was made glorious had no glory at all by reason of the glory that excelleth. . . . Although their abode and home is on earth, the priests are entrusted with the management of things in heaven, and receive an authority such as God never granted either to angels or archangels: to whom it was never said, 'Whatsoever ye shall bind on earth shall be bound in heaven, and whatsoever ye shall loose on earth shall be loosed in heaven.' For though even temporal rulers have authority to bind, their power reaches only to the body; whereas this bond penetrates the very soul, and passes up into the heavens, where God ratifies the act of his priests. What, indeed, has He really given them but the whole authority of Heaven? For He says, 'Whosesoever sins ye remit, they are remitted unto them, and whosesoever sins ye retain, they are retained.' What authority can be greater than this? 'The Father hath committed all judgement unto the Son.' But now I see this judgement delegated by the Son to the priests; for they are advanced to this office with as absolute a commission as if they had been already translated into the heavens, as if they were already exalted above human nature and exempted from the dominion of our passions. . . . Out upon the madness which would despise an office so important, without which it is impossible for us to obtain either salvation or the blessings which are promised! For if, except a man be born again of water and of the Spirit he cannot enter into the kingdom of God, and if he who does not eat the flesh of the Lord and drink His blood is rejected from eternal life, and if all these blessings are dispensed only by the holy hands of the priest, how can any one without their ministry either escape the fire of hell or obtain the crowns which are laid up for us? . . . Wherefore those who despise the priestly office commit a greater crime, and are worthy of a sorer punishment, than even the followers of Dathan."[1]

Surely this is building in wood and stubble! It is by no such pretensions or denunciations as these that the truth is commended or the Church edified. Far otherwise was the mind of the Apostle Peter himself, who, writing to his brethren of the Dispersion, called them all, without distinction, "a royal priesthood."[2]

Not less repugnant to New Testament teaching is the picture which presents itself to the preacher's fervid imagination when the priest blesses and distributes the bread and wine. "When you see the Lord sacrificed and laid upon the altar, and the priest standing and praying over the sacrifice, and

---

[1] *On the Priesthood*, b. iii.   [2] 1 Pet. ii. 9.

all the people empurpled with his most precious blood, do you then fancy yourself still among men, or are you not instantly transported into the heavens, so as laying aside every fleshly sentiment to look around with naked soul and disembodied spirit on celestial objects? O the wondrous loving-kindness of God! He who sits above with the Father is at that instant holden in the hands of every one, giving Himself to those who clasp and embrace Him, as all may clearly see with the eyes of faith.... Then, too, there are angels standing near the priest; and all the order of the heavenly powers raise their voice in honour of the victim. I once heard a certain person relate what an aged and venerable man accustomed to revelations told him, namely, that when the sacrifice was offered he suddenly beheld a multitude of white-robed angels encompassing the altar and bowing down their heads, as soldiers do homage to their prince; and I believe it."[1]

---

[1] *On the Priesthood*, b. iii., vi. In the *Order of the Divine Sacrifice*, in the Liturgy of the Church of Constantinople, the "bloodless sacrifice," as the Fathers loved to call it, is made to resemble the Offering on the Cross. The bread was fashioned cross-wise, or in four limbs, and impressed with the sign of the cross on each limb. The priest taking a "holy spear," performed various touchings and piercings of the cruciform cake, elevated it, and replaced it in the charger. Then the deacon, addressing the priest, says, "Slay, Sir;" and the priest immolates the "holy cake," saying, "The Lamb of God is slain who taketh away the sin of the world." Then the deacon says, "Prick, Sir;" and the priest pierces the cake on the right side with the "holy lance": at the same moment the deacon pours wine and water into the chalice.—Isaac Taylor's *Ancient Christ.*, i. p. 549. This *Order*, however, it should be stated, although appended to the works of Chrysostom, is, at least in its actual

Per. I.
Chap. 10.

The communicants, however, were not always thus transported. Chrysostom has often to reprove them for occupying the very moment of the consecration with worldly business and merriment. Many also, he tells us, presented themselves only on great festivals, and then in a most disorderly manner. They hustled one another in their eagerness first to reach the table; and as soon as they had partaken of the bread and wine, hurried out of the church without waiting for the conclusion of the service. Many who came to partake of the "awful and terrific table," passed their days on the race-ground, or hastened away to the forbidden spectacles of the stage. "You leave the well of blood, the terrific cup, to go to the Devil's well,[1] where your own soul suffers shipwreck. If souls were visible, how many could I show you floating there, like the corpses of the Egyptians in the Red Sea."[2]

It was a common belief in that age, as now

---

form, of a very much later date.—*Dict. Christ. Antiq.*, art. Liturgy, pp. 1024, 1025.

The bishop of Salford (Roman Catholic), citing part of the above passage from Chrysostom, prefaces the quotation with these words: "It has been a universal belief in the Church, that holy angels assist at every mass that is celebrated. And no wonder; nothing greater or more sacred is ever done in heaven. The oblation of Jesus Christ in the mass intimately affects the whole heavenly Court, for while it gives grace and pardon to us, it is an infinite act of adoration and thanksgiving, sounding like a blessed voice of praise throughout creation."—*On the Holy Sacrifice of the Mass*, p. 54. London, 1878.

[1] The allusion is to certain obscene spectacles at the theatre.

[2] Isaac Taylor, ii. p. xxx.; Stephens, p. 135.

in the Romish Church, that heaven is to be purchased by good works and self-mortification. Such a doctrine is almost inseparable from the ascetic life; Chrysostom thus gives it shape. "As those who are in a foreign country, when they wish to return to their own land, take pains, a long time beforehand, to collect means sufficient for their journey, so surely ought we, who are but strangers on this earth, to lay up a store of provisions through spiritual virtue, that when our Master shall command our return into our native country, we may be prepared, and may carry part of our store with us, having sent the other in advance."[1] In one of his letters to Olympias, he

---

[1] Since the above was written, a card has come into our hands, which has been widely circulated :—

NOTICE TO TRAVELLERS GOING TO HEAVEN.

Trains leave: At all hours.	Arrive: When God wills.
Limited Express, 1st Class.—Poverty, Chastity, Obedience.	*Price of Tickets.*
Express, 1st and 2nd Class.—Piety, Devotions, Sacraments.	1st.—Love and Crosses.
Accommodation, 1st, 2nd, and 3rd Class.—Commandments, Duties of State of Life.	2nd.—Desire and Combat.
	3rd.—Fear and Penance.

ADVICE.

1. There are no return tickets.
2. No excursion trains.
3. Children who have not attained the use of reason do not pay any thing, provided they are held on the lap of their Mother—the Church.
4. Travellers are advised to bring no other baggage but *good works* if

invites her to count over her own perfections, and to dwell with complacency on the heavenly reward which is in store for her. The sufferings of life, no less than good works, were similarly assigned to our credit in the celestial ledger. When Chrysostom was driven out of Cæsarea and dragged by night along the mountain path, he wrote to Olympias: "Were not these calamities sufficient to blot out many sins, and suggest to me a hope of future glory?"[1] But when Olympias, pursuing this mistaken notion to its legitimate issue, wrote, "My only thought is how I may increase my suffering," Chrysostom seems to have become conscious of having ventured too near the precipice. He thus admonishes her: "I regard it as something highly sinful that thou professest, voluntarily and designedly, to encourage thoughts which bring sorrow with them. Thou certainly art in duty to thyself bound to contrive everything to obliterate sadness from thy mind, but thou dost what is agreeable to Satan by augmenting thy grief and trouble."[2]

---

they do not wish to miss the train, or meet with a delay at the next to the last station.

5. Travellers can take passage on any part of the road.

[1] There is an obvious confusion of ideas in these words. That "our light affliction, which is for the moment, worketh for us more and more exceedingly an eternal weight of glory," is one thing; that our sins can be purged by calamities or sufferings, is another, and a wholly unscriptural doctrine.

[2] Stephens, pp. 371, 407; Roberts, pp. 151, 152. The reflections of the latter author on Chrysostom's letters (all written from Cucusus) are very

Section III. We turn with pleasure from the legal and ritualistic side of Chrysostom's character to the spiritual and Christlike. On the vanity of mere outward observances he says: "We go to the church, not merely for the sake of spending a few moments there, but that we may come away with some great gain in spiritual things. If a child goes daily to school and learns nothing, is his regular attendance an excuse for him? Does it not rather aggravate his fault? ... When you have sung together two or three psalms and gone through the ordinary prayers and return home, you suppose this is sufficient for your salvation. Have you not heard what God says: 'This people honour me with their lips, but their heart is far from me'?" "In our prayers we pay less respect to God than a servant does to his master, a soldier to his general, or even a friend to his friend. For we speak to our friends with attention, but whilst we are on our knees asking pardon for our sins and treating with God about

A.D. 107.

---

pertinent. "One shade of melancholy rests upon them all, but the melancholy of a mind receiving every dispensation as the work of mercy, and the discipline of grace. He bore his banishment, not indeed without occasional complaint, but in general with the cheerful fortitude of a Christian soldier. ... Still in these letters we do not perceive, in their just and beautiful proportions, those supports under affliction which we look for in a sainted Father of the Church of Christ. There are not found in them any distinct references to the Cross of Jesus, or to the love and sympathy of that Divine Participator in human sorrows, who has offered the refreshment of his hallowed rest to the weary and heavy-laden. If we do not find in Chrysostom too high an opinion of his own deserts, we cannot but discover in his letters a tendency to claim the rewards of Heaven on a title simply based on his sufferings and persecutions."—Pp. 153, 154.

the business of our salvation, our mind is at court, or at the bar, and there is no correspondence between our thoughts and our words."[1]

Like Gregory Nazianzen, Chrysostom deprecated the intolerance of that uncharitable age. "To anathematize," he says, "is presumptuous; it is as great a usurpation of Christ's authority as for a subject to put on the Imperial purple. The part of a Christian is 'to instruct in meekness those who oppose themselves, if God peradventure will give them repentance to the acknowledging of the truth.' But if any man refuse to accept thy counsel, do not hate him, turn not from him, but catch him in the net of sincere charity. He whom thou anathematizest is either living or dead; if living, thou dost wrong to cut off one who may still be converted; still more so if dead, for 'to his own master he stands or falls.'" Nevertheless, in this as in other things, he was not always consistent with himself. We shudder as we read the following to Olympias:—"If in addition to the rewards of her chastity, her fasts, her vigils, her prayers, her boundless hospitality, Olympias wishes to enjoy the sight of her adversaries, those iniquitous and blood-stained men, undergoing punishment for their crimes, that pleasure also shall be hers. Lazarus saw Dives tormented in flames. This thou too wilt experience. For if he,

---

[1] Du Pin, iii. p. 44.

who neglected but one man, suffered such punishment, what penalty will be exacted of men who have overturned so many churches and surpassed the ferocity of barbarians and robbers?"[1]

In words no less apt now than when they were spoken does Chrysostom urge upon his hearers the debt of Christian love which every man, lay as well as clerical, owes to his fellow. "There are many who possess farms and fields, but all their anxiety is to make a bath-house to their mansion, to build entrance courts and servants' offices: *how the souls of their servants are cultivated they care not.* . . . Ought not every Christian landholder to build a church, and to make it his aim before all things else that his people should be Christian? . . . Nothing can be more chilling than the sight of a Christian who makes no effort to save others. Neither poverty, nor humble station, nor bodily infirmity, can exempt men and women from the obligation of this great duty. To hide our Christian light under pretence of weakness is as great an insult to God as if we were to say that He could not make His sun to shine." Every house should be a church, and every father of a family a shepherd over his household, responsible for the welfare of all its members, even of the slaves, whom the Gospel places in their relation to God on the same level with their owners. Whilst "in early days the

---

[1] Stephens, pp. 133, 372.

Per. I.
Chap. 10.

house was by the love of heavenly things turned into a church, now the church itself, through the earthly mind of those who attend it, is become an ordinary house."[1]

The commentaries of Chrysostom on Scripture are, as already said, among the choicest of his works. "One of his maxims was, that sound doctrine cannot be extracted from Holy Scripture except by a careful comparison of many passages not isolated from their context. . . . He had a clear conception of the essential coherence between the Old and the New Testament. 'The very words, Old and New,' he used to say, 'are relative terms: New, implies an antecedent; Old, preparatory to it.' . . . The commandment, 'Thou shalt not kill,' attacks the fruit and consequence of sin; the precept, 'Whosoever is angry with his brother without a cause,' strikes at the root." He held that the entire Bible was written under Divine inspiration, and that no passage, no word even, is to be disregarded. "Men wrote as they were moved by the Holy Spirit; yet this was not independent of their own human understanding and personal character. The prophet retained his peculiar faculties and style; only all his powers were quickened, energized by the Spirit, to the utterance of words which, unassisted, he could not have uttered."[2] In the

---

[1] Stephens, pp. 230, 231.

[2] Augustine gives an equally full testimony to the Divine authority of Scripture. "All the sacred writings which are called canonical I have

sound method Chrysostom adopted of interpreting Scripture, he was preceded by his tutor Diodorus, bishop of Tarsus, and supported by his fellow-pupils, the historian Theodoret and Theodore of Mopsuestia.[1] Before their time the fanciful allegorical method of Origen and the Alexandrian school had been predominant, in which the object was to discover, not what the passage of Scripture was intended to mean, but what it might by some ingenious process be made to mean; what recondite lessons or truths might be wrung from it by mystical interpretations.[2]

Chrysostom was accustomed to impress on all his hearers the duty of reading the Bible for themselves. This was a point on which the Church teachers of this age were unanimous, thus unconsciously rebuking and condemning the times which succeeded, when those who were appointed to teach the Truth took away the Book from their flock, and sealed it up as though it were a fountain of error. "Give yourselves to the reading of Holy Scripture; not merely hearing it at church, but when you return home take your Bible in hand and dive into the meaning of what is written

---

learned to regard with such reverence that none of the writers according to my belief erred in anything; and if I meet with anything which appears to be opposed to truth it is I doubt not to be imputed to a blunder of the transcriber, or an error of the translator, or my own defective understanding of the passage."—Epistle to Jerome, quoted in Roberts' *Church Memorials*, p. 276.

[1] See *ante*, p. 179.

[2] Stephens, pp. 423–425. See *Early Church History*, pp. 273, 274.

Per. I.
Chap. 10.

therein.[1] . . . Seating yourselves, as it were, beside these waters, even although you may have no one at hand to interpret them, yet will you by the diligent perusal of them acquire great benefit. . . . Divine Providence ordained that the Scriptures should be written by publicans, fishermen, tentmakers, shepherds, goatherds, in order that the things written should be readily intelligible to all, that the artificer, the poor widow, the slave might derive advantage from them; . . . as says the prophet, 'They shall be all taught of God.'" "If," he says again, "after repeated perusal, the meaning of the text is still obscure, have recourse to some one wiser than thyself, to a teacher; God, seeing thy fervour, will Himself, even if man does not, open the meaning to thee." . . . Elsewhere he does not shrink from fully setting forth the truth on this matter: "Holy Scripture does not need the aid of human wisdom for its true understanding, but only the revelation of the Spirit." The common excuse of the absorbing occupation of the present life he thus answers: "Let no one give the cold reply, 'As for me, I am fully occupied with business in court, or the interests of the State or my craft; I have a wife to care for, children to maintain, a household to manage; I

---

[1] It was Chrysostom's practice to give out his text beforehand, in order that the congregation might prepare themselves for the sermon by Scripture searching and reflection. Augustine likens the zealous Christian who stores up Scripture in his memory, against a time of need, to the industrious ant.—Neander, iii. pp. 398, 399.

am a man of the world, and it is not for me to read the Scriptures. This duty belongs to those who have betaken themselves to the mountains for that very purpose.' How! is it not forsooth because thou art surrounded with worldly cares that thou hast more need than they to read thy Bible? . . . Ignorance of Scripture is a great precipice and a deep pit. It begets heresies, leads to a corrupt life, and throws everything into confusion." " Better the light of the sun should be extinguished than that David's words should be forgotten."¹

Often did his admonitions remain unheeded. Commencing his lectures on the Acts of the Apostles, he asserts that many of his hearers were not aware of the existence of such a book. " We find draughts and dice, but books nowhere, except among a few. And even these lock them away in cases, all their care being for the fineness of the parchment and the beauty of the letters. For they did not buy them to be benefitted, but to show their wealth and pride." " Gentlemen," he says again, " are acquainted with the characters, families, and native cities of charioteers and dancers, and can tell the breeding, training, sires and dams of the horses that run in the races; but not one probably knows the titles of Paul's Epistles."²

---

¹ Isaac Taylor, ii. pp. 436-439; St. Chrysostom's *Picture of his Age*, p. 79.

² Id., pp. 128, 130. The Scriptures at this time were not so scarce as we

Per. I.
Chap. 10.

Chrysostom is clear and emphatic on the nature of sin. "There is only one thing," he writes to the faithful Olympias, "which is really terrible; there is only one real trial, and that is Sin. Spoliation of goods is freedom; banishment is but a change of abode; death is but the discharge of nature's debt, which all must pay. These, and all other evils, when compared with Sin, are but as dust and smoke." Sin is "a terrible pit, containing fierce monsters, and full of darkness; as fire, which when once it has got a hold on the thoughts of the heart, if it is not quenched, spreads further and further; as a weight, heavier and more oppressive than lead." He combats the error of supposing that sin is more pardonable in a man of the world than in a monk. Anger, uncleanness, swearing are equally sinful in all. "Nothing," he says, "has inflicted more injury on the moral tone of society than the supposition that strictness of life is demanded of the monk only."[1]

But on Repentance our author is not equally sound. In his nine homilies on this duty delivered at Antioch, he enumerates the several paths which lead to it. They are (1) Confession; (2) Mourning for sin; (3) Humility; (4) Almsgiving (the queen of virtues, the readiest of all ways of getting to heaven, and the best advocate

---

sometimes imagine. Copies were greatly multiplied and widely diffused. "Even Britain," says Chrysostom, "abounds with the word of Life."—Isaac Taylor, i. p. 460.   [1] Stephens, pp. 80, 396.

there); (5) Hourly prayer; (6) Fasting (which makes angels of men). The confession here spoken of was not the auricular confession of the Romish Church, now required as a necessary condition of Communion, but was usually public, and when private, was always voluntary. On this point Chrysostom's testimony is of great value. "I do not require thee to discover thy sins to men, but to show thy wounds unto God, who will not reproach but only heal thee. . . . Is it to a man that thou confessest, to a fellow-servant, who might expose thee? Nay, it is to the Lord, thy physician, thy friend, who says, 'Confess thy sin to Me alone, and I will deliver thee.'"[1]

The reader of the *Early Church History* may remember the beautiful passages from Tertullian, Clement of Alexandria, and Origen on the subject of Prayer.[2] Chrysostom is not unworthy to be placed beside them. "The effect of prayer on the heart is like that of the rising sun on the natural world. The wild beasts come forth by night to prowl and devour, but the sun arises, and they get them away and lay them down in their dens; so, when the soul is illuminated by prayer, the irrational and brutal passions are put

---

[1] Isaac Taylor, *Ancient Christianity*, i. p. 251, et seqq.; Bingham's *Antiquities*, b. xviii. § 2, where Basil, Hilary, Ambrose, and Augustine are cited to the same purpose.

[2] *Early Church History*, pp. 134–137.

to flight. Prayer is the treasure of the poor, the security of the rich; the poorest of men is rich if he can pray, and the rich man who cannot pray is miserably poor. . . . It is impossible that a man who with becoming zeal calls constantly on God, should sin; he is proof against temptation so long as the effect of his praying endures, and when it begins to fail he must pray again. And this may be done anywhere, in the market or in the shop, since prayer demands the outstretched soul rather than the extended hands. Avoid long prayers which give opportunity to Satan to distract the attention; prayers should be frequent and short; it is in this way we can best comply with Paul's direction to pray without ceasing."

Notwithstanding his legality, Chrysostom could preach salvation by Christ free and full. "What reward shall I render unto the Lord for all His benefits? Who shall express His glorious acts, or show forth all His praise? He abased Himself that He might exalt thee; He died to make thee immortal; He became a curse that thou mightest obtain a blessing. . . . Say not, I have sinned much; how can I be saved? *Thou art not able, but thy Master is able so to blot out thy sins that no trace even of them shall remain. In the natural body, though the wound be healed yet the scar remains; but God does not suffer the scar even to remain, but together with release from punishment, grants righteousness also, and makes the sinner to be equal to him who has not sinned. He makes the sin neither to be, nor to have been.¹ . . . Sin is drowned in the ocean of God's mercy, just as a spark is extinguished in a flood of water." ²

We will pluck one more leaf from his spiritual meditations. The subject is thanksgiving. " Let us give thanks to God continually. For it is monstrous that, enjoying as we do his bounty in *deed* every day, we should not so much as in *word* acknowledge the favour; and that too, although the acknowledgment again yields all its profit to *us*, since *He* needs not anything of ours, but we stand in need of all things from Him. . . . But let us be thankful, not for our own blessings alone, but also for those of others; for in this way we shall be able both to destroy our envy, and to strengthen and purify our charity; since it will not be possible for thee to go on envying those in behalf of whom thou givest thanks to the Lord."³

It is evident that two opposite influences strove together in Chrysostom, the ritual and the spiritual. Isaac Taylor, remarking on the impossibility of holding the two in equipoise, and on the vain endeavour of certain of the Fathers to do this, adduces Chrysostom as the most illustrious example

---

¹ It is doubtful whether Scriptural warrant can be found for these latter sentiments in the extreme form in which they are put.

² Stephens, pp. 406, 408.

³ *Homily on Matthew.*

of failure. "How does he toil and pant in this bootless task! Personally too much alive to the spiritual and vital reality of the Christian scheme, to be quietly willing to let it disappear; and yet far too deeply imbued with the Gnostic and the Brahminical feeling, and too intimately compromised as a public person with the Church doctrines of the times, he could never rest. . . . Few great writers offer so little repose; few present contrasts so violent; as if his cynosure had been a binary star, shedding contrary influences upon his course. And so it was in fact. Scarcely is there a homily all of a piece; hardly are there two consecutive passages that can be read without a surprise, amounting to a painful perplexity, until the secret of all this contrariety is understood; and then it becomes manifest enough that, within the writer's soul, a spiritual Christianity, which *should* have been uppermost, was ever wrestling with Church doctrines and Gnostic sentiments, which *would* be uppermost."[1]

---

[1] *Ancient Christianity*, i. pp. 249, 250.

CHAPTER XI.

JEROME.

SECTION I. Eusebius Hieronymus was born about the year 346[1] at Stridon, near Aquileia, at the head of the Adriatic. At the age of seventeen[2] he was sent to Rome to complete his studies: his teacher was the famous grammarian Aelius Donatus. Here Jerome used on Sundays to visit the catacombs;[3] he also began to collect a library, which he afterwards carried with him wherever he went.[4] He relates that he yielded to the temptations which the great capital so plentifully presented, and fell into sin.[5]

A.D. 346-371.

At the age of five and twenty we find him at Aquileia, one of a circle of young men who devoted themselves to sacred studies and to the ascetic life. The most celebrated of these was the historian

---

[1] *Dict. Christ. Biog.*, iii. p. 29, art. Hieronymus (4) St. Jerome. Schaff says about A.D. 340; p. 967. The dates assigned greatly vary; some writers place it so early as 329.

[2] Or fourteen.   [3] See *Early Church History*, p. 482.

[4] "The Alexandrian manuscripts," he says, "emptied my purse." When he was permitted to use the library of Pamphilus in Cæsarea, containing all the works of Origen, he thought himself richer than Crœsus.—Schaff's *Nicene Christianity*, p. 968, note.

[5] *Dict. Christ. Biog.*, iii. pp. 29, 30.

Per. I.
Chap. 11.

Rufinus, between whom and Jerome there sprang up so ardent a friendship that they were compared to Damon and Pythias. But Jerome was as violent in his antipathies as in his friendships; and he gave full scope to the acerbity of his nature when, on his retirement with his brother Paulinian to lead a hermit life on their paternal estate at Stridon, he had fallen under the displeasure of the bishop. In his correspondence with that dignitary, his language was most abusive, and it was now that he commenced the offensive practice of holding up his antagonist to ridicule by fastening upon him an opprobrious epithet, a practice which unhappily he followed through life.[1]

There floated before Jerome's imagination an alluring vision of the East, the cradle and paradise of monasticism; and in 373 the two brothers with a few intimate friends directed their course thither. Passing through Cæsarea in Cappadocia, they made the acquaintance of Basil, who by the recent death of Athanasius had become the leading churchman of the Catholic party in the East.[2]

At Antioch, Jerome fell sick and had a strange vision or dream connected with his classical studies which sat uneasy on his conscience. What he saw he related long afterwards in a letter to a noble Roman lady:—"When, years ago, I had torn myself from home, and parents, sister and

---

[1] *Dict. Christ. Biog.*, iii. pp. 29, 30; see also *St. Jerome*, by Dr. Cutts, pp. 30-32.   [2] Ibid., p. 33.

friends, for the kingdom of heaven's sake, I could
not part with the books which with very great
care and labour I had collected at Rome. And
so, unhappy man that I was, I followed up my
fasting by reading Cicero; after a night of watching, after shedding tears, which the remembrance
of my past sins drew from my inmost soul, I
took up Plautus. If sometimes, coming to myself,
I began to read the prophets, their inartistic
style repelled me. When my blinded eyes could
not see the light, I thought the fault was in the
sun, not in my eyes. While the old serpent
thus deceived me, about the middle of Lent a
fever seized me, and so reduced my strength that
my life scarce cleaved to my bones. They began
to prepare for my funeral. My whole body was
growing cold, only a little vital warmth remained
in my breast; when suddenly I was caught up
in spirit, and brought before the tribunal of the
Judge. So great was the glory of his presence,
and such the brilliancy of the purity of those who
surrounded Him, that I cast myself to the earth,
and did not dare to raise my eyes. Being asked
who I was, I answered that I was a Christian.
'Thou liest,' said the Judge, 'thou art a Ciceronian
and no Christian, for where thy treasure is there
is thy heart also!' Thereupon I was silent. He
ordered me to be beaten, but I was tormented
more by remorse of conscience than by the blows:
I said to myself, 'Who shall give thee thanks in

hell?' Then I cried, with tears, 'Have mercy upon me, O Lord, have mercy upon me!' My cry was heard above the sound of the blows. Then they who stood by, gliding to the knees of the Judge, prayed Him to have mercy on my youth, and He gave me time for repentance on pain of more severe punishment if I should ever again read pagan books. I, who in such a strait would have promised even greater things, made oath and declared by his sacred Name, 'O Lord, if ever I henceforth possess profane books or read them, let me be treated as if I had denied Thee!' After this oath they let me go, and I returned to the world. To the wonder of all who stood by, I opened my eyes, shedding such a shower of tears, that my grief would make even the incredulous believe in my vision. And this was not mere sleep, or a vain dream, such as often deludes us. The tribunal before which I lay is witness, that awful sentence which I feared is witness, so may I never come into a like judgment. I protest that my shoulders were livid, that I felt the blows after I awoke, and thenceforward I studied divine things with greater ardour than ever I had studied the things of the world."[1]

Jerome appears to have kept this vow for many years. On his settlement at Bethlehem he resumed his classical studies; and in later life he

---

[1] Cults, pp. 45, 46.

seems to have treated the vision either as a solemn reality or an idle fancy, just as for the moment it suited him.¹

A.D. 374.

In Syria he met with an aged hermit named Malchus, whose romantic history intensified his desire for the ascetic life. The desert which he made choice of was that of Chalcis, some fifty miles east of Antioch. It was peopled by monks and hermits, in the midst of whom Jerome took up his abode, supporting himself by his own labour. At first he seems to have been charmed with the solitude. One of his companions having gone back to Aquileia, Jerome wrote to him in a tone of reproach: "What art thou doing in thy home, O effeminate soldier? Where are the rampart and the fosse, and the winter spent in the tented field! . . . O desert, blooming with the flowers of Christ! O wilderness, where are shaped the stones of which the city of the Great King is built! O solitude, where men converse familiarly with God!"²

But a letter written after he had left the desert tells another and a very different tale. "I sat alone, I was filled with bitterness; my limbs were uncomely and rough with sack-cloth, and my squalid skin became as black as an Ethiop's. I spent whole days in tears and groans; and if ever the sleep which hung upon my eyelids overcame my

---

¹ Schaff, p. 28. ² Cutts, pp. 38-41.

resistance, I knocked against the ground with my bare bones which scarce clung together. I will not speak of my meat and drink, since the monks, even when sick, take nothing but cold water, and regard cooked food as a luxury. Through fear of hell I had condemned myself to such a dungeon, with scorpions and wild beasts as my companions." With all this, however, he could not escape from himself. Solitude served only to inflame his passions, and his imagination carried him back to the forbidden delights of Rome. "Though my face was pallid with fasting, yet my soul glowed with carnal desire in my cold body. My flesh had not waited for the destruction of the whole man, it was dead already, and yet the fires of the passions boiled up within me. I often imagined myself in the midst of girls dancing." At times, however, hope and peace would break through the gloom, although the false notion of penance as the necessary price at which the Divine favour is to be purchased deprived him of the full and abiding assurance of faith. "Destitute of all help, I cast myself at the feet of Jesus; I bathed them with my tears, I wiped them with my hair. I tried to conquer this rebellious flesh by a week of fasting. I often passed the night and day in crying and beating my breast, and ceased not until, God making Himself heard, peace came back to me. Then I feared to return to my cell, as if it had known my thoughts, and full of anger against myself I plunged alone into the desert. Sometimes, after shedding floods of tears, with my eyes lifted up to heaven, I believed myself transported into the midst of the choirs of angels, and, filled with confidence and joy, I sang, ' Because of the savour of thy perfumes, we will run after Thee.' "[1]

During the four or five years spent by Jerome in the desert, he studied and wrote diligently. In one of the nearest monasteries was living a converted Jew, of whom he learnt Hebrew, as a means, he said, of self-mortification.[2] He also disputed on the ecclesiastical politics of the see of Antioch with the neighbouring monks and solitaries, by whom he was persecuted as a heretic. The hatred indeed was mutual.[3]

Weary of the desert, he returned to Antioch in 379. The Church in that city was split up into three parties, each of which had its own bishop, of whom Jerome says: "I know nothing of Vitalis; I reject Meletius; I do not acknowledge Paulinus." Nevertheless he accepted ordination as a priest at Paulinus' hands, but on the condition that he should not be required to leave his monastic life, or to perform any functions of the priestly office.[4]

---

[1] *Dict. Christ. Biog.*, iii. pp. 31, 32; Cutts, pp. 43, 44.

[2] He complains that its grating sound destroyed the elegance of the Latin speech.

[3] Cutts, p. 46; Schaff, p. 970; Thierry, *St. Jérome*, pp. 69, 70. The monks took away his paper, so that he was obliged to write on an old rag. His Western companions said, "We had rather live with wild beasts than with such Christians as these."—Ibid.

[4] Cutts, p. 50; Du Pin, iii. p. 74.

In the year 380 Jerome went to Constantinople, where, as has been related, he placed himself under the instruction of Gregory Nazianzen. He remained in the Eastern metropolis during the council of 381, and must have been a spectator of Gregory's fall; but to these events he makes no allusion. Thence he removed to Rome, which at this time he calls "The light of the world, the salt of the earth, the only place where the Gospel remains uncorrupted." (!) Here his reputation as a scholar became established. Two main objects henceforth shared his affections, scriptural study, and the promotion of the ascetic life. The former drew him into his most celebrated work, a new translation into Latin of the Old and New Testaments from the original languages, of which we shall speak presently. Of asceticism, which was introduced into Rome nearly forty years before, by Athanasius and the Egyptian monks,[1] Jerome was now the foremost champion.[2]

In Rome he became the guest of Marcella, a widow of illustrious birth and great wealth, who had consecrated her ancestral palace on Mount Aventine to the service of religion. His companion, our old acquaintance Epiphanius, bishop of Cyprus,[3] was entertained by Paula, another Roman matron, equally noble and wealthy. These ladies were the centre of a society of religious

---

[1] See *ante*, p. 26.   [2] *Dict. Christ. Biog.*, iii. pp. 32, 33.
[3] See *ante*, pp. 208-210.

women which was being formed when Jerome was a student in Rome. Some of them he knew by person, all were acquainted with him through his letters, and he soon became " the soul of this patrician circle. He answered their questions of conscience; he incited them to celibate life, lavish beneficence, and enthusiastic asceticism; and flattered their spiritual vanity by extravagant praises. He was their oracle, biographer, admirer, and eulogist." But he was not a safe guide. "The letters which he wrote to these ladies," observes Maitland, "are a fearful monument of the social effects of the monastic system. Amidst elaborate and far from spiritual interpretations of Solomon's Song—amidst fulsome eulogies of the nuns and dissertations upon their peculiar relationship to the Bridegroom—the religion and the Christ of the New Testament seem missing. The Lord of life is departed, the grave-clothes alone remain to show the place where He lay."[1]

Marcella was as intellectual as she was pious. "All the while I was in Rome," writes Jerome, "she never saw me without putting some question on history or theology; nor was she ever satisfied by authority only, without examination; and often my place was changed from teacher to learner." "Paula was descended on one side from the Scipios

---

[1] Schaff, p. 211; Cutts, p. 76; Thierry, pp. 121, 122; Maitland, *Church in the Catacombs*, p. 206.

and the Gracchi, on the other from the half fabulous kings of Sparta and Mycenæ. Left a widow at thirty-five, by the death of her Greek husband Toxotius, she carried mourning in her heart more than on her garments, and for a time her grief was so violent that her life was in danger. She had four daughters—Blesilla, Paulina, Julia-Eustochium, and Rufina. To exalted and refined sentiments Paula joined an excessive delicacy of body and softness of habitude. Half a Greek, brought up in an opulence which had no equal in the West, she lived an Asiatic life, nearly always reclining, and when she walked, she was supported or rather carried on the arms of her eunuchs. Nevertheless she possessed an invincible strength of mind in resisting tyranny and wrong. Her understanding was solid and well-cultivated; she spoke Greek as a family language, and knew Hebrew well enough to read and sing the Psalms of David in the original." [1]

"Paula's daughter Eustochium, then barely sixteen years of age, was a pattern of calm reflective will, and of firmness, even stubbornness in her resolutions; her education had fully developed the innate germ of Christian stoicism in her heart. Entrusted in infancy by her mother to the care of Marcella, she had breathed a serene and peaceful atmosphere, not always to be found in her own

---

[1] Thierry, pp. 130-132.

home. She early announced her intention not to marry, but to assume the virgin's veil. It was the first example of such a resolution given by a girl of her rank, and all the world believed she would change her mind when she became of age. But when the time arrived and Eustochium prepared to take the vow, a cry of surprise and exasperation arose; her friends exerted themselves by alternate threats and caresses to turn her from her purpose, but in vain. Her father's sister Prætextata was a zealous pagan, and with her husband saw in their niece's determination a disgrace to their name and a sacrilege against their gods. Finding all their warnings and entreaties fruitless, they tried to entrap her on the side of feminine coquetry. They invited her to their house. As soon as she entered her aunt's apartment, some women, who had been engaged for the purpose, stripped off her woollen garments, and letting down her long hair, braided it and frizzled it in the newest fashion, painted her eyes, lips, and neck, clothed her in a magnificent silk robe, and covered her with jewels. Eustochium quietly submitted to the metamorphose, listened with her habitual serenity to all the blandishments which were lavished upon her, and then, when the hour came to return to Marcella, put on again her old serge dress and went her way."[1]

---

[1] Id., pp. 132-134.

"Less difference existed between Paula and her eldest daughter Blesilla. Both were weak in body, and subject to alternate mental depression and exaltation; but the latter wasted her energy in vain agitations and pleasures. A widow after seven months of married life chequered with cares, although scarcely twenty years of age, she rejected all proposals for a second union. This resolution was not like her sister's, prompted by love for the ascetic life; she chose rather thenceforth to live for herself, for the daily round of pleasure, and the charms of the toilet; she might almost be said to have passed her life before the mirror. In this condition she was attacked by fever, but recovered when at the very point of death. She believed her cure to be miraculous, and renouncing the world, assumed the habit of a church widow. Her pagan friends were scandalized; Jerome seized the pen in her defence: 'She stank somewhat of negligence, and was buried in the graveclothes of riches, and lay in the sepulchre of this world, but Jesus groaned in spirit, and cried, "Blesilla come forth," and she arose and came forth, and now sits at the table with Christ.'"[1] His letter provoked answers from Helvidius, a lawyer, and the monk Jovinian. Of his controversy with the latter we shall speak in a future chapter.

Jerome's advocacy of the ascetic life was as

---

[1] Id., pp. 134, 135; Cutts, pp. 77, 78.

violent as it was blind. "I love to praise marriage because it supplies us with virgins; of these thorns we gather roses." "Although your little nephew should hang about your neck; although your mother with hair dishevelled and garments rent, should show you the breasts at which she nourished you; although your father should lie on the threshold; trample on your father and set out! Fly with dry eyes to the banner of the cross! The only kind of piety is to be cruel in this matter." "Peter," he has the audacity to say, "was only an apostle, but John, because he was a virgin, was apostle, evangelist, and prophet. John the single, expounds what the married could not: 'In the beginning was the Word,' etc. To him, a virgin, was committed the charge of the virgin-mother by his virgin Lord; and for the same cause was he more beloved of the Lord, and reclined on his bosom."[1]

When Eustochium took the veil, Jerome addressed a letter to her, which was in effect an elaborate eulogy of virginity. In his defence of Blesilla he had lashed the manners of the high *pagan* society; his letter to Eustochium contained "a scathing satire on the vices of the *Christians*." "How many virgins daily fall! 'Why,' say they, 'should I abstain from food which God created to

---

[1] Maitland, pp. 201–205; Robertson, i. p. 334. Although Jerome speaks of this letter as written when he was a young man, he praises Fabiola (see below) for having learnt it by heart, and acted on it.—Ibid., note.

be used?' And when they have flooded themselves with wine, they add sacrilege to drunkenness, and say, 'Be it far from me that I should refrain from partaking of the blood of Christ!' And when they see any one pale and sad, they call her a wretch and a Manichæan." The clergy were not spared. "All their anxiety is about their dress, whether they are well perfumed, whether their shoes of soft leather fit without a wrinkle. Their hair is curled with the tongs, their fingers glitter with rings, and they walk on tiptoe lest the wet road should soil the soles of their shoes. You would take them for bridegrooms, rather than for clerics; their whole thought and life is to know the names and houses and doings of the rich ladies."[1]

Blesilla's health again gave way, and now her disorder terminated in death. The world insisted that Jerome and her mother had killed her with austerities. Her relations gave her a pompous funeral; and a vast crowd collected to see the procession pass along the Appian Way to the family mausoleum. Paula, who followed the bier, was overcome with grief, and fainted. This incident produced a strong sensation. "See this mother," cried the spectators, " who weeps for the daughter she has killed with fasting. Let us drive the cursed race of monks out of the city; let us stone them; let us throw them into the Tiber."[2]

---

[1] Cutts, pp. 90, 94, 95, 103.   [2] Id., pp. 106, 107.

A month after these occurrences bishop Damasus A.D. 385. died. Jerome, now become the first ecclesiastic in Rome and the acknowledged leader of the most influential circle, aspired to the vacant chair; but he was obnoxious to many of the clergy, and his temper entirely unfitted him for so responsible an office. His rival, Siricius,[1] was elected. This disappointment was aggravated by a calumnious story regarding his relations with Paula, which took such hold of the public mind that he was hooted in the streets.[2]

Section II. Jerome now began to suspect that he had been mistaken in coming to Rome, and that his true vocation after all was the desert. He therefore determined to shake off the dust of the great city, and return to a solitary life. On the eve of his departure he wrote to one of his friends: "In haste, dear Lady Acella, whilst the vessel is spreading her sails, I write these lines between my sobs and my tears, giving thanks to God that I am found worthy of the hatred of the world. Pray for me that, leaving Babylon, I may arrive at Jerusalem; that, escaping the dominion of Nebuchadnezzar, Ezra may lead me back to my country. Fool that I was, to wish to sing the Lord's songs in a strange land, to abandon Mount Sinai, and ask help from Egypt!" Paula resolved to be

---

[1] As fierce an advocate of celibacy as Jerome himself.
[2] Id., pp. 113, 114.

Per. I.
Chap. 11.

Jerome's companion. With Eustochium and a band of maidens taken from all classes, she set sail for Antioch A.D. 385. At Cyprus they made a stay of ten days, receiving from Epiphanius the same hospitality which Paula had shown him in Rome. Jerome, with his brother and a friend, travelling by another route, reached Antioch before them. On the ladies' arrival the two parties formed a caravan, the ladies riding on asses, with their luggage on pack-mules. They arrived in Jerusalem early in 386.[1]

Paula was profoundly affected as she approached the scene of the Saviour's passion. "The whole city," says Jerome, "was witness of her tears and groans. In the church of the Sepulchre she threw herself on the stone with which the tomb was supposed to have been closed, and embraced it so vehemently that we could scarcely disengage her. But when she entered the sepulchral chamber, when her knees felt the ground which the limbs of the Saviour had touched, and her hands pressed the stone couch on which his Divine body had lain, she fainted away. Regaining consciousness she covered those lifeless relics with kisses, clinging to them with her lips, as one parched with thirst at a long sought spring, as though she purposed to dissolve the rock by her tears and kisses."[2] Such a demonstration on the part of this noble Roman

---

[1] Thierry, pp. 178, 179; Cutts, pp. 121-123. [2] Thierry, pp. 205, 206.

lady may seem strange to us, and the outcome of a morbid excitement, but we shall do well to consider whether our love to the same Saviour equals hers.

A.D. 386.

The pilgrims made the round of the Holy Places, from Mamre and the Dead Sea southward to Nazareth and the Lake of Galilee in the north; after which they went down into Egypt. "At the monasteries of Nitria they were received with great honour. They heard the strange tales of the monks, assisted at all their services, ate their hard fare, lay in their hard cubicles, and were indeed almost persuaded to take up their abode in the Egyptian desert. But the superior attractions of Palestine prevailed, and returning thither the whole company settled at Bethlehem in the autumn of the same year. There Jerome spent the remaining thirty-four years of his life, pursuing unremittingly the two great objects to which he had devoted himself."[1]

The first work of the pilgrims was to build a monastery, and three convents over which Jerome and Paula presided. They erected a church also, in which the inmates of all the houses met, and a hospice or house of entertainment for the pilgrims, who came from all parts of the world to visit the holy places. "Now," cried Paula, "if Joseph and Mary should again come to Bethlehem, they would have a place to lodge in." Jerome took posses-

---

[1] *Dict. Christ. Biog.*, iii. p. 35.

sion of a cave or grotto next to that "of the Nativity,"[1] where he surrounded himself with his books, papers, amanuenses, and other appliances of study: he called it his paradise. "I find myself," he wrote to Augustine, "well hidden in this hole, to weep for my sins whilst waiting for the Day of Judgment." As soon as he was settled he opened a free school for the inhabitants of Bethlehem, to whom he taught Greek and Latin. Thus carried back to the books he had so passionately loved in his youth, he forgot his dream, and eagerly drank again at the forbidden fountain. Virgil, the lyric and comic poets, Cicero, Plato, Homer, became again his daily delight, and he never wearied of expounding them to his pupils.

In figure and visage Jerome was spare, his naturally pale complexion embrowned by the

---

[1] Jerome's grotto is one of the well-known objects of curiosity at Bethlehem. The genuineness of the cave which now bears his name is a question which depends on that of "The Grotto of the Nativity," both being rock-hewn and situated underneath the present church of St. Mary. That the stable where our Saviour was born was a *grotto* was an article of early belief (Justin Martyr, *Dialogue with Trypho*, c. lxxviii.; Origen, *Against Celsus*, b. i. c. i.); and it was in this belief that Jerome took up his abode there. That he did live in one or other of the several rock-hewn chambers here existing (and which have since undergone much alteration) may be considered as certain, but whether in that which is now called the Chapel of St. Jerome, is much less so. The earliest mention of this chapel is in 1449. It is entirely hewn out of the rock except on the north side, where a window looks towards the cloisters of the church. There is a painting in the chapel representing Jerome with a Bible in his hand. Constantine, in 330, erected a basilica over the "Grotto of the Nativity," and it is pretty generally agreed that the present church is substantially identical with that basilica.—Baedeker's *Palestine*; Tischendorff's *Travels in the East*, p. 193.

Eastern sky: he wore his hair short and straight. His inner and outer garment were those of the hermit, of a dark brown colour, the same he had worn even in Rome; and if we may judge by his directions to others, they were not over-cleanly.[1] He fasted till sunset, when he supped on vegetables and bread; he allowed himself flesh and wine only in sickness.[2]

No inconsiderable part of Jerome's time was taken up with the care and discipline of the monastery, and with the crowds of monks and pilgrims who flocked to the hospice. Yet Scriptural studies were his main pursuit, and his diligence in these is almost incredible. Sulpicius Severus, who visited Bethlehem, says: "The presbyter Jerome who rules the Church there is so well versed in Latin, Greek, and even Hebrew learning, that no man can stand before him. He devotes himself wholly to books and study, resting neither night nor day. I staid with him six months, and when I parted, his household accompanied me

A.D. 386-395.

---

[1] Thierry, pp. 119, 120. "Cleanliness of body," so he wrote to some of his lady friends, "is the filth of the soul. A mean sombre garment is the index of a mind at peace." "No one of the Roman matrons," he says elsewhere, "was ever able to command my homage, except she mourned and fasted and appeared in squalid clothing." Sometimes however he expresses himself more reasonably: "Shun equally sordid and showy garments. Foppery and filth are alike to be avoided; the one as redolent of voluptuousness, the other of vain-glory." "Thy clothes," he tells Eustochium, "should not be exactly clean, yet not filthy."—Maitland, p. 303. Chrysostom commends the squalid attire of his beloved Olympias.—Stephens, p. 372.

[2] Thierry, pp. 255-257.

along the road, and I returned with a light heart to Alexandria."[1] He wrote, or rather dictated, with great rapidity. The translation of the three books of Solomon was the work of three days, when he had just recovered from a severe illness; and he rendered the book of Tobit from the Chaldee in a single day. When confined to his couch with sickness he would take down from his shelves one volume after another, and dictate to an amanuensis.[2]

Of the manner of life at Bethlehem we have a picture from the hands of Paula and Eustochium, coloured by their own fervid feelings and imagination. It is in a letter to Marcella at Rome. "It would take too long to recount who of the bishops, the martyrs, the doctors of the Church, have visited Jerusalem, esteeming themselves imperfect in religion and knowledge until they had received the finishing touch, and adored Christ in those places where first the Gospel shone forth from the cross. . . . We do not say this because we deny that the 'kingdom of God is within us,' and that there are holy men in other quarters; but they who are foremost in all the world are gathered together here. . . . The Gaul, and even

---

[1] Sulpicius Severus, *Dialogues*, i. § 4.

[2] Smith, *Dict. of the Bible*, iii. p. 1701; *Dict. Christ. Biog.*, iii. p. 36. Jerome's reputation was spread throughout the Christian world. One day six strangers presented themselves at his cell; they were sent by a pious and wealthy Spaniard, who desired to possess copies of all his works. —Gilly's *Vigilantius*, p. 124.

the Briton, severed from the rest of the world, whosoever among them has made any progress in religion, hastens hither, eager to see for himself the places mentioned in the holy Scriptures; not to speak of the Armenians and Persians, the people of Arabia and Ethiopia, Egypt teeming with monks, Pontus, Cappadocia and Mesopotamia. . . . There are almost as many choirs of choristers as there are different nations. There are no distinctions amongst them; the only strife is who can be most humble. . . . In what words," they continue, "can we place before thee the cave of the Saviour and the manger in which He uttered his first cry? Here one does not see the broad porticoes, the gilded ceilings, the palace halls which wealth erects, that man's worthless little body may walk about more sumptuously. See, in this little hole of earth the maker of the Heavens was born; here He was wrapped in swaddling clothes; here visited by the shepherds; here pointed out by the star; here adored by the Magi. . . . In this little city of Christ all is rustic. The silence is only broken by psalms. Wherever one turns, the ploughman holding the plough sings alleluias; the toiling reaper cheers his labour with psalms; the vine-dresser, pruning the vine with his hook, sings something of David. These are the ballads of this country; these the love-songs; this the shepherd's pipe; these its rustic sports." Jerome added a short letter to theirs. "Here bread and herbs, the

Per. I.
Chap. 11.

produce of our own hands, with milk, afford us plain but wholesome food. Living thus, sleep does not overtake us in prayer, satiety does not interfere with study. In summer the trees afford us shade; in autumn the air is cool, and the fallen leaves afford us a quiet resting place; in spring the fields are clothed with flowers, and we sing our psalms the sweeter amid the singing of the birds; and when the winter's cold and snow come we have no lack of wood, and I watch, or sleep warm enough."[1]

The repose of the community at Bethlehem was, in the year 395, rudely interrupted by a threatened invasion of the Huns, who had overrun Syria, laid siege to Antioch, and were directing their course towards Palestine. The monasteries were broken up. Jerome and Paula hurried down to the sea at Joppa, where they erected a temporary camp for the protection of the sisterhood, and hired ships to carry them to a place of safety. At this juncture, news was brought that the Huns had changed their course, and instead of crossing Lebanon had turned to the north and west.[2]

About this time Fabiola, one of the group of noble ladies who remained in Rome, was on a visit at the convent. She had come to consult Jerome on a case of conscience. Ill-treated by her husband, she had sought relief in divorce, and to

---

[1] Cutts, pp. 157–161.   [2] Id., pp. 187, 188.

escape the temptations of her unprotected state she had married again. Could she, without performing penance, be in communion with the Church, her first husband being still alive? She returned to Rome without having conferred with Jerome; but the case being made known to him by a priest of her company, he sent his judgment in writing. On the plea that she married a second time from necessity, he says: "We all favour our own vices, and what we have done of our own will we attribute to the necessity of nature." On the question of her second marriage while her husband was living, he quotes the Apostle's sentence: "'The woman is bound by the law to her husband so long as he liveth, but if, while her husband liveth, she is married to another man she shall be called an adulteress.' Therefore, if this sister wishes to receive Christ's body and not to be called an adulteress, let her do penance." Fabiola accepted the conditions, and "Rome beheld a daughter of the ancient and illustrious house of the Fabii kneeling amongst the penitents on the steps of the Lateran church in mourning habit, with dishevelled hair, and sprinkled with ashes."[1]

---

[1] Id., pp. 187-190.

CHAPTER XII.

JEROME (*concluded*).

SECTION I. During his residence at Bethlehem, Jerome was involved in several long and bitter controversies. The earliest of these was his contest with his old friend Rufinus respecting the doctrines of Origen. Like Basil and Gregory, Jerome and Rufinus had early been captivated by the philosophy of that profound Christian thinker. But as time went on the former became convinced that some of Origen's dogmas could not be defended, and that his own reputation for orthodoxy was in danger. So that when the question again agitated the Churches of Palestine, A.D. 395, Jerome hastened to repudiate the charge of being one of Origen's disciples. This produced an acrimonious correspondence between himself and Rufinus, and although after a while they professed to be reconciled, and took each other's hands over the Saviour's tomb in the church of the Resurrection, yet on Rufinus' removal to Rome in 397, the quarrel broke out afresh. For several years an exchange of controversial, or more properly speaking, abusive tracts took place between the two angry disputants. Augustine was deeply pained to witness such strife between men of advanced age, of reputation for learning and piety, and who had once been familiar friends and fellow-students of Scripture. "I am pierced through," he writes to Jerome, "by darts of keenest sorrow when I think how between Rufinus and thee, to whom God has granted to feast together on the honey of the Holy Scriptures, the blight of such exceeding bitterness has fallen. This, too, at a time when you were living together in that very land which the feet of our Lord trod when He said, '*Peace* I leave with you, my peace I give unto you.' If I could anywhere meet you both together (which, alas! I cannot hope to do), so strong is my agitation, grief and fear, that I think I would cast myself at your feet, and there weeping till I could weep no more, would, with all the eloquence of love, appeal first to each of you for his own sake, then to both for each other's sake, and for the sake especially of the weak, for whom Christ died, imploring you not to scatter abroad these hard words against each other, which if at any time you were reconciled you could not destroy, and which you could not then venture to read, lest strife should be kindled anew." Sad to say, this pathetic pleading was ineffectual; even Rufinus' death did not disarm Jerome.[1]

A.D. 395-410.

---

[1] Robertson, i. pp. 375-377; Neander, iv. pp. 459-462: Augustine, Letters, lxxiii. § 8, Clark. "The scorpion," wrote Jerome, "is buried under the soil of Sicily, with Enceladus and Porphyrion; the many-

Per. I.
Chap. 12.

With Augustine himself, slightly his junior in age, Jerome had a curious correspondence, which only escaped embitterment owing to the patience displayed by the latter. Jerome, in his commentary on the Epistle to the Galatians (chap. ii.), had put forward the strange hypothesis that the dispute between the apostles Peter and Paul, there described, was merely feigned. Peter, he asserted, only pretended to separate himself from the Gentiles the more forcibly to bring out the incongruity of a Christian continuing to keep the Mosaic law. This appeared to Augustine as imputing to the apostle an acted lie, and he accordingly wrote to Jerome, A.D. 394,[1] showing what evil consequences must ensue if it could possibly be supposed that any teaching of the apostles was illusory. He asks, with a sly hit at Jerome's extravagant notions on celibacy, if we are to consider that the passages in which Paul eulogises marriage are fictitious. Unfortunately the presbyter to whom Augustine committed his letter, together with some of his own writings for Jerome's perusal, died before he had set out on his errand, but not before he had shown the letter to several persons, and copies had been taken. A second letter, which Augustine wrote three years later, when he discovered that the first had

---

headed hydra has ceased to hiss against us."—Robertson, *loc. cit.* Of Jerome's controversies with Jovinian and Vigilantius, we shall speak when we come to the history of those reformers.   [1] Or 395.

never been received, also miscarried: the messenger to whom it was committed never started, alleging that he was afraid of the sea. But of this letter, too, copies were taken, and a deacon, who had met with one on an island of the Adriatic, bound up with other writings of Augustine, either brought a copy, or described its contents to Jerome. Soon afterwards, some pilgrims returning from the Holy Land, informed Augustine that it was the talk of the monasteries of Bethlehem how he had attacked Jerome in a letter which he had not sent to him. Augustine hastened to exculpate himself, and to point out that what he had written was never intended for publication. He also begged Jerome to use an equal freedom in criticism, and concluded with the earnest desire that he could have personal intercourse with his correspondent. "In Jerome's reply, friendship struggles with suspicion and resentment." He professes to know little of Augustine's works, concerning which, nevertheless, he might have something to say in the way of criticism, and insinuates that Augustine was seeking to increase his own reputation at his expense. Augustine's rejoinder opens with language of profound respect, and after explaining how his first letter had miscarried, he enters again on questions of Biblical interpretation. He commends Jerome's version of the New Testament, but, with the mistaken reverence of the times for the Septuagint, entreats him not to

Per. I.
Chap. 12.

continue the translation he had begun of the Old Testament from the original Hebrew. Jerome again complains that he had not received Augustine's original letter. "Send me," he says, "your letter signed by yourself, or else cease from attacking me, and let me beg you, if you write to me again, to take care that I am the first whom your letter reaches." Augustine now (some ten years after his first letter was written) sent to Jerome authentic copies of both his letters, at the same time begging that the matter might not, through the mishaps which had occurred, grow into a feud like that between Jerome and Rufinus. On the receipt of this packet Jerome returned an immediate and full reply. He touched on all the points raised, appealing, on the question of Peter's conduct at Antioch, to Origen and other Eastern expositors of Scripture to bear him out.[1] It would seem, however, that Jerome was at last convinced, for Augustine, writing at a later date, cites a passage from him, in which he admits that no bishops are immaculate, since Paul found something to blame even in Peter. The correspondence was carried on some time longer with increasing good-will on both sides.[2]

In 403 Paula died, at the age of 56. Her health

---

[1] The Eastern Churches continued to maintain Jerome's interpretation of Peter's conduct; the Western followed Augustine.—Cutts, p. 220.

[2] *Dict. Christ. Biog.*, iii. pp. 44, 45; Augustine's and Jerome's Letters. In this, as in all the correspondence of the time, we are struck with the adulatory titles made use of. We have seen the commencement of this

had been undermined by years of excessive austerities. "She was," says Jerome, "always mourning and fasting; and had become almost blind with weeping." As she was departing she murmured in Hebrew some verses in Psalms xxvi. and lxxxiv., commencing, "O Lord, I have loved the beautiful order of thy house and the place of the habitation of thy glory." Then applying her finger to her mouth, she made the sign of the cross upon her lips. "There were present at her death the bishops of Jerusalem and other cities, and an innumerable company of priests and deacons, virgins and monks. There was no doleful cry, but a universal chant of the Psalms. Her body was carried to the tomb by the hands of bishops, and laid in the midst of the church of the Nativity. The cities of Palestine came to her funeral; the widows and the poor, after the example of Dorcas, showing the clothes that she had given them. . . . During the whole week the Psalms were sung in order in Hebrew, Greek, Latin and Syriac." . . . "If," writes Jerome, "all my being should become

A.D. 403.

---

weakness in Cyprian's days.—See *Early Church History*, p. 310, note. As the honour paid to the bishops became more profound, the style of address became more fulsome. Augustine salutes Jerome as "My lord most beloved and longed for," "My venerable lord Jerome;" and addresses him and others as "Your charity, your holiness." Jerome in reply styles Augustine "My lord truly holy and most blessed father (*papa*)," and calls him "Your excellency," "Your grace." At the Council of Ephesus, A.D. 431, Cyril is styled "Most saintly, most sacred, most devoted to God, our father and bishop." The bishops were saluted with bowing the head, kissing the hand, and even kissing the feet.—See Augustine's and Jerome's Letters; *Dict. Christ. Antiq.*, i. p. 238.

Per. I.
Chap. 12.

tongue and voice, I should still be unable worthily to declare her virtues.' Noble by birth, she was yet more noble by her sanctity; once powerful by her wealth, she became still more powerful by her poverty in Christ; the descendant of the Gracchi and the Scipios, she preferred Bethlehem to Rome, and a mud roof to the gilded ceiling of a palace. Never," he adds, " from the death of her husband to the day of her own going to sleep, did she eat with any man however holy, not even if he were a bishop. She never entered the bath unless she was sick; even in a dangerous fever she used no soft bed, but rested on the hard ground with a scanty covering of hair-cloth, if indeed that is to be called rest, which joined days and nights together by almost ceaseless prayers. . . . Farewell," he exclaims, " O Paula, and help by thy prayers the old age of him who bears thee a religious reverence. Thy faith and works have joined thee to Christ, and being now present with Him thou wilt more easily obtain what thou desirest. 'I have raised to thee a monument more durable than brass,'[1] which time shall never destroy. But," he adds, "we do not weep that we have lost her; we thank God that we once possessed her. What do I say? We possess her still, for the elect who ascend to God still remain in the family of those who love them."[2]

"The picture of Paula's death," writes Joseph

---

[1] Exegi monumentum œre perennius.—Horace, *Odes*, b. iii. carm. 30.
[2] Cutts, *St. Jerome*, pp. 202-208; Thierry, p. 398.

" Bevan Braithwaite, "gains nothing in our eyes from the ascetic colouring spread over it. Yet we may be instructed as we trace in her self-denying faith, her care for the poor, her patience in tribulation, her child-like trust in God, the genuine marks of the followers of Jesus. We would especially notice her love for the Scriptures. She had stored them in her memory. The facts of the Bible were to her the foundation of truth; and she still sought after an insight into the spiritual meaning for the edification of her soul. Much as we must deplore the evils of monasticism, we cannot mark the conduct of these devoted women in laying aside the wealth and honours of earth for what they believed to be the service of Christ, without, in some measure at least, entering into the feelings of Jerome as he watched by the couch of the dying Paula, and listened to the descendant of so many illustrious heathens testifying of her longing to depart and to be with Christ; and breathing forth her spirit in language more ancient than the earliest triumphs of Rome, but which is for ever new in the experience of the children of God: 'How amiable are thy tabernacles, O Lord of Hosts! my soul longeth, yea, even fainteth for the courts of the Lord.'" [1]

It was now that the nations of the north of Europe—Goths, Vandals, Sueves, and Alans—having broken down the military barriers of the

---

[1] *Unpublished Memoir of Jerome.*

Empire, poured their hordes over her fairest provinces. In 405 the Isaurians laid waste the north of Palestine; the monasteries of Bethlehem were beset with fugitives, and Jerome and his friends were brought into great straits for the means of living. But another and a sorer calamity was at hand. Already the Goths were ravaging the northern provinces of Italy; and in 410 Rome was taken by Alaric. Many of the inhabitants were massacred; a far greater number were suddenly reduced to the miserable condition of captives and exiles. The city was given up to pillage; the booty was immense.[1] "The acquisition of riches served only to stimulate the avarice of the rapacious barbarians, who proceeded by threats, by blows, and by torture, to force from their prisoners the confession of hidden treasure. The noble Marcella, the venerable head of the religious sisterhood in the city, was verging upon extreme old age. The blood-stained Gothic soldiers who rushed into her house expecting large spoils from so stately a palace, eagerly demanded that she should surrender the treasures which they were persuaded she had buried. She showed her mean and threadbare garments, and told them how it came to pass that she, a Roman matron, was destitute of wealth. The words 'voluntary poverty' fell on unbelieving ears. They beat her with clubs; they scourged her; she

---

[1] See *ante*, pp. 22, 23.

bore the strokes with unflinching courage, but fell at their feet and implored them not to separate her from the youthful Principia, her adopted daughter, dreading the effect of these horrors on the maiden, if called to bear them alone. At length their hard hearts softened towards her. They accepted her statement as to her poverty, and escorted her and Principia to the basilica of St. Paul.[1] Arrived there she broke forth into a song of thanksgiving, 'that God had at least kept her friend for her unharmed, that she had not been made poor by the ruin of the city, but that it had found her poor already, that she would not feel the hunger of the body, even though the daily bread might fail, because she was filled with all the fulness of Christ.' But the shock of the cruelties she had endured was too great for her aged frame, and after a few days she expired, the hands of her adopted daughter closing her eyes, and her kisses accompanying the last sigh."[2]

Many of the fugitives took refuge in Africa and Syria, and some even found their way to Bethlehem. "Jerome describes himself as struck dumb with amazement at the capture of the city that had conquered the world; and as the intelligence followed in quick succession, of the desolation of

---

[1] Alaric had given orders that the right of asylum in the churches should be respected, especially in the two great basilicas of St. Peter and St. Paul.

[2] *Dict. Christ. Biog.*, iii. p. 45; Hodgkin, *Italy and her Invaders*, i. pp. 372, 373.

the provinces, and of the ruin which foreshadowed the breaking up of the Empire in the west, he often sought relief in the words of his own translation of Psalm cxx. 5, 'Woe is me that my pilgrimage is lengthened out!'" . . . "It was," he says again, " as though the end of the world was come. Who would have believed that obscure Bethlehem would see begging at its gates nobles lately laden with wealth? The daughters of the queenly city wander from shore to shore; her ladies have become servants; her most illustrious personages ask bread at our gate, and when we cannot give bread to them all, we give them at least our tears. In vain I try to snatch myself from the sight of such sufferings by resuming my unfinished work, I am incapable of study; I feel that this is the time for translating the precepts of Scripture, not into *words* but *deeds*, and not for saying holy things, but doing them." [1]

SECTION II. We have spoken of the Vulgate, the celebrated translation of the Bible into Latin from the original languages. It arose out of Jerome's

---

[1] J. B. Braithwaite, ubi suprà; Cutts, pp. 222-224. "The fall of Rome," says Thierry, "turned men's brains as with a vertigo and delirium. There was no longer any government, pity, or justice, and for many men no longer a God. 'The world crumbles away, and our head knows not how to bow down,' cried Jerome in terror. 'That which is born must perish, that which has grown must wither. There is no created work which rust or age does not consume:—but Rome! Who could have believed, that, raised by her victories above the universe, she would one day fall, and become for her people at once a mother and a tomb?'"—*St. Jerome*, p. 479.

connection with the Roman bishop Damasus. Whilst he resided in Rome, a council was held in the city, to which he was appointed secretary, and when it was dissolved the bishop retained his services for himself in the same capacity. During their intercourse on matters of Scripture interpretation, Damasus urged Jerome to undertake a thorough revision of the Latin Gospels. Jerome recognized the need of such a work. "Mistakes," he says, " have been introduced by false transcription, by clumsy corrections, and by careless interpolations, so that there are almost as many forms of text as copies." This revision was accomplished whilst he was in Rome; and after he removed to Bethlehem, at the urgent request of Paula and Eustochium, he extended his labours to the Old Testament.[1] He had, as has been said, already commenced the study of Hebrew;[2] and now he engaged as his teachers, at much difficulty and expense, three Rabbis, one of them from Lydda and another from Tiberias.[3] Great preparation was needed for the

---

[1] Eustochium, as well as Paula, understood Hebrew. They used to go to Jerome's cave at certain hours to read the Hebrew Bible with him; and from the conversations which arose on these occasions many a passage in his version of the Vulgate was settled.—Cutts, pp. 148, 149.

[2] Jerome's knowledge of Hebrew was much greater than that of Origen, Epiphanius, or Ephrem, the only other Fathers who understood it at all. —Schaff, *Nicene Christianity*, p. 970.

[3] It is said of the Jew of Lydda, that his thirst for gold was equal to his love of knowledge. To read Daniel and Tobit, Jerome was obliged to change his instructor for one who understood Chaldee. The Rabbi rendered the text into Hebrew, which Jerome dictated in Latin for his scribes to write down.—Thierry, p. 261.

work. He consulted Biblical students; he searched every library in Palestine and Egypt, especially those of Alexandria and Cæsarea; he made use of the Hexapla of Origen; by the help of linguists he made himself acquainted with the Ethiopic and Syriac versions; and he availed himself of the traditional knowledge of his Jewish instructors on orthography, vowel sounds and interpretations, as well as on Biblical topography. On the last point he was not satisfied with information at second-hand, but made a tour of Palestine, identifying, as well as he was able, the sites of the cities and villages, mountains, and sacred spots of the Old and New Testaments. This was not all. He exercised his sound and penetrating judgment in replacing passages which had been omitted, and rejecting such as had been interpolated. Nor were learning and genius alone necessary for the accomplishment of this vast undertaking; it required a rare intrepidity to call in question the authority of the Septuagint, and to restore to its proper place the original Hebrew. It must also be borne in mind, that the task was undertaken and completed by one man on his own individual responsibility. "No scholar, for fifteen hundred years," remarks Westcott, "was so fitted to accomplish it." In the words of Milman: " Whatever it may owe to the older and fragmentary versions of the sacred writings, Jerome's Bible is a wonderful work, still more as achieved by one man, and that a Western

Christian, even with all the advantage of study and of residence in the East. It almost created a new language. The inflexible Latin became pliant and expansive, naturalizing foreign Eastern imagery, Eastern modes of expression and of thought and Eastern religious notions, most uncongenial to its own genius and character; and yet retaining much of its own peculiar strength, solidity and majesty. If the Northern, the Teutonic languages, coalesce with greater facility with the Orientalism of the Scriptures, it is the triumph of Jerome to have brought the more dissonant Latin into harmony with the Eastern tongues. The Vulgate was, even more perhaps than the Papal power, the foundation of Latin Christianity."[1]

Like all innovations, however good, the labours of Jerome were received at first with an outcry of alarm. He was accused of disturbing the repose of the Church, and shaking the foundations of the faith. Even Augustine, as we have seen, was carried away by the popular prejudice, and in order to deter him from pursuing his work related an occurrence which took place in a church in Africa. In his new version of the book of Jonah, Jerome had

---

[1] Cutts, pp. 68-72; Smith's *Dictionary of the Bible*, art. Vulgate, where will be found a complete history of the older Latin versions and of Jerome's great work in all its stages; *Encyclop. Brit.*, 8th edition, art. Bible; Milman, *Latin Christianity*, i. p. 74; see also his *History of Christianity*, iii. p. 352.

Per. I.
Chap. 12.

thought fit to translate the Hebrew word (c. iv. 6), which in the LXX., the old Latin, and our own English version, is rendered *gourd*, by the word *ivy*.[1] "One of our bishops," so wrote Augustine, "reading thy version, came upon this rendering so different from that which was familiar to the senses and memory of all the worshippers, and which had been rehearsed for so many generations. Thereupon arose such a tumult in the congregation, especially among the Greeks, correcting what had been read, and denouncing the translation as false, that the bishop was compelled to ask the testimony of the Jewish residents. These, whether from ignorance or spite, answered that the Hebrew word was correctly rendered in the Greek version, and in the Latin taken from it. What further need I say? The bishop was compelled to correct thy version as if it had been falsely translated, as he desired not to be left without a congregation, a calamity which he narrowly escaped."[2]

The Vulgate was an appeal from tradition to truth, but in course of time it came itself to represent that very idolatry of tradition which it had sought to overthrow. Barely tolerated during the life-time of its author, its intrinsic merit made way for it, until by the seventh century it had entirely superseded the older versions. Its daily

---

[1] Et præparavit Dominus Deus *hederam* (instead of *cucurbitam*).
[2] Letters of Augustine, lxxi. c. 3, lxxxii. c. 4.

and hourly use in all the churches and monasteries of Europe, coupled with ignorance of the original languages on the part of the clergy, raised its authority in time to the place of an article of faith; so that the Council of Trent, in 1546, declared: " The Vulgate edition shall be held for authentic in public lectures, disputations, sermons and expositions, and none shall dare to refuse it." [1]

Although Augustine occupies the chief place in the Pelagian controversy,[2] the part taken in it by Jerome requires some notice here. In 414, Orosius, a disciple of Augustine, came to reside at Bethlehem, fresh from the Council of Carthage, and full of the thoughts and doings of his teacher. The next year Pelagius himself came thither; and thus Jerome found himself, without seeking it, in the very heat of the battle. He was not prepared to go so far in defence of the doctrine of grace as Augustine, but in order to maintain his reputation for orthodoxy, he published (A.D. 415) a *Dialogue* against the Pelagians, which raised him up many enemies. The new heresy had met with much favour in Palestine, and Jerome became a marked man. One night, in 416, a mob of Pelagian monks from Jerusalem made an assault upon the colony at Bethlehem. Some attacked the houses

---

[1] *Dictionary of the Bible*, loc. cit.; Father Paul's *History of the Council of Trent*, Brent, pp. 148-152. On the invention of printing, the Vulgate was the first book of any considerable size which was issued from the press.

[2] See below, chap. 15.

of the men, which were successfully defended; others assailed the convents of the women, forced the doors and set fire to the buildings. The nuns fled for protection to a tower which had been erected at one end of a pile of buildings as a stronghold against the Arabs; Jerome and his monks made a sally to cover their retreat, and with the aid of the people of the village, the assailants were driven off.[1]

A long period of sickness preceded Jerome's death. By the help of a cord fixed to the ceiling of his cell, he used to raise himself from his couch whilst he recited his *Hours*.[2] He was attended in his last illness by the younger Paula (grandchild of his friend Paula), and another of the nuns. He died 419 or 420 A.D., at the age of seventy-four.[3]

All critics agree in extolling Jerome's learning and sound theology. "What Jerome was ignorant of," said Augustine, "no mortal has ever known." The words of Erasmus are: "The divine Jerome is among the Latins so incontestably the first of

---

[1] *Dict. Christ. Biog.*, iii. p. 46; Cutts, pp. 227, 228.

[2] The prayers and psalms repeated at stated times were thus named.

[3] Cutts, pp. 229, 230. The earlier dates to which his birth is assigned by some would make him much older. The well-known master-piece of Domenichino, painted in 1614, and now in the Vatican, represents the dying Jerome receiving the Sacrament from the hands of Ephrem the Syrian (see *ante*, p. 71), in the church at Bethlehem. Paula is kneeling to kiss Jerome's hands. It is curious that this picture, now accounted second only (in Rome) to Raphael's "Transfiguration" (opposite to which it stands), was painted for fifty scudi (ten guineas), and was so despised by its first owners that they wanted to use the canvas for another painting.

theologians that we have scarcely another worthy the name. What a pitch of Roman eloquence in him! How great a skill in languages! What a depth of acquaintance with the history of all antiquity! How retentive a memory! How happy a union of all qualities! How absolute a knowledge of mystic science! Above all things, how ardent a spirit, and how admirable an inspiration!" "His commentaries on Scripture," says Roberts, "are among the best which the Fathers have bequeathed to us. His *Letter to Demetrias* is valuable for the clear and sound exposition it contains of Divine Grace as the gift of gratuitous mercy."[1]

Although his notions were at least as superstitious, and his prejudices more violent than those of his contemporaries, yet his powerful intellect often grasps the truth with singular firmness, and holds it up to view unsullied and luminous. The traditions of the Church had become by this time of equal authority with Holy Scripture. "Of the dogmas which are preserved in the Church," writes Basil, "there are some which we have from Scripture, and others from the tradition of the Apostles, and both have the same force. What written precept have we, for instance, for signing believers with the cross? or for turning to the east in our prayers? The words of invocation, when the bread of the Eucharist and cup of

---

[1] Schaff, p. 206, note; Roberts' *Church Memorials*, p. 204.

Blessing are consecrated, which of the saints has left to us in writing? We bless both the water of baptism, and the oil of unction, and the person who is baptized—out of what Scripture? Is it not on the authority of the silent mystical tradition?" However inconsistent he may have been in practice, Jerome disposes in a few words of all such pretensions. "Do not suffer yourselves to be seduced by pretended apostolical traditions. Hypocritical priests require men to worship their traditions and statutes as other nations worship idols; but to us God has given the law and the testimony of the Scriptures. . . . I place the Apostles apart from all other writers; they always speak the truth; others err like men. We ought not, like the scholars of Pythagoras, to regard the prejudicated opinion of the teacher, but the weight and reason of the thing taught."[1]

But the case is far otherwise when we come to consider Jerome's spirit and temper, and his influence on his own and succeeding ages. There is too much ground for the protest of Isaac Taylor against the "vile legendary trash" of which Jerome's *Life of the Hermit Paul* largely consists. "It is not," he adds, "without an emotion profoundly painful, that one turns from the turbid, frothy, and infectious stream of Jerome's ascetic writings, to the pellucid waters of Plato, Xenophon, and Cicero, reason darkened indeed, but

---

[1] Smith's *St. Basil the Great*, pp. 120, 121; Roberts, p. 235.

struggling toward the light, and exempt from virulence, from hypocrisy and from absurdity. Such a contrast powerfully impresses the mind with a sense of the infinite mischief that has been done to mankind by men, who, when Christianity, with its simple grandeur and its divine purity, was fairly lodged in their hands and committed to their care, could do nothing but madly heap upon it, and often for selfish purposes, every grossness and folly which might turn aside its influence, and expose it to contempt. It may be a Christian-like and kindly office to palliate the errors, and to cloak the follies, and to give a reason for the false notions, of the Nicene divines; but when, on the other side, one thinks of the long centuries of woe, ignorance, and persecution, and religious debauchery, which took their character directly from the perversity of these doctors, it is hard to repress emotions of the liveliest indignation."[1]

We will conclude with the masterly analysis of Jerome's character in the *Dictionary of Christian Biography*. "He was vain and unable to bear rivals; extremely sensitive as to the estimation in which he was held by his contemporaries, and especially by the bishops; passionate and resentful, but at times becoming suddenly placable; scornful and violent in controversy; kind to the weak and the poor; respectful in his dealings with women; entirely without avarice; extraordinarily diligent

---

[1] Taylor's *Ancient Christianity*, i. pp. 345, 346.

Per. I.
Chap. 12.

in work, and nobly tenacious of the main objects to which he devoted his life . . . His writings contain the whole spirit of the Church of the Middle Ages, its monasticism, its contrast of sacred things with profane, its credulity and superstition, its subjection to hierarchical authority, its dread of heresy, its passion for pilgrimages. To the society which was thus in a great measure formed by him, his Bible was the greatest boon which could have been given. But he founded no school and had no inspiring power; there was no courage or width of view in his spiritual legacy, which could break through the fatal circle of bondage to received authority which was closing round mankind." [1]

---

[1] Vol. iii. pp. 49, 50.

CHAPTER XIII.

AUGUSTINE.

SECTION I. Of Augustine, "the tenderest, most devout, and in all respects most noble-minded of the Christian Fathers,"[1] more is known than of any other, chiefly because he has left an autobiography, the well-known *Confessions*, written when he was about forty-three years old. The son of a pagan citizen of Thagaste in Numidia,[2] he was born A.D. 354. His mother Monnica, "the pattern of mothers," was a Christian, and to her patience and faithfulness her husband mainly owed his conversion, and her son his character and greatness.[3]

Augustine was sent first to an elementary school in his native town, "where," as he tells us, "*one and one are two, two and two are four*, was a hateful singsong" to him, and when he did not learn, he was beaten. He calls this discipline "a great and grievous ill," and in his distress he used earnestly to pray to God that he might not be so punished. "We boys," he says, "wanted not memory or capacity, but we delighted only in play,

A.D. 354–370

---

[1] *British Quarterly Review*, Jan. 1881, p. 83.
[2] Now Tajilt. [3] *Dict. Christ. Biog.*, art. Augustinus, i. p. 217.

AUGUSTINE AT SCHOOL.

Per. I.
Chap. 13.

and for this we were punished by those who were doing the same things themselves. But the idleness of our elders is called business, whilst boys who do the like are punished by those same elders."[1]

In due time he was promoted to a higher school in the neighbouring large town of Madaura, where the majority of the inhabitants were pagans, and the statues of the gods still stood uninjured in the forum. Here Virgil delighted him,—"the wooden horse full of armed men, and the burning of Troy, and the spectral image of Creusa;" but although Homer contained the same "sweetly vain fiction," the difficulty of mastering Greek embittered all the romance of the Iliad. To make the youthful scholar comprehend the Greek poet, harsh threats and blows were freely used.[2]

It is worthy of notice that when Augustine in after years looked back upon his school days with a ripened judgment, and from a Christian standpoint, he condemned the classic method of instruction, that "torrent of hell" as he calls it, by which learning was poured into the boyish mind through the obscene fables of heathenism. He also brings out into strong relief the scrupulous care with which the scholars were trained in the niceties of grammar, whilst moral truth and practice were neglected; so that as he expresses it, "it

---

[1] *Confessions*, b. i. cc. 9, 14. We have availed ourselves of the admirable translation in Clark's edition, generally collating it with the original.

[2] Id., cc. 13, 14; *St. Augustine*, by Dr. Cutts, p. 28.

was accounted a greater offence for a scholar to drop the aspirate and say '*ominem,* instead of *hominem* (man), than if, in opposition to the divine commandments, he, a man, should hate a man." [1]

At the age of sixteen he returned home to his parents, and the next year was sent to college at Carthage to complete his education. During this period, notwithstanding his mother's loving counsel and entreaties, he fell into dissolute habits. "My mother's admonitions to chastity appeared to me but womanish counsels which I should blush to obey." . . . "Blindly" (he says again) "I rushed on headlong; when I heard my equals pluming themselves on their disgraceful deeds, I made myself out worse than I was that I might not be dispraised. . . . A cauldron of unholy loves bubbled up around me; and yet foul and dishonourable as I was, I craved, through an excess of vanity, to be thought elegant and urbane." He and his companions, *habitués* of the theatre and the circus, prided themselves on their gallantry, and practised shameful tricks and rough jokes in the public streets. But in the midst of all this dissipation he found time for study, and his natural genius asserted itself so strongly that he became head scholar in the school of rhetoric.[2]

---

[1] *Confessions,* b. i. cc. 16, 18. Ut qui illa sonorum vetera placita teneat aut doceat, si contra disciplinam grammaticam, sine aspiratione primæ syllabæ *ominem dixerit,* displiceat magis hominibus, quam si contra tua præcepta *hominem oderit,* cum sit homo.

[2] Id., b. ii. c. 3: b. iii. c. 1; Cutts, pp. 33–35.

In the course of his studies he lighted upon the "Hortensius" of Cicero, a dialogue in praise of philosophy, of which fragments only remain. "This book," he writes, "changed my affections, and turned my prayers to Thee, O Lord.[1] Suddenly all my vain hopes became worthless, and with an incredible warmth of heart, I yearned for the possession of immortal philosophy, and began to arise that I might return to Thee.... One thing alone checked my ardour, that the name of Christ was not in the book. For this name had my tender heart piously drunk in, even with my mother's milk, and whatever was without that name, though never so erudite, polished and truthful, could not take complete hold of me." But he was not yet humble enough to receive the spiritual teaching of the Scriptures. "They were such as the lowly can understand; but they appeared to me unworthy to be compared with the dignity of Cicero; my full-blown pride shunned their simple style, nor could the sharpness of my wit penetrate their inner meaning."[2]

In this condition of mind he met with the Manichæans,[3] whose rationalistic system entangled him like "bird-lime," and for a long time held him a willing prisoner. Years afterwards, when he had

---

[1] His *Confessions* are throughout addressed to God.
[2] *Confessions*, b. iii. c. 4.
[3] See a brief notice of their rise and doctrines in *Early Church History*, p. 401.

escaped, and had come into the reality of the Gospel, he saw how deceitful had been the illusion which had been put upon him. "O truth, truth, how did the marrow of my soul pant after thee! They sounded out thy name to me, but it was but a voice. As fictitious dishes served up to one in hunger, so instead of Thee they served up to me thy sun and moon, thy beauteous works, but not Thyself; and glowing phantasies and empty fictions; and I fed upon them, but was not nourished but famished. For I hungered and thirsted, not so much after thy works, but after Thee Thyself, the Truth, with whom is no variableness, neither shadow of turning; and far from Thee was I wandering, cut off even from the husks of the swine whom with husks I was feeding."[1]

Augustine returned from Carthage an avowed Manichæan, and not content with holding these opinions himself, he used all his trained skill as a disputant to win converts to the same error. His pious mother (his father was then dead) "wept for him more than mothers weep the bodily death of their children." She did more than grieve. Shrinking from, and detesting the blasphemies of his heresy, she began to doubt whether it was right in her to allow her son to live with her and to eat at the same table. From this perplexity she was delivered by a dream. She saw herself stand-

---

[1] *Confessions*, b. iii. c. 6.

ing on a wooden rule,[1] bowed down with grief, when a shining youth advanced towards her, and with a smile inquired the cause of her sorrow. She answered that she was lamenting her son's perdition; he bade her be comforted, and told her to behold and see that where she was, there was her son also. She looked, and saw Augustine standing near her on the same rule. On her relating to him the vision he pretended that it signified she should not despair of being some day what he was. "No," she replied promptly and decidedly, "it was not told me, where he is, thou shalt be, but where thou art, he shall be." He confesses that his mother's answer, showing that she was not deceived by his sophistry, moved him more than the dream itself.[2]

About the same period his mother in her distress applied to a bishop, reported to be well skilled in refuting errors and teaching sound doctrine, entreating him that he would have some talk with her son. He refused, alleging that Augustine was as yet unteachable, being puffed up with the novelty of the heresy he had embraced, and with having already silenced many by his arguments. "Leave him alone for a time," he said, "only pray for him; he will of himself, by reading, discover his error; for I myself, when a youth, was by a misguided mother be-

---

[1] *Regula:* symbolical of the rule of faith.
[2] *Confessions,* b. iii. c. 11.

trayed to the Manichæans, and not only read but wrote out almost all their books; and yet I came to see, without argument or proof from any one, how that sect was to be shunned." But Monnica could not be satisfied; she besought the good bishop still more earnestly and with many tears, that he would see and discourse with her son. A little displeased at her importunity he exclaimed, " Go thy way and God bless thee, for it is not possible that the son of these tears should perish." She went away comforted, accepting his answer as a voice from heaven.[1]

A.D. 374.

Augustine now commenced to teach rhetoric at Carthage. His pupils were mostly studying for the law. "In those years I made sale of the art of victorious loquacity. Yet I preferred to have honest scholars, as they are esteemed, to whom I without artifice taught artifices, not to be practised against the life of the guiltless, although sometimes for the life of the guilty." Many heathen notions and practices still lingered, and amongst them that of soothsaying. "When I would compete for a theatrical prize," Augustine continues, "a soothsayer demanded how much I would give him to make me win. He was to sacrifice certain living creatures, and so induce the devils to favour me. I answered him: 'Although the garland I was to win should be made

---

[1] Ibid., c. 12.

of imperishable gold, I would not suffer a fly to be destroyed to secure it.' But I said this not out of pure love for Thee, O God of my heart, for I knew not then how to love Thee, but because I detested and abominated such foul mysteries, although I myself was sacrificing to devils by the superstition in which I was enthralled." Accordingly he did not hesitate to consult another kind of impostors, the astrologers, or " mathematicians," who observed the stars, but offered no sacrifices and invoked no spirit in their divinations.[1]

At twenty, Augustine had mastered nearly all the science of the age. Whilst others were scarcely able to understand Aristotle with the aid of skilful tutors, he read him unassisted. " Whatever was written on rhetoric, logic, geometry, music, or arithmetic, I understood without an instructor, because of the quickness of intelligence and acuteness of observing which Thou, O my God, gave me."[2]

By degrees Augustine discovered that the professors of Manichæism could not solve the questions which sprang up in his astute mind, and that what Manes had taught regarding the universe was contradicted by science. His confidence was further shaken by the most renowned bishop of the sect. who discerned Augustine's genius, requesting to become his pupil. All this time, during which he

---

[1] Id., b. iv. cc. 2, 3.
[2] Ibid., c. 16.

was wandering in the labyrinth of a false religion, Augustine was in bondage also to the indulgence of his unsubdued appetites.[1]

Amongst the pupils in his school of rhetoric was Alypius, a youth of great promise, but "the vortex of Carthaginian customs had inveigled him into the madness of the games." Although not yet himself converted, Augustine perceived clearly the folly of such a manner of life. "One day," he writes, "when I was sitting in my accustomed place, with my scholars before me, Alypius came in, saluted me, sat down, and fixed his attention on the subject I was handling. Whilst I was explaining there occurred to me a simile borrowed from the circus, as likely to make what I wished to convey pleasanter and plainer, imbued at the same time with a biting gibe at those who were enthralled by that madness. I had no thought at the moment of curing Alypius of that plague. But he applied my words to himself, and thought I spoke them only for his sake. And what any other would have made a ground of offence against me, this worthy young man took as a reason for being offended at himself, and for loving me more fervently." But although Augustine's sharp reproof brought Alypius for the time to his senses, he was not in reality "cured of his plague." In Rome, not long afterwards, he was one day met

---

[1] Id., b. v. cc. 6, 7; Cutts, p. 46.

Per. I.
Chap. 13.

by a knot of acquaintances and fellow-students returning from dinner, who with friendly violence drew him towards the amphitheatre, he all the while resisting. "You may," he protested, "drag my body thither and seat me there, but you cannot force me to lend my mind or my eyes to the spectacle." Nevertheless they carried him in with them and took their places. Soon the customary excitement seized the vast crowd. For a while Alypius kept his eyes firmly closed, but on the fall of one of the combatants, there arose so mighty a cry, that, overcome by curiosity, his resolution gave way, and he looked on the scene before him. Instantly the sight of the blood brought back all the old craving; he fixed his gaze until he was intoxicated with the sanguinary pastime, and joined in the universal shout. "From all this, didst Thou," adds Augustine, "with a most powerful and a most merciful hand pluck him, and teach him not to trust in himself but in Thee."[1]

The schools of rhetoric at Carthage were very disorderly, and although that of Augustine enjoyed a high reputation, he longed for a more quiet chair, where discipline still held something of her ancient sway. He resolved to go to Rome. This resolution was a great grief to Monnica. Unable to part with him, she went down to the harbour, deter-

---

[1] *Confessions*, b. vi. co. 7, 8.

mined either to prevent his voyage, or to bear him company. To free himself from her, he pretended that he had a friend whom he desired to see off, and who was waiting for a favourable wind. "By the help of this device, I hardly persuaded her to remain that night in a place close to our ship, where there was an oratory in memory of the blessed Cyprian." During the night, whilst she was weeping and praying that he might not be permitted to leave her, the wind rose, filled the sails, and bore Augustine out of sight of land. His reflections in after-years on the events of this sad night are full of tenderness and wisdom. "I lied to my mother, and such a mother, and got away. Thou, O God, mysteriously counselling and hearing the real purpose of her desire, granted not what she then asked, that Thou mightest make me what she was ever asking." When the next morning she came to the shore and found the ship was gone, "she was wild with grief."[1]

SECTION II. Augustine came to Rome in 383. He had been there only six months when the city of Milan applied to Symmachus, the prefect (that upright and eloquent pagan whom we have met with in the life of Ambrose), for a teacher of rhetoric.[2] Augustine, through some Manichæan friends, made application for the appointment;

---

[1] Id., b. v. c. 8. [2] *Ante*, p. 161.

Per. I.
Chap. 13.

and Symmachus, having satisfied himself of his fitness, sent him to Milan at the public expense. Alypius would not leave him. "He clave to me," writes Augustine, " by a most strong tie, and went with me to Milan, both that he might not leave me, and that he might practise something of the law he had studied, more to please his parents than himself. At Rome," he continues, "he had thrice sat as assessor with much uncorruptness, wondered at by others, he wondering that they should prefer gold to honesty."[1]

The great attraction for Augustine at Milan was Ambrose. "To Milan I came, and to Ambrose the bishop,[2] thy devout servant, known to the whole world as among the best of men, whose eloquent discourse did at that time strenuously dispense unto thy people the flour of thy wheat, the gladness of thy oil, and the sober intoxication of thy wine. To him was I unknowingly led by Thee, that by him I might knowingly be led to Thee. He received me as a father, and I began to love him, not at first indeed as a teacher of the Truth, which I utterly despaired of finding in thy Church, but as a man friendly to myself. I studiously hearkened to him preaching to the people, but not with the intent I ought to have done, for of the matter I was careless and scornful, but testing his eloquence whether it came up to

---

[1] *Confessions*, b. v. c. 13: b. vi. c. 10.
[2] He had then occupied the see nine years.

its fame. Yet all the time, little by little, I was unconsciously drawing nearer to him. For although I took no pains to learn *what* he spoke, but only to hear *how* he spoke, yet along with the words which I prized there entered into my mind also the things about which I was indifferent; for I could not separate them: so that whilst I opened my heart to admit how *skilfully* he spoke, by degrees there entered also the conviction how *truly* he spoke. In the end I resolved to become a catechumen in the Catholic Church."[1]

Augustine found but little opportunity of private intercourse with the bishop. "It would seem that Ambrose, after the fashion of hot countries, sat habitually in a corner of the cloister or verandah which surrounded the open court of the house, so that those who wished to speak to him could watch for an opportunity of finding him disengaged." "When," writes Augustine, "he was not occupied with the crowds of busy people to whose infirmities he devoted himself, he was either refreshing his body with necessary sustenance, or his mind with reading. Often when we had come and seen him thus intent, and had sat long silent, we were fain to depart, inferring that he was unwilling to lose the little time he thus secured for replenishing his mind."[2]

Monnica could not long remain absent from her

---

[1] *Confessions*, b. v. cc. 13, 14.
[2] Id., b. vi. c. 3; Cutts, pp. 56, 57.

beloved and erring son, but followed him to Milan. The vessel in which she sailed was in danger of shipwreck, and the sailors themselves were alarmed, but Monnica, so Augustine relates, was comforted by a heavenly vision and able to predict a safe termination to their voyage.[1]

Shortly before her arrival Augustine and Alypius were joined by another young man, Nebridius, "who left Carthage and his fine paternal estate, his house and his mother, and came to Milan for no other reason but that with me he might live in a most ardent search after truth and wisdom. So," he continues, "were there three indigent persons sighing out their wants one to another, and waiting upon Thee that Thou mightest give them their meat in due season." These three, with a few others of like mind, formed the project of separating themselves wholly from the turmoil of the world. Each was to throw his possessions into the common stock; and the cares of the household were to be committed to two of them as stewards, that the rest might devote themselves undisturbed to the pursuit of wisdom. But an important element had been left out in their calculation. "We began to ask whether the wives whom some of us possessed already, and others hoped to have, would give their consent, and all our plans which had been so skilfully framed

---

[1] *Confessions*, b. vi. c. 1.

broke to pieces, and were utterly wrecked and cast aside. So we fell again to sighs and groans, and our steps again followed the broad and beaten tracks of the world."[1]

Augustine found himself still under the shackles of his old sins. He had brought with him to Milan his son Adeodatus, and the youth's mother. Monnica was very solicitous that he should break off the unlawful connexion, and contract an honourable marriage. A maiden was even chosen for him and his consent obtained; but, alas, the time of reformation was not yet come; he fell back again into his former mode of life.[2]

He had now cast off the doctrines of the Manichæans, and had allied himself with the Neo-Platonists, with whom, however, he did not long remain. "Being," he says, "warned to return to myself, I entered into my inward parts, Thou leading me on; and with the eye of my soul I saw above my mind the unchangeable light. Not this common light which all flesh may look upon, nor a greater one of the same kind, though much more resplendent, but very different from these. Neither was it above my mind as oil is above water, nor as heaven is above earth, but it was above me because it made me, and I was below it because I was made by it. He who knows the truth knows that light, and he who knows that

---

[1] Ibid., cc. 10, 14.   [2] Ibid., c. 15.

light knows eternity. Love knows it. O eternal truth, and true love and beloved eternity! . . . I found not the way to enjoy Thee, until I embraced that Mediator between God and man, the Man Christ Jesus, who is over all God blessed for ever, and who called to me saying, 'I am the way, the truth, and the life!'"[1]

There was at Milan a good man named Simplician,[2] one who had been spiritually helpful to Ambrose, and who is described by him "as having traversed the whole world to acquire divine knowledge, and given his entire life to holy reading, night and day." "Thou God!" exclaims Augustine, "didst put into my mind, and it seemed good in my eyes, to go to this man. I went therefore and unfolded to him the tortuous course of my errors." Simplician related to him the history of Victorinus, who after worshipping idols all his life, became in his old age a child of Christ, and made a public confession of his name. As Augustine listened—"I burned," he says, "to imitate Victorinus, and when I heard that in the time of the Emperor Julian a law was made forbidding Christians to teach grammar and rhetoric, and that this man chose rather to relinquish the school of words than to give up thy word, he appeared to me not more courageous than happy

---

[1] Id., b. vii. cc. 10, 18.
[2] He succeeded Ambrose as bishop of Milan.—See *ante*, p. 173.

in having thus discovered an opportunity of serving Thee only;—which thing I also sighed for in my bonds; bonds not imposed by another, but by my own iron will. The enemy being master of my will had made a chain of it, and bound me with it. Out of a perverse will came lust; and lust indulged became custom; and custom unresisted became necessity. And that new will which had begun to rise in me, freely to serve Thee and to wish to enjoy Thee, O God, the only sure delight, was not as yet able to overcome my former wilfulness made strong by long indulgence. Thus did my two wills—one old, the other new; one carnal, the other spiritual—strive within me, and by their discord undid my soul."[1]

Another hand of help was extended to him by his fellow-countryman Pontitianus. This man, coming to the house where Augustine and Alypius dwelt, saw on the table a volume of Paul's Epistles; and in the conversation which ensued he related to them the anecdote of the two gentlemen, who were turned from the pursuit of worldly honour to embrace the ascetic life by reading Athanasius' *Life of St. Anthony*.[2] The narrative sank deep into Augustine's soul. "Thou, O Lord, whilst he was speaking didst turn me towards myself, taking me from behind my back where I

---

[1] *Confessions*, b. viii. cc. 2, 5, and note in Clark's edition, p. 175.
[2] See *Early Church History*, p. 532, note.

Per. I.
Chap. 13.

had placed myself, and setting me before my face that I might see how foul I was, how crooked and defiled, bespotted and ulcerous. I beheld and loathed myself, and whither to flee from myself I found not. And whenever I sought to turn away my gaze from myself, Thou again didst set me over against myself, and thrustedst me before my own eyes that I might find out my own iniquity and hate it. . . . Pontitianus," continues Augustine, "having finished his story and the business he came for, went his way, and I withdrew into myself. With what scourges of rebuke did I not lash my soul to make her follow me, struggling to go after Thee! Yet she drew back, she refused. All her arguments were spent and confuted; there remained only a mute shrinking; she dreaded, as if it were death itself, the plugging of that flow of habit whereby she was wasting to death. I grasped Alypius, and exclaimed, 'What ails us? What is it? The unlearned start up and take Heaven by force, while we with our learning, but wanting heart, behold! where we wallow in flesh and blood.' Some such words I uttered, and in my excitement flung myself from him, while he gazed after me in silent amazement."[1]

"There was," he goes on to relate, "a little garden belonging to our lodging, of which we had the use. Thither the tempest within my breast

---

[1] *Confessions*, b. viii. cc. 6–8.

hurried me, where no one might check the fiery struggle in which I was engaged with myself, until it came to the issue which Thou knewest, though I did not." Alypius followed, "for his presence did not destroy my privacy, and how could he desert me so troubled? We sat down as far from the house as we could."[1]

The fever which consumed Augustine's soul communicated itself to his body; he tore his hair; he smote his forehead; with close-knit fingers he clasped his knee. The two natures, the two wills within him, the good drawing this way, the evil that way, were locked together in a death-struggle for the mastery. "The very toys of toys and vanities of vanities, my old mistresses, held me in their thrall; they shook my fleshly garment and whispered softly, Dost thou part with us? From this moment shall we no more be with thee for ever? What they said I did not so much as half hear, for they did not openly show themselves and contradict me, but muttering as it were behind my back, furtively plucked me as I was departing, to make me look back upon them. For on that other side toward which I had set my face and whither I still trembled to go, the chaste dignity of continence shone upon me full of cheerfulness, honestly alluring me to come and doubt nothing, and extending her holy hands, full of

---

[1] Ibid.

Per. I.
Chap. 13.

a multiplicity of good examples, to receive and embrace me." [1]

At length he could contain himself no longer; the storm which raged within him found vent in a torrent of tears. Feeling entire solitude to be the fittest place for weeping, he stole away from Alypius, and flung himself under a fig-tree, where his heart found relief in words. "'Thou, O Lord, how long? How long, Lord, wilt Thou be angry for ever? O remember not against us former iniquities. How long, how long? To-morrow, to-morrow? Why not now? Why not this hour an end to my uncleanness?' Thus I said, and wept in the most bitter contrition of my heart, and behold I heard the voice, as of a boy or girl, I know not which, coming from a neighbouring house, chanting and oft repeating, *Tolle, lege; tolle, lege;*' 'Take up and read, take up and read.' Instantly my countenance altered; I began to think most intently whether children were wont in any kind of play to sing such words; and I could not remember ever to have heard the like. So checking my tears I rose up, interpreting it to be no other than a command to me from Heaven, to open the book and read the first chapter I should light upon. . . . Eagerly, therefore, I returned to the place where Alypius was sitting, for there I had laid the volume of the Apostles. I

---

[1] Ibid., cc. 8, 11.

seized, I opened, and in silence read that paragraph on which my eyes first fell: 'Not in rioting and drunkenness, not in chambering and wantonness, not in strife and envying; but put ye on the Lord Jesus Christ, and make no provision for the flesh to fulfil the lusts thereof.'[1] No further would I read, nor needed I, for instantly as the sentence ended, by a serene light as it were infused into my heart, all the darkness of doubt vanished away. Then putting my finger, or some other mark, in the place, I closed the book, and with a tranquil countenance made known to Alypius what had passed. He asked to see what I had been reading. I showed him; he looked further and read, 'Him that is weak in the faith, receive ye,' which he applied to himself and was strengthened. Thence we go in to my mother. We tell her; she rejoices; we relate how it all took place; she leaps for joy, and triumphs and blesses Thee, who art able to do exceeding abundantly above all that we can ask or think, for she saw that Thou hadst given her for me more than she was wont to ask in her pitiful and most sorrowful groanings. For Thou didst so convert me to Thyself, that I sought neither a wife nor any other of this world's hopes, standing on that rule of faith where Thou hadst showed me to her in a vision so many years before."[2]

---

[1] Rom. xiii. 13, 14.   [2] *Confessions*, b. viii. c. 12.

SECTION III. It was only in accordance with the spirit of the age that Augustine, having now given himself to the Lord, should take the vow of perpetual celibacy and withdraw altogether from secular concerns. Throwing up his professorship, he retired to a country house at Cassiacum,[1] which was placed at his disposal by one of his Milanese friends. There he passed the seven months which intervened till his baptism. He was accompanied by his mother and his son, then not quite fifteen, Alypius and Nebridius, and six other chosen friends. To this select company the time spent at Cassiacum was the realization of the happy life of which some of them had already dreamed. They rose early, sometimes passed the morning in reading, dined frugally together, and in the afternoon assembled under a spreading tree in the meadow, for pleasureable and profitable conversation. When it rained they removed to a hall of the baths which were attached to the villa. "Of these *réunions* Augustine was the life and soul; it was a little school of Christian philosophy of which he was the professor. Some had their tablets always ready, and with the stylus noted down rapidly what was said. When the discussion was prolonged into the twilight, a servant brought a lamp that the writers

---

[1] Now Cassago de Brianza, twenty miles from Milan. The site of the villa has been occupied for centuries past by the palace of the Visconti of Modrone.—Cutts, p. 76.

might not lose any of the master's words." These conversations were the germ of several of Augustine's philosophical treatises.[1]

A.D. 387.

After his baptism, which was performed (A.D. 387) by Ambrose himself, his son and Alypius being baptized at the same time, Augustine and Monnica proceeded to Rome, intending to return to Africa. But the sweet prospect of again living together in their native country was not to be realized: Monnica's earthly race was nearly run. It was whilst they rested at Ostia, recruiting their strength for the voyage, that a memorable conversation took place between the mother and son concerning the Kingdom of Heaven. "The day now approaching on which she was to depart this life (which day Thou knewest, we knew not) it came to pass—Thou as I believe by thy secret ways so ordering it—that she and I were alone leaning in a certain window which looked into the garden of the house. We were discoursing together very pleasantly, and forgetting those things which are behind and reaching forth to those which are before, were inquiring between ourselves in the presence of the Truth which Thou art, of what nature the eternal life of the saints is to be, which 'eye hath not seen nor ear heard, nor hath it entered into the heart of man to conceive.' And when our discourse was

---

[1] Cutts, pp. 75-78.

Per. I.
Chap. 13.

brought to that point, that the very highest delight of the bodily senses is, in respect to the sweetness of that life, not only not worthy of comparison, but not even of mention, we, lifting ourselves with a more glowing affection towards the Self-same, did by degrees pass through all corporeal things, even the very heavens, yea, we soared higher yet, by inward musing and discourse and admiration of thy works. We came to our own minds, and went beyond them, advancing up to that region of unfailing plenty, where Thou feedest Israel for ever with the food of truth; and we said, If to any the tumult of the flesh were hushed, hushed the images of earth and waters and air of heaven, yea, the very soul hushed to herself and by not thinking of self surmounting self; hushed all dreams and imaginary revelations and tongues and signs, since all these say, We made not ourselves, but He made us, who abideth for ever:—If then, having uttered this, they too should now be hushed and He alone speak, not by them but by Himself, that we might hear his word, not through any tongue of flesh, nor angel's voice, nor sound of thunder, nor in the dark riddle of a similitude, but might hear Him, whom in these things we love, might hear his very Self without these—as we two now strained ourselves, and in swift thought touched on that Eternal Wisdom which abideth over all—could this be sustained and other discordant visions withdrawn, and the beholder be ravished and absorbed and wrapped up amid these inward joys, so that life might be eternally like that one moment of understanding which now we sighed after, would not this be, 'Enter thou into the joy of thy Lord?'[1]

"Such things was I saying, although not perhaps in these very words, when my mother spoke: 'Son, for my part I have no further delight in anything in this life, what I do here any longer, and to what end I am here I know not, now that my hopes in this world are accomplished. One thing there was for which I desired to tarry for a while in this life, that I might see thee a Catholic Christian before I died. My God has done this for me more abundantly, since I now see thee despising all earthly felicity and become his servant. What do I longer here?'"[2]

Five days afterwards, Monnica fell sick of a fever. "We hastened to her. Looking intently upon us she said, 'Here shall you lay your mother.' My brother remarked that it is a happier lot to die in one's own country. She replied, 'Lay this body anywhere; let not care for that disquiet you at all. This only I request, that you will remember me at the Lord's altar wherever you may be.' . . . I heard afterwards that one day when I was absent, some friends asking whether she did not

---

[1] *Confessions*, b. ix. cc. 6, 8, 10; Cutts, p. 88.
[2] *Confessions*, ibid.

Per. I.
Chap. 13.

dread to leave her body so far from her own city, she replied, 'Nothing is far from God, nor need I fear lest at the end of the world He should not recognize the place whence He is to raise me up.' On the ninth day then of her sickness, and the fifty-sixth year of her age, and the three and thirtieth of mine, was that religious and holy soul set free from the body. I closed her eyes. A mighty sadness flowed into my heart and was passing into tears, when my eyes by the violent control of my mind drew back the fountain dry, and woe was me in such a struggle. That which grievously pained me was the newly-made wound wrought through the sudden wrench of that most sweet and dear custom of living together.... Evodius [a young man newly converted who had joined their party] took up the Psalter and began to sing, the whole house responding, 'I will sing of mercy and judgment unto Thee, O Lord;' which, when they heard, many brethren and religious women came together; and whilst they whose office it was made ready for the burial, I, together with those who thought not fit to leave me, discoursed on what was suited to the occasion, and by this alleviation of truth mitigated the anguish known unto Thee alone.... And when her dead body was carried forth, we went and returned without tears. For not even in those prayers which we poured forth unto Thee when the sacrifice of our redemption was offered for her, the corpse being now placed by the grave-side previous to its being laid therein, did I weep; yet was I the whole day in secret heavily sad, and with troubled mind prayed Thee, as I was able, to heal my sorrow."[1].

A.D. 387.

---

[1] *Confessions*, b. ix. cc. 11, 12, and note in Clark, p. 211.

CHAPTER XIV.

AUGUSTINE (continued).

Per. I.
Chap. 14.

SECTION I. Augustine tarried nearly a year in Rome before returning to Africa. In 388 he took up his dwelling in his native town, Thagaste. Distributing half of his patrimony to the poor, he retired with a few chosen friends, of whom Alypius was one, to his own house, and entered upon a life of fasting, prayer, meditation, and study. Like Basil and Jerome, he exerted himself for the establishment of monastic houses, but it was chiefly the lower classes and liberated slaves whom he persuaded to take the vows.[1]

At the end of three years, having occasion to go to Hippo, he was present in the church when the bishop Valerius was discoursing on the necessity of appointing an additional priest for the Catholic service. He was recognized and laid hold of, and notwithstanding his resistance, presented to the bishop, who ordained him on the spot. When he removed to Hippo[2] he took with him his brother-

---

[1] Cutts, p. 94; Ruffner's *Fathers of the Desert*, ii. p. 301.

[2] The modern seaport town of Bona, in the east of Algeria, is built out of the ruins of the ancient Hippo, the site of which lay a mile to the

hood, and settled his monastery in the gardens adjoining the church. In a few years Valerius, finding his strength decline, associated Augustine with him in his episcopal duties, and at his death in 396 Augustine became bishop. He thus meditates on his new position. "Nothing is better than the study of Divine wisdom without distraction; but to preach, to refute, to reprove, to edify, to take care for each individual soul, is a heavy burden and toil. Who would not shun it? But the Gospel makes me afraid when I think of the slothful servant who buried his Lord's talent." The episcopal residence now became both a cloister and a school of theology. Many who were there trained for the priesthood rose to offices of rank and influence.[1]

Augustine required his clergy to live with him as a religious community in celibacy and poverty. There was, however, no display of asceticism. He himself wore the black dress of the Eastern cœnobites, but retained his linen and shoes. "I applaud your courage," he said to those who went barefoot; "do you bear with my weakness." The

---

south. Hippo Regius, a royal city of the Numidian kings, was a strong and warlike town, commodiously situated both for trade and for the chase; with a beautiful air, and commanding a fine view of the sea, the spacious harbour, the forest-clad mountains and plains cut through with rivers.—Shaw, *Travels in the Levant*, 1738, p. 97.

[1] Cutts, pp. 106–108; Lloyd, *North African Church*, p. 205. Combining the clerical life with the monastic, Augustine became unwittingly to himself the founder of the Augustinian order, which 1100 years afterwards gave Luther to the world.—Schaff, pp. 993, 994.

table service was of wood, earthenware and marble, and the spoons of silver. Hospitality was freely maintained. The diet of the brotherhood was mostly vegetable; but flesh and wine were provided for the visitors, of whom there was a continual succession. On the dining-table was carved a Latin distich:—

"He who slanders the absent is forbidden to sit at this board."[1]

If any one infringed this rule, Augustine used to tell him that either the verses must be effaced, or he must leave the table. Another reprehensible custom in conversation was the frequent taking of the name of God to witness the truth of what was said. The penalty which the bishop imposed on his guests for this offence was to go without wine at dinner.[2]

Augustine was a powerful and very diligent preacher; often preaching five days in succession, sometimes twice a day. The fire which burnt in his own soul kindled a corresponding flame in the souls of his hearers. Like all true Christian preachers, he depended for success on the help of the Holy Spirit. "The Christian orator," he says, "will succeed more by prayer than by gifts of oratory. Before he attempts to speak he will pray for himself and his hearers. And when the

---

[1] Quisquis amat dictis absentum rodere vitam
Hanc mensam vetitam noverit esse sibi.

[2] Cutts, p. 167; Lloyd, p. 270; Schaff, p. 994.

time is come, before he opens his mouth, he must lift up his thirsty soul to God to drink in what he is about to pour forth, and to be himself filled with what he is about to dispense. For who knows what it is expedient at any given moment for us to say, or to be heard saying, except God who knows the hearts of all? And who can enable us to say what we ought, and in the way we ought, but He in whose hand are both ourselves and our words? He therefore who would both know and teach, should learn all that is to be taught, and acquire a faculty of speech, suitable to his office; but when the hour for speech arrives let him give heed to our Lord's words, 'Take no thought how or what ye should speak, for it shall be given you in that same hour what ye shall speak; for it is not ye that speak but the Spirit of your Father that speaketh in you.' If the Holy Spirit speaks thus in those who for Christ's sake are delivered to the persecutors, why not also in those who deliver Christ's message to those who are willing to learn?"[1]

At the same time he has a word of reproof for such as from sloth or a fanatical spirit despised the helps which God has provided. "If any one says we need not direct men how or what they should teach, since it is the Holy Spirit that makes them teachers, he might as well say we need not pray,

---

[1] *On Christian Doctrine*, b. iv. c. 15; Schaff, *loc. cit.*

Per. I.
Chap. 14.

since our Lord says, 'Your Father knoweth what things ye have need of before ye ask Him;' or that the apostle Paul should not have given directions to Timothy and Titus as to how or what they should teach to others. These three apostolic epistles ought to be constantly before the eyes of every one who has attained to the position of a teacher in the Church."[1]

Augustine's practice agreed with his precepts. "One day he had prepared an eloquent discourse, designed to produce a strong impression on cultivated minds. Suddenly in the midst of his preaching he broke the thread of his argument, and turned abruptly to a more simple and popular subject. On his return home he related how he had yielded to an impulse of the Holy Spirit which had driven him to set aside the original plan of his sermon. Hardly had he spoken, when a man knocking at the door, entered,

---

[1] *On Christian Doctrine*, b. iv. c. 16. With all this wisdom, Augustine, like most of the Fathers, indulged in a symbolism often fanciful and sometimes absurd. See for example his comment on the healing of the impotent man at the Pool of Bethesda. "The pool is the Jewish people shut in by the five books of Moses as by five porches. The law only brought forth the sick, it could not heal them. Christ, by his teaching and mighty acts, troubles sinners, troubles the water, and arouses it to his own death. To descend into the troubled waters means to believe in the Lord's death. That only one was healed signifies unity; those who came afterwards were not healed, because he who is outside unity cannot be healed. Christ found in the impotent man's age the number of infirmity. The number forty is consecrated by a kind of perfection. Why should we wonder that he was weak and sick whose years fell short of forty by two? Finding the man thus lacking, Christ gave him two precepts, ordered him to do two things, 'Take up thy bed—and walk.' Thus filling up that which was lacking of the perfect number."—*On St. John*, Tractate xvii.

bathed in tears. He had been arrested by the diverted portion of the discourse, and now confessed himself to be won over to the Gospel."[1]

A.D. 397.

SECTION II. It was early in Augustine's episcopal life that he came into conflict with the Donatists.[2] This sect, confined to the North African province, had increased rather than diminished under the successors of Constantine, and its adherents were here as numerous as the Catholics. Hippo was a very hotbed of the schism. With the same faith, the same worship, and nearly the same discipline, there were two rival communities, each claiming to be the true Church. This was a condition of things which Augustine could not endure to behold. He not only yearned to bring all men to what he looked upon as the peculiar privileges of the Catholic Church; he sincerely believed that outside her pale there is no salvation.[3] He confounded the authority of Christ with that of the visible Church, and claimed for the latter the same absolute obedience as for Christ Himself. From the moment therefore when he became

---

[1] *Dict. Christ. Biog.*, i. p. 219.

[2] For an account of the rise of the Donatists, see *Early Church History*, pt. ii. c. 10.

[3] "Why," he asks, "should any hesitate to throw themselves into the arms of that Church, which has always maintained herself by the succession of bishops in apostolic sees, by the faith of the people, the decisions of councils, and the authority of miracles? It is either a matchless impiety or a foolish arrogancy not to acknowledge her doctrine as a rule of faith."—Du Pin, iii. p. 192.

bishop of Hippo, no object lay nearer to his heart, than to bring back the Donatists into the Catholic communion. His confidence in his own theological principles induced him to believe that if the bishops of that party could only be brought calmly to investigate the questions at issue, they would acknowledge their error. In 397 a public disputation took place between himself and an aged Donatist bishop, named Fortunius, which however led to no practical result. In 403 another effort was made. At a Council held at Carthage the Donatists were invited to choose delegates prepared to discuss the contested points with delegates of the Catholic party. The invitation seems to have been prompted by the spirit of love, but its terms were not conciliatory, it was the language of men who believed themselves the sole possessors of the truth, addressed to men in error, and whose errors moreover it was their business to correct. The Donatists rejected this overture.[1]

It happened several years afterwards (410) that some Donatist bishops who had been summoned before the higher civil authorities, let fall the assertion that they would be well able to prove the truth of their cause if they were but allowed a patient hearing. The Catholic bishops, or Augustine on their behalf, seized eagerly upon the words; and the next year the Emperor Hono-

---

[1] Neander, iii. pp. 280, 281; Cutts, pp. 143-145.

rius gave orders for a conference to be held at Carthage between the two parties. The Pro-consul of Africa, Flavius Marcellinus, a man of ability, and friendly with Augustine, was appointed to preside. The terms on which the Donatists were invited to meet their opponents had the sound of extreme liberality. The Catholics declared themselves ready to surrender their bishoprics to the Donatists if these should be able to prove their case. But there is little merit in the profession of great sacrifices when there is not the remotest chance of these being called for. More feasible was another proposal, that if the Donatists should lose their cause, and should be willing to return to the Catholic Church, their bishops should be recognized as such; or, if preferred, the bishops of both parties should resign, and Donatists and Catholics unitedly choose new officers. "Be brothers with us in the Lord's inheritance," pleaded Augustine, "let us not for the sake of preserving our own dignities hinder the peace of Christ." He endeavoured at the same time to inspire his Catholic brethren with the charity that animated his own breast: "The eyes of the Donatists are inflamed, they must be treated tenderly. Let no one defend his faith by disputation, lest the spark let fall should kindle a great fire. If you should hear reviling language, endure it; be as though you had not heard it; be silent. 'Shall I be silent,' you may ask, 'when charges are brought against

A.D. 410.

Per. I.
Chap. 14.

my bishop?' Yes, be silent, not that you are to allow the charges, but to bear them."[1]

Accordingly there met at Carthage (A.D. 411) 286 bishops of the Catholic, and 279 of the Donatist party.[2] The latter, who stood in awe of the superior logic of Augustine, came to the conference reluctantly and full of distrust: this was manifest from the first. As the numbers were so great, Marcellinus directed that seven disputants from each side should be chosen. To this the Donatists objected; and the greater part of the first day was spent in debate on this point, and on other questions of a formal nature. At length they yielded, and nominated their representatives, of whom Petilian was the chief spokesman. Augustine of course was the leader on the Catholic side; and amongst his colleagues were Alypius and Possidius.[3]

When the deputies met again on the second day, the Donatists refused to be seated, saying: "The divine law forbids us to sit with the wicked."[4] No notice was taken of this most offensive remark; but the Catholics declining out of courtesy to sit whilst their opponents were standing, Marcellinus also ordered his own chair to be removed. Two

---

[1] Neander, iii. pp. 284-286.

[2] One hundred and twenty Catholic bishops are said to have been absent, and sixty-four sees were vacant. Many of the Donatist bishops also were absent.—Gibbon, iv. p. 217, note. It must be borne in mind that many villages of this province, as well as towns, were then presided over by bishops.

[3] Neander, ibid.   [4] Ps. xxvi. 5.

subjects chiefly occupied the conference. The first related to an historical question of a hundred years before, viz., the traditorship of Felix[1] and the validity of Cæcilian's consecration: into this we need not here enter. The other resolved itself into the great theological problem: What is the Church?[2]

A.D. 411.

That which had been the apple of discord between Cyprian and Novatian,[3] the definition of the Church, was now keeping the Catholics and the Donatists asunder. Both parties confounded the visible with the invisible Church, the cup with that which it contains. The Catholics maintained that, apart from the communion with the one visible Catholic Church, derived from the Apostles through the succession of bishops, there can be no communication of the Holy Spirit, and no salvation. Augustine thus confounded what Christianity had effected through the Church, with the Church itself as an outward institution. He did not see that the mighty effects brought about by the Gospel had been due to its inherent divine power; nay, that it might have produced far purer and mightier effects, had it not been in so many ways disturbed and checked in its operation by the imperfect vehicle of its transmission.

---

[1] See *Early Church History*, pp. 389, 392. The *traditores*, or betrayers, were those who in the Diocletian persecution gave up to the magistrates their copies of the New Testament to be publicly burnt.—Id., p. 352.

[2] Neander, iii. p. 286.

[3] See *Early Church History*, pp. 322-324.

Per. I.
Chap. 14.

In his exclusion of dissenters from the benefit of the Gospel, Augustine does not come behind Cyprian: "No one," he says, "attains to salvation, and eternal life, who has not Christ for his Head. But no one can have Christ for Head, who does not belong to his body, which is the Church. The entire Christ is the Head and the Body; the Head is the only-begotten Son of God, and the body is the Church. He who agrees not with Scripture in the doctrine concerning the Head, although he may stand in external communion with the Church, belongs not to the Church; and he who holds fast to all that Scripture teaches respecting the Head, and yet cleaves not to the unity of the Church, belongs not to the Church." Whenever the Donatists appealed to miracles, answers to prayer, visions, and the holy lives of their bishops, as evidences that the true Church was with them, Augustine met them by a reference to such passages of Scripture, as Matt. xxiv. 24: "There shall arise false Christs, and false prophets, and shall show great signs and wonders." "Let them not try to prove the genuineness of their Church by the councils of their bishops, or by deceitful miraculous signs, seeing that our Lord has put us on our guard against such proofs, but let them confine themselves to the Law and the Prophets, and the word of the only Shepherd."[1]

---

[1] Neander, iii. pp. 287-290.

The Donatists, like the Novatians, held that A.D. 411. every Church which tolerates unworthy members within it, is itself polluted by communion with them, and thus ceases to be a true Christian Church; and by a natural but mistaken egotism, they took it for granted that they were themselves the true Church, and that the rest of Christendom was apostate and corrupt. Petilian argued that religious acts are operative only in a pure Church; that none but a blameless priest can administer the " sacraments." Augustine replied : " Often the conscience of man is unknown to me, but I am certain of the mercy of Christ."

Petilian: Whoever receives the faith through an unbeliever receives not faith but guilt.

Augustine: But Christ is faithful, from whom I receive faith and not guilt.

Petilian: The character of a thing depends on its origin and root; a genuine new birth can come only from good seed.

Augustine: My origin is Christ; my root is Christ; my head is Christ. He alone makes me free from guilt, who died for our sins and rose again for our justification; for I believe not in the minister by whom I am baptized, but in Him who justifies the sinner, so that my faith is counted to me for righteousness.[1]

It was a foregone conclusion that Marcellinus

---

[1] Ibid., pp. 291, 293, 298, 299.

Per. I.
Chap. 14.

should give sentence against the Donatists. They were adjudged to have lost their cause and to be guilty of heterodoxy. It was determined that the sect should be utterly blotted out; that all who would not conform should be deprived of both place and name, so that the whole province might be brought back into the Catholic unity. To this object, unhappily, Augustine lent the weight of his eloquence, learning, and character. The pro-consul forbade the Donatists thenceforth to assemble for worship, and ordered them to give up their church-buildings to the Catholics; at the same time admonishing the bishops to return to the one true Church. Appeal to the Emperor proved useless. Honorius, in 412, issued a decree enacting severe penalties against the sect. The malcontents were to be heavily fined in proportion to their rank, and if obstinate were to forfeit all their property. Slaves and peasants were to be scourged into conformity, and their Catholic masters who should neglect to act on this order were to be punished as Donatists. Bishops and clergy were to be banished, and the church property confiscated.[1]

Very many yielded; whole communities even, as at Cirta, returning bodily to the Catholic Church. A greater number, however, nobly preferred to suffer the loss of all things rather than do violence to their consciences. Three hundred bishops and

---

[1] Robertson, i. pp. 408, 409.

thousands of the inferior clergy were torn from their churches and banished to the islands. "The persecution," says Julius Lloyd, "was as unrelenting as that by which Louis XIV. coerced the Huguenots. Some yielded through fear of the Imperial Edict, others through the extraordinary ability and fascinating influence of Augustine. Not Francis de Sales, Bossuet and Fenelon together, exercised over the Protestants of France a greater influence than Augustine alone, in winning to his side all who were accessible to eloquence or argument."[1]

The measures adopted were only too successful. The remnant of the Donatist Church, on the irruption of the Vandals, sided with the conquerors against the Empire, and were taken under their protection, but this Church never regained its influence. The Donatists lingered, however, till the pontificate of Gregory the Great at the end of the sixth century, but after his adverse edicts they disappear from history.[2]

During this long controversy Augustine vacillated between gentle and forcible methods of overcoming the Donatists. At one time we find him

---

[1] *North African Church*, p. 222; *Dict. Christ. Biog.*, i. p. 894; Gibbon, iv. pp. 217, 218; Robertson, i. p. 409. A section of the Donatists, the Circumcelliones, burned the churches, maltreated the Catholic clergy, committed many other outrages, and laid wait for Augustine himself. The moderate Donatists looked on in horror, but were powerless to check these excesses.—*Dict. Christ. Biog.*, i. p. 891; see *Early Church History*, p. 398.

[2] Roberts, *Church Memorials*, p. 257.

Per. I.
Chap. 14

appealing to the example of Elijah, who slew with his own hand the prophets of Baal; at another protesting against the penal measures by which it was proposed to coerce the schismatics: "You must go forward," he said, "simply with the word of truth; you must seek to overcome by argument, else all the effect will be that instead of open and avowed heretics you will have hypocritical Catholic Christians."[1]

In a letter assigned to the year 408, Augustine defends with sophistical arguments the principle of coercion. "If any one saw his enemy running headlong to destroy himself, when he had become delirious through a dangerous fever, would he not in that case be much more truly rendering evil for evil if he permitted him to run on thus than if he took measures to have him seized and bound? . . . Who can love us more than God? And yet God quickens us by salutary fear, and the sharp medicine of tribulation; afflicts with famine even the patriarchs, disquiets a rebellious people by severe chastisements, and refuses though thrice besought to take away from the Apostle the thorn in the flesh. . . . Whatever the true Mother does, even when something severe and bitter is felt by her children at her hands, she is not rendering evil for evil, but is applying the benefit of discipline to counteract the evil of sin, not with the hatred

---

[1] Neander, iii. pp. 282, 283.

which seeks to harm, but with the love which seeks to heal." [1]

At the Conference this question was necessarily uppermost in the minds of the Donatist leaders over whose heads the sword of the magistrate hung suspended by a hair. "Did the Apostles," asked Petilian, "ever persecute any one, or did Christ ever deliver any one over to the secular power? In dying for men he has given Christians the example to die, but not to kill." Another Donatist bishop, Gaudentius, pleaded: "The Saviour of souls sent fishermen, not soldiers, to preach his faith. What must that man think of God who defends Him with outward violence?"[2] To these unanswerable arguments Augustine had nothing to reply but the same kind of sophism: "It is no doubt better to be led to God by instruction than by fear of punishment or affliction. But although the former is better, the other is not to be neglected. Bad servants must be reclaimed by the rod of temporal suffering." No atrocities, alas, will be wanting when for the sake of the supposed good, either of the whole or of individuals, the question, What is right? comes to be thus subordinated to the question, What is expedient? With a strange perversity of interpretation, Augustine adduced as a Scriptural warrant for the most flagrant acts of oppression, our Saviour's command in the parable

---

[1] Letter to Vincentius (xciii.), c. i. § 2: c. ii. § 4, 6.
[2] Compare the words of Athanasius, *ante*, p. 37.

of the Supper, "*compel* them to come in."[1] His sanction of persecution became from this time forward a precedent of great authority in the Church. In it is to be found the germ of that whole system of spiritual despotism and intolerance which culminated in the Inquisition.[2]

---

[1] Luke xiv. 23.   [2] Neander, iii. pp. 301–308.

CHAPTER XV.

AUGUSTINE (*concluded*).

SECTION I. Whilst persecution was raging against the Donatists, Augustine embarked in the Pelagian controversy. Hitherto the doctrinal differences which agitated the Church had come from the East; this arose in the West.[1]   A.D. 412.

About the end of the fourth century Pelagius,[2] a British monk, a man of learning and reputation,

---

[1] The *germ* of the Pelagian doctrine had however for some time existed in the Eastern Church. Marius Mercator asserts that it had its birth in the Antiochian School, chiefly with Theodore of Mopsuestia (A.D. 392), and was carried to Rome by Rufinus, who, not daring himself to publish it, taught it to Pelagius. But it is to be noted that the cardinal doctrine of Pelagianism, man's natural goodness, is put by Athanasius, half a century earlier, into the mouth of Anthony. In his sermon to the monks the anchorite is made to say: "Virtue needs only the consent of the will, since it is within us, and originates in the mind, for the soul was created beautiful and upright. If it turn from its original nature, this is called vice. The thing therefore is not difficult; for if we remain as we were originally created, we are in a state of virtue. Now if this had to be obtained from without, there would be real difficulty; but since it is within us, let us guard the soul as a precious deposit which the Lord has committed to our keeping, in order that He may acknowledge his work to be as He made it. . . . In this we have the Lord for our fellow-worker." Upon which Ruffner observes, "The origin of this doctrine was not the Bible, nor even apostolical tradition, but the Platonism of the Fathers from the time of Justin Martyr. Plato taught the entire moral ability of man to purify his soul from sin."—*Fathers of the Desert*, i. pp. 261, 262, and note; Du Pin, iv. p. 36.

[2] This name is the Greek form for Morgan—i.e., *sea-born*.

Per. I.
Chap. 15.

took up his abode in Rome, where he became the disciple of Rufinus. Amongst his acquaintances was Cælestius,[1] a native of Ireland, who had forsaken the profession of an advocate for the ascetic life. The two friends began to put forth views in direct contradiction to those of Augustine, who had for some time taught that man is by nature wholly evil, and in himself impotent to embrace and pursue good. They remained, however, unmolested until the sack of the city in 410, when Cælestius fled to Carthage. Here his doctrines excited alarm, and were condemned by a Council held in 412. Augustine brought his powerful intellect to bear upon the infant heresy, refuting it both by preaching and writing.[2]

Pelagius, meantime, had gone to Palestine,[3] where (415) he was charged with heresy before bishop John of Jerusalem, and a synod of his clergy. Orosius, a young Spanish ecclesiastic, who had been living with Jerome, stood forth as his accuser. When Orosius supported his charge by a reference to Augustine, Pelagius contemptuously asked, "What is Augustine to me?" Orosius answered, that a man who presumed thus to speak of the bishop to whom the North African Church owed her restoration, deserved to be excommuni-

---

[1] Jerome describes Cælestius as *Scotorum pultibus prægravatus*, "heavy with Scotch porridge." The term Scot at that time signified a native of Ireland.

[2] Robertson, i. pp. 411-413; Schaff, pp. 791, 792.

[3] See *ante*, p. 295.

cated. John, who also made little account of the authority of Augustine, exclaimed, "I will be Augustine," and undertook himself the defence of Pelagius.[1] The synod, on the ground of jurisdiction, referred the question to the bishop of Rome. In the same year, before a synod at Diospolis, the ancient Lydda, Pelagius was tried and pronounced innocent. A doctrinal heresy took easy root in the East.

Cælestius, who had returned to Rome, seized this occasion to appeal against the sentence of the Carthaginian synod. A council was called by Zosimus, the Roman bishop; and on Cælestius disavowing all dogmas which the Roman See had condemned, he was exculpated, Zosimus sending a letter of reproof to the Africans, for listening too readily to charges against good men. But Augustine and the African prelates were not to be thus trifled with. They assembled again in synod at Carthage (A.D. 418), asserted their independence of Rome, and passed nine canons, which came to be regarded as the bulwark of the Church against Pelagianism. The Emperor Honorius now interposed, declared the Pelagians to be heretics, and subjected them to disabilities and penalties. Upon this Zosimus, pressed by the Court and by the anti-Pelagian party, re-opened the matter, and summoned Cœles-

---

[1] John spoke only Greek, Orosius only Latin, but Pelagius both languages.—Schaff, p. 796.

Per. I.
Chap. 15.

tius before a fresh council. But Cælestius quitted Rome; and Zosimus excommunicated him and Pelagius as heretics; at the same time requiring all bishops to subscribe the African canons. Pelagius and his adherents were banished.[1]

The Pelagian doctrine may be thus stated. Adam was created mortal and would have died, even if he had not sinned; and men come now into the world in the same state in which Adam was created. Adam's sin brought injury to his descendants, not by transmission, but by the influence of example. As man is able to discern good from evil, so he has power to will and to work what is good; as by our own free will we run into sin, so by the same free will are we able to repent and reform, and raise ourselves to the highest degree of virtue and piety. Pelagius, indeed, spoke of grace, but by it he understood that knowledge of his will which God has given—the law and the Gospel, the example of the Saviour's life. He denied that the help of the Holy Spirit is necessary to man's salvation. He professed to follow Scripture, but when Scripture crossed his path he forsook that safe guide, and gave himself up to the beguiling direction of his own reason.[2]

Augustine's teaching was the very opposite of

---

[1] Robertson, i. pp. 413-418; Schaff, pp. 798, 799. Cælestius went to Constantinople, where he was kindly received by Nestorius.

[2] Roberts, pp. 259-261; Robertson, i. pp. 421, 422.

all this. He held that death, temporal and eternal, with all the diseases of the body, are the consequences and penalty of sin. He denied, sometimes absolutely, sometimes in a modified sense, the freedom of the will, and taught that without grace man can do only evil. Original sin, derived from Adam's transgression, he held to be a cardinal doctrine of the Gospel, and that God exacts the penalty due to his broken law, even from the heathen and from infants of the tenderest age if unbaptized. In intimate connection with this doctrine he maintained the existence of an eternal decree, separating antecedently to any difference of merit one portion of the human race from another —ordaining one to everlasting life, abandoning the other to everlasting misery. This he allowed to be a perplexing mystery, and repugnant to our natural ideas of God's justice, but defended it on the ground of his inscrutable and sovereign will. Predestination, moreover, implied irresistible grace and final perseverance.[1]

Augustine did not all at once arrive at these conclusions; and even when he had matured his system he shrank from its legitimate consequences. His charity was better than his logic. We find him reproving some who asserted that God has predestinated the wicked, not only to suffer eternal punishment, but also to commit sin, their

---

[1] Roberts, *loc. cit.*; Robertson, i. p. 426; Cutts, p. 208.

Per. I.
Chap. 15.

sinful actions being determined by an inevitable necessity. And in a letter (A.D. 426) he writes, "We have been visited by two young men who report that your monastery has been agitated by dissension. Some, they told us, entertained such exalted views of grace as wholly to deny free-will, and even maintained that in the day of judgment God will not render to every one according to his works. Most of you, however, hold a different opinion, maintaining that man's free-will is assisted by God's grace, and by it disposed to what is right; and that when the Lord shall come to render to every one according to his works, He will judge those works only to be good which he has prepared for us to walk in; and this I pronounce to be the right opinion. . . . If there be no grace of God, how does He save the world, if there be no free will, how is He to judge the world?"[1]

Augustine erred from supposing that divine truth can be fully grasped by human reason, and was obliged to explain away a host of clear and positive statements of Scripture, which controverted his positions.[2] "His was the error," observes Canon Mozley, "of those who follow without due consideration the strong first impression which the human mind entertains, that

---

[1] Letter 214; Roberts, pp. 261-263.

[2] For instance, he distorts the plain words in 1 Tim. ii. 4, "Who willeth that all men should be saved," into "all manner of men," rich and poor, learned and unlearned, and he makes the sense to be, that all who are saved, are saved only by the will of God.—Schaff, p. 856.

there must be some definite truth to be arrived at on the question, and who therefore imagine that they cannot be doing other than good service if they only add to what is defective, enough to make it complete, or take away from what is ambiguous, enough to make it decisive. . . . If revelation as a whole does not speak explicitly, revelation did not intend to do so; and to impose a definite truth upon it when it designedly stops short of one, is as real an error of interpretation as to deny a truth which it expresses."[1]

Dr. Schaff refers the two systems to the characters of their authors. "Pelagius was an upright monk, who, without inward conflicts, won for himself in the way of tranquil development a legal piety which knew neither the depths of sin nor the heights of grace. Augustine passed through sharp convulsions and bitter conflicts, till he was overtaken by the unmerited grace of God. He had a soaring intellect and a glowing heart, and only found peace after he had long been tossed by the waves of passion; he tasted all the misery of sin, and then all the glory of redemption. . . . The Pelagian controversy turns upon the mighty antithesis of sin and grace. . . . It comes at last to the question whether redemption is chiefly a work of God or of man; whether man needs to be born anew, or merely improved. The soul of the

---

[1] *On the Augustinian Doctrine of Predestination*, p. 147.

Per. I.
Chap. 15.

Pelagian system is human freedom; the soul of the Augustinian is Divine Grace. The one system proceeds from the liberty of choice to legalistic piety; the other from the bondage of sin to the evangelical liberty of the children of God. The one loves to admire the dignity and strength of man; the other loses itself in adoration of the glory and omnipotence of God. The one flatters natural pride, the other is a gospel for penitent publicans and sinners. Pelagianism begins with self-exaltation, and ends with the sense of self-deception and impotency. Augustinianism casts man first into the dust of humiliation and despair, in order to lift him on the wings of grace to supernatural strength, and lead him . . . up to the heaven of the knowledge of God." [1]

For his clear setting forth of the doctrine of Divine Grace, apart from the presumptuous theory of Predestination, the Church owes to Augustine a debt of lasting gratitude. In his enunciation of this Evangelical truth he stood opposed to the traditional principle of salvation by good works, which was taught by almost every writer of the time. And although it was left for the Reformed Church fully to endorse his Apostolic teaching on this point, yet in every century, thoughtful and humble disciples accepted it for themselves, and were edified by his Christlike spirit. But the

---

[1] *Nicene Christianity*, pp. 786-718.

Catholic Church, through her doctors and councils, continued to uphold the efficacious merit of good works, on which the Council of Trent, in 1546, set its seal, ruling that "If any one shall say that justifying faith is none other than a trust in the Divine mercy forgiving our sins for Christ's sake, or that it is that trust alone by which we are justified, let him be accursed."[1]

SECTION II. Hitherto the North African province had escaped the scourge of the Northern hordes which had laid Europe waste. Its turn was now come. Genseric, King of the Vandals, the most terrible of all the barbarian leaders, crossed from Spain in 429, and ravaged the country with all the atrocities in which uncivilized races indulge when let loose upon a wealthy and luxurious population. The miseries the Catholics had inflicted on the Donatists were now multiplied upon themselves.[2]

After overrunning nearly the whole province, the invading army laid siege to Hippo. During several months the city was successfully defended by the Roman general Count Boniface. Augustine was old and infirm. "The devastation of his country," says his biographer Possidonius, "embittered his days. He saw the towns ruined, the country houses destroyed, the inhabitants slain or fugitives, the churches destitute of priests, the

---

[1] Session VI., canon 12.   [2] Gibbon, iv. pp. 215-218.

Per. I.
Chap. 15.

virgins and monks dispersed. Some had succumbed to torments, others had perished by the sword, others again were taken captive, and served hard and brutal masters."

Several bishops, with the remnant of their flocks, took refuge in Hippo, and found shelter in Augustine's house. "The misfortunes," writes Possidonius, "of which we were witnesses were the topic of our daily conversation. We pondered the terrible judgments which the Divine justice was accomplishing before our eyes, and we said: 'Thou art just and good, and thy judgments are true.' We mingled our griefs, our groans and our tears, and offered them to the Father of all mercies and God of all comfort, beseeching Him to deliver us from the evils we endured and those we feared." "What I ask of God," said Augustine one day at table, "is, that He would be pleased to deliver this city from the enemies who besiege it; or if He has otherwise ordained, that He will give his servants strength to endure the evils He shall permit to befall them; or at least that He will withdraw me from this world and call me to Himself." This last prayer was soon to be granted.[1]

In the third month of the siege Augustine was attacked with fever. A man brought to him his sick son, and entreated him to lay his hands upon him. The dying bishop asked why, if he had

---

[1] Cutts, pp. 235, 236.

the power to heal the sick, he should not exercise it first upon himself? The father replied that he had had a dream in which he heard a voice say: "Go seek the bishop Augustine, ask him to lay hands on thy son, and he shall be healed." Upon this, Augustine did as the man requested, and (so Possidonius relates) the youth immediately recovered.[1]

It was a maxim with Augustine that even the most experienced Christian ought not to die without a season of penitential retirement. Accordingly, as he felt death approaching, he begged his friends to leave him entirely to himself, and not to enter his chamber, except with his physician or the attendants. He caused the penitential psalms to be written out large, and hung before him upon the wall, and in this manner, in solitude and prayer, he passed the last six days of his life. He died on the 28th of August, 430, aged seventy-six years.[2]

With Augustine departed the glory of the North African Church. "Rising with Tertullian towards the end of the second century, it ran a fervid course like its own ardent sun, and set almost as precipitately in the early part of the fifth." The name of Christian still survived, but little more was left than the dregs of Christianity, to withstand, two centuries later, the fury of the Mohammedan invasion.[3]

---

[1] Cutts, p. 237.   [2] Id., pp. 237, 238.
[3] At the time of the Vandal conquest the province numbered 500 Catholic

Per. I.
Chap. 15.

Since the apostles no man has occupied a more important place in the Church than Augustine, or has exercised more lasting influence on mankind. "He was," says Schaff, "a philosophical and theological genius of the first order, towering like a pyramid above his age, and looking down commandingly upon succeeding centuries. He had a mind uncommonly fertile and deep, bold and soaring, and with it, what is better, a heart full of Christian love and humility. He stands of right by the side of the greatest philosophers of antiquity and of modern times. . . . With royal munificence he scattered ideas in passing which have set in mighty motion other lands and later times."[1]

"The same part," writes Neander, "which Origen had borne in directing the theological development of the Eastern Church, was sustained by Augustine with reference to the Western; but his influence was in many respects still more general and enduring. To remarkable acuteness and depth of intellect, he united a heart filled and thoroughly penetrated with Christianity, and a life of the most manifold Christian experience. . . . Augustine's scientific discipline, as well as Origen's, came from Platonism; but whilst in the case of the latter the Platonic element was sometimes confounded with the Chris-

---

bishops; in A.D. 457, less than eighteen years afterwards, only three remained.—*North African Church*, pp. 282, 291. There appears no bishop of Hippo after Augustine.—Schaff, p. 996, note.

[1] *Nicene Christianity*, p. 997.

tian, and Christianity subordinated to Platonism, Augustine's theology disentangled itself from Platonism, and the forms of Christian intuition and thought were expressed in an independent manner. . . . But even in his case the philosophical element of his speculative intellect unconsciously mingled itself with the Christian and theological; and it was from him that this mixture of elements was transmitted to the scholastic theology of the Middle Ages, which stood in immediate connection with his own. . . . By him was the great principle first established in a logically consistent manner 'Faith precedes understanding.'[1] We find, therefore, in him two tendencies by which he exerted a special influence on the development of Christian knowledge in this and the succeeding centuries:—a tendency to assert the dignity and independence of faith, as opposed to a proud speculative spirit which severs itself from the Christian life; and the tendency in opposition to the advocates of a blind faith to maintain the agreement of faith with reason, the development of faith within itself by means of reason. But it is necessary to add that Augustine assumed as that on which faith must fix, and from which it must take its departure, everything given in the tradition of the Church. Hence he was led to admit into his *reason* many foreign elements as though they sprang from *faith*.

---

[1] Fides præcedit intellectum.

Per. I.
Chap. 15.

His system of faith wanted that historical and critical direction whereby alone, returning at all periods of time to the pure and original fountain of Christianity, it could make and preserve itself free from the foreign elements which continually threaten to mix in with the current of impure temporal tradition."[1]

Want of courage, no less than an undue reverence for tradition, hindered Augustine from standing forth as a Church Reformer. He confesses that Christianity which God made free, appointing few sacraments and easy to be observed, had in his time become more burdened with ceremonies than the Jewish Church itself; and he professes himself ready to abolish those customs which are neither contained in Scripture, nor enjoined by councils, nor confirmed by universal practice. But here he stops. The more flagrant abuses of the age were left untouched. "I dare not," he says, "condemn more freely many things, because I must take care not to offend the piety of some and the pugnacity of others."[2]

It is with no desire to dwell with harshness on the defects in Augustine's character, but because his surpassing gifts must not blind us to his deficiencies, that we add Isaac Taylor's words. "Every one must allow this eminent man to have been a fervent and heavenly-minded Christian. That

---

[1] *Church History*, iii. pp. 501, 502, 509, 510.
[2] Letter (lv.) to Januarius, c. xix. § 35.

grace which prevails over nature, rendering whoever receives it a new creature in Christ Jesus, shone in him conspicuously; and his devotional writings come home to the heart of every spiritually-minded reader. . . . No moment in the history of the Church can be named more fearfully critical than when the bishop of Hippo stood before Christendom in the prime and vigour of his religious course. The fate of Europe was trembling on the point between an abyss of ignorance and anarchy and a possible renovation. . . . There was a downward rush toward all those follies and abuses which rendered Christianity an object of contempt to the Saracen conquerors of the next century. Yet was there at the same time a rising movement towards reform; more than two or three raised a remonstrant voice against the frauds and illusions of the age. . . . Who better than Augustine might have led this early reformation? . . . O, that it had been whispered to him at that dark moment, to think, and speak, and act as a true father of the Church! . . . Fruitless regrets! Augustine, the last hope of his times, joined hands with the besotted bigots around him who would listen to no reproofs. Superstition and spiritual despotism, illusion, knavery, and abject formalism, received a new warrant from the high seat of influence which he occupied." [1]

---

[1] I. Taylor's *Ancient Christianity*, i. pp. 442-445. Augustine not only endorsed Ambrose's discovery of the buried martyrs under the altar at

SECTION III. Augustine was a most voluminous writer. His *Confessions* have been freely used in the foregoing narrative. The treatise *On the Trinity* is associated with a well-known legendary anecdote. As he was walking to and fro on the sea-shore of Hippo, he saw what appeared to be a little boy busily employed in digging a hole in the sand and then filling it with water, which he fetched in a cockle-shell from the sea. Augustine paused and spoke to him: "What art thou doing, my child?" "I am trying to empty the sea into this hole which I have dug." "My child, it is impossible to get the great sea into that little hole." "Not more impossible, Augustine," replied the angel, "than for thy finite mind to comprehend the mystery of the Trinity."[1]

His most famous work is entitled *The City of God*. "The later opponents of Christianity among the heathen charged the misfortunes and the decline of the Roman Empire on the overthrow of idolatry. Augustine answered the charge in his immortal work *The City of God*, that is, the Church of Christ, upon which he laboured twelve years, from 413 to 426, amidst the storms of the great migration, and towards the close of his life. He was not wanting in appreciation of the old Roman virtues, and he attributes to

---

Milan (see *ante*, p. 158), but himself presents us with a tissue of miraculous cures wrought by the bones of the martyr Stephen, quite as incredible. See below, pp. 395-398.

[1] Cutts, p. 183.

these the former greatness of the empire, and to the decline of them he imputes her growing weakness. But he rose at the same time far above the superficial view which estimates persons and things by the scale of earthly profit and loss, and of temporary success. *The City of God* is the most powerful, comprehensive, profound, and fertile production in refutation of heathenism and vindication of Christianity, which the ancient Church has bequeathed to us, and forms a worthy close to her literary contest with Græco-Roman paganism. It is a grand funeral discourse upon the departing universal empire of heathenism, and a lofty salutation to the approaching universal order of Christianity. While even Jerome deplored in the destruction of the city the downfall of the empire, as the omen of the approaching doom of the world, the African Father saw in it only a passing revolution preparing the way for new conquests of Christianity. Standing at that remarkable turning-point of history, he considers the origin, progress and end of the perishable kingdom of this world, and the imperishable kingdom of God, from the fall of man to the final judgment, where at last they fully and for ever separate into hell and heaven." [1]

We conclude our notice of Augustine with two more excerpts from his writings. In the first he

---

[1] Schaff, *Nicene Christianity,* pp. 85, 86.

Per. I.
Chap. 15.
describes the Memory, a faculty he had in his own case trained in no common degree.

"I come to the fields and spacious palaces of my MEMORY, where are the treasures of countless images brought into it from all manner of things by the senses. There is stored up, also, whatsoever we think, either by enlarging or diminishing, or any other way varying those things which the senses apprehended: yea, and whatever else has been committed to it which forgetfulness has not yet swallowed up and buried. When I enter this store-house, I require what I will to be brought forth, and some things come instantly; others must be longer sought for, and are fetched, as it were, out of some inner receptacle; others, again, rush out in troops, and whilst something else is desired and inquired for, start forth, as who should say, 'Is it perchance we?' These I drive away with the hand of my heart from before the face of my remembrance, until what I wish discovers itself and comes to view out of its secret place. Other things present themselves without effort, and in continuous order as they are called for, those in front giving place to those that follow, and as they make way returning to their hiding-place ready to come forth again when I will. All which takes place when I repeat a thing from memory. All these things, each of which entered by its own avenue, are severally and under general heads there laid up, being received into that great storehouse of the memory, in her numberless secret and inexpressible windings to be forthcoming at need. Yet it is not the things themselves that enter in, but only the images of the things, which how they are formed who can tell? Even when I dwell in darkness and silence, in my memory I can produce colours if I will, and discern betwixt black and white; sounds also are there lying dormant, and laid up as it were apart. For these, too, I call, and forthwith they appear; and though my tongue be still and my throat mute, yet can I sing as much as I will. The same with the other things piled up by the other senses; so that I discern the scent of lilies from violets, though smelling nothing. In that vast court of my memory there are present also with me heaven, earth, sea, and whatever I can think upon in them. There also meet I with myself and recall myself, and when, where, and what I have done, and under what feelings. Out of the same store do I myself with the past combine fresh and fresh likenesses of things which I have experienced or have believed, and thence again infer future actions, events and hopes, on all which I reflect as if present. Excessive great is this power of memory, O my God, a large and boundless chamber; who has ever sounded the depths of it? Men go abroad to admire the height of the mountains, the mighty billows of the sea, the broad flow of the rivers, the compass of the ocean, and the courses of

A.D. 430.

the stars, and yet they omit to wonder at themselves."[1]

Our last quotation shall be from the closing words of his great work, *The City of God*. His own days on earth were drawing toward their end, when he wrote thus of the glories of the heavenly city.

"How great shall be that felicity which shall be tainted with no evil, and shall lack no good! . . . Along with the other great and marvellous discoveries which shall then kindle rational minds in praise of the great Artificer, there shall be the enjoyment of a beauty which appeals to the reason. . . . What power of movement such incorruptible bodies shall possess, I have not the audacity rashly to define, as I have not the ability to conceive. One thing is certain, the body shall be wherever the spirit wills, and the spirit shall will nothing which is unbecoming either to the spirit or the body. . . . God Himself shall be the end of our desires, who shall be seen without end, loved without cloy, praised without weariness. . . . In that blessed city no inferior shall envy any superior. Along with his gift, greater or less, each shall receive this further gift of contentment to desire no more than he has. Neither are we to suppose that because sin shall have no power to delight, free will must be withdrawn. On the contrary, it will

---

[1] *Confessions*, b. x. §§ 8-17.

be all the more truly free, because set free from delight in sinning to take unfeigned delight in not sinning. For whereas the first freedom of will, which man received when he was created upright, consisted in an ability not to sin, but also in an ability to sin, this last freedom of will shall be superior, inasmuch as it shall not be able to sin. And this shall not be a natural ability, but the gift of God; for as the first immortality which Adam lost by sinning, consisted in his being able not to die, while the last shall consist in his not being able to die, so the first free will consisted in his being able not to sin, the last in his not being able to sin. And so piety and justice shall be as certain as happiness. There shall be then in that city free will in all her citizens, delivered from all ill, filled with all good, enjoying secure from change the delights of eternal joys, sins forgotten, pains forgotten, and yet not so forgetful of deliverance as to be ungrateful to the Deliverer. . . . The city shall have no greater joy than to sing the glory of the grace of Christ, who redeemed us by his blood. There shall be that Great Sabbath which has no evening, on which God rested from all his works, and which He blessed and sanctified; for we shall ourselves be the Seventh Day, when we shall be filled and perfected with his blessing and sanctification. There shall we be still, and see that He is God. . . . There we shall be still and we shall see, we shall see and we shall love, we shall love

Per. I.
Chap. 15.

and we shall praise. Behold, this shall be in the end which hath no end. For what other end have we than to reach the kingdom which hath no end?"[1]

Sentences from Augustine.

The New Testament lies hid in the Old; the Old is opened up in the New.

Distinguish the times, and Scripture will agree with itself.

Thou hast made us for Thyself, and our heart is restless till it rests in Thee.

To serve God is true freedom.

Adversity can never subdue him whom prosperity cannot corrupt.

To talk well and to live badly is nothing else than to condemn one's-self with one's own lips.

That which is new in time is not new with God, who made all times.

Truth only is victorious, and the victory of truth is love.[2]

---

[1] *The City of God*, b. xxii. c. 30.

[2] Novum Testamentum in Vetere latet, Vetus in Novo patet.
Distingue tempora, et concordabit Scriptura.
Fecisti nos ad Te, et inquietum est cor nostrum donec requiescat in Te.
Deo servire vera libertas est.
Nulla infelicitas frangit, quem felicitas nulla corrumpit.
Benè loqui et malè vivere, nihil aliud est quam sua se voce damnare.
Id quod in tempore novum est, non est novum apud Deum, qui condidit tempora.
Non vincit nisi veritas, victoria veritatis est caritas.
Schaff, p. 998, note; Prosper Aquitanus, Augustini Opera, Bened. ed. x., Appendix, p. 223, seqq. The famous maxim, "In essentials unity, in non-essentials liberty, in all things charity" (in necessariis unitas, in dubiis libertas, in omnibus caritas), does not come from Augustine, but is of comparatively recent date.—Schaff, ibid.

CHAPTER XVI.

The Spirit of the Age.

SECTION I. PUBLIC WORSHIP.—" Three centuries and more," says Cardinal Newman, " were necessary for the infant Church to attain her mature and perfect form and due stature. Athanasius, Basil, and Ambrose are the fully instructed doctors of her doctrine, morals and discipline."[1] Strange interpretation of Church History! The presumptuous forbidding to marry, the plagiarism of Brahminical self-torture, the invocation of the martyrs and adoration of their bones and ashes, the fond belief in lying wonders, the exaltation of priestly rule to the prejudice of the civil power, instead of the unworldly kingdom of Jesus, are these the tokens of fully instructed teaching in doctrine, morals and discipline?[2]

The preceding biographies have presented in some fulness the state of the Church in the fourth and fifth centuries. It will only be necessary here to make a few additions.

IV.-V. Cent.

---

[1] Quoted in *The Church in the Middle Ages*, p. 65.
[2] Augustine would have been far from agreeing with Cardinal Newman. —See *ante*, p. 358.

Per I.
Chap. 16.

To begin with the order of public worship, as it was conducted in Constantinople and other great cities. "A stranger on entering the spacious open court in front of the church, which was flanked on either side by cloisters, beheld the fountain where the worshippers were expected to wash their hands before entering the divine presence. Lingering in these cloisters, and pressing around the faithful to solicit their prayers, he would observe men, pale, dejected, and clad in sack-cloth. These were the first class of penitents, men of notorious guilt, whom only a long period of humiliating probation could admit even within hearing of the service. As he advanced to the church door, he had to pass the scrutiny of the doorkeepers, who guarded admission, and distributed the several classes of worshippers to their proper seats. Nearest to the door were placed the catechumens and the less guilty penitents of the second order. Amongst these also Jews and heathens were admitted, that they might profit by the religious instruction. He would see the walls of the church lined with marbles; the roof often ceiled with mosaic, and supported by lofty columns with gilded capitals; the doors inlaid with ivory or silver, the distant altar glittering with precious stones. In the midst of the nave stood the pulpit or reading desk, around which were arranged the choristers. When the chanting was ended, one of the inferior clergy ascended the pulpit, and read the portion of Scripture for the day. He was succeeded by the preacher, a presbyter, or a bishop, selected for his learning and eloquence, whose discourse was frequently interrupted by the plaudits of the auditory.[1] Around the pulpit, also, was the last order of penitents, who prostrated themselves in humble reverence during the prayers and the benediction of the bishop. Here the steps of the uninitiated stranger must pause. He might only behold at respectful distance the striking scene: first of the baptized worshippers in their ranks, the women in galleries above; beyond, in still further secluded sanctity, on an elevated semi-circle, the bishop in the midst of his attendant clergy. Even the gorgeous throne of the Emperor was below this platform.[2] Before it stood the altar, spread with a cloth of fine linen, and in some churches overhung with a richly-wrought canopy. In the East, embroidered curtains or light doors altogether hid it from view. Such was the ceremonial as it was addressed to the multitude. But as soon as the liturgy commenced, the catechumens were dismissed, and the church doors were closed.[3] To add to the impressiveness,

---

[1] See *ante*, pp. 185-187.   [2] See *ante*, p. 172, note.

[3] The dismissal of the uninitiate was called *Missa Catechumenorum*, that of the baptized at the end of the service came in later ages to be known as *Missa Fidelium*. By degrees the word *Missa* was retained only for the latter, and was applied, not to the act of dismissal, but to the service itself; and thus in its slightly altered form of *Mass* it came to signify the consecration and oblation of the *Host* (*hostia*, victim or sacrifice).—*Dict. Christ. Antiq.*, ii. pp. 1193, 1194.

night was sometimes chosen for the Christian, as it had formerly been for the pagan mysteries."[1]

How unlike all this to the simplicity of the primitive worship! If, however, the stranger had happened upon the birthday of some popular Saint, he would have beheld a still greater contrast. "As soon as he passed the door his senses would be greeted by the perfume of flowers,[2] and the noon-day glare of lamps and tapers. He would see the floor covered with a prostrate crowd of pilgrims, imprinting their devout kisses on the walls and pavement, and directing their prayers to the relics of the saint, which were usually concealed behind a linen or silken veil." Suspended on the walls or on the pillars of the church he would see the votive offerings of the faithful, the model in gold, silver or wood, of an eye, a hand, a foot, the picture of a shipwreck, the memento of some special blessing. How early this imitation

---

[1] Milman's *History of Christianity*, iii. pp. 310–315.

[2] The use of flowers, whether for strewing the graves of the dead, or adorning the churches, dates from the latter part of the fourth century. The former of these two customs (they would not have dreamed of the latter) was repudiated by the Early Christians as a heathen observance (see the *Octavius* of Minucius Felix, xii., xxxviii.). One of the earliest passages in which it is alluded to is in Ambrose : "I will not sprinkle his tomb with flowers, but with the sweet scent of Christ's spirit; let others scatter baskets of lilies; our lily is Christ." Jerome says: "Some husbands strew over the tombs of their wives, violets, roses, lilies, and purple flowers." The practice was soon extended to the churches, first to those of the martyrs, which in their origin were only enlarged sepulchres, and then to the basilicas. Jerome commends Nepotianus for decorating both kinds of buildings with flowers, foliage, and vine leaves.—*Dict. Christ. Antiq.*, i. p. 679.

of a pagan usage was first practised, cannot be said with certainty, but it was already in vogue, both in the East and West, at the period we are now reviewing.[1]

The truth is that the public worship of the Christians had approached perilously near to that of the ancient Greeks and Romans. Thus there were in both rituals splendid robes, mitres, tiaras, croziers (identical with the *lituus*, or crook of the augur), processions, lustrations, images, gold and silver vessels, and, in the course of the fifth century, incense. The heathens supposed that their country would be more prosperous in proportion as the temples of the gods and heroes were multiplied, and this notion descended to the Christians. New churches were continually being dedicated to Christ and the saints, in order to render heavenly assistance more powerful and certain.[2]

It was not to be expected that the idea of sanctity which had become attached to places of worship should lose anything of its force. On the

---

[1] Gibbon, iii. pp. 538, 539. The classic student is familiar with this custom. Many offerings, arms, legs, and other parts of the body, in metal, stone, or clay, which were formerly hung up in the temples, are still preserved in museums and cabinets. Persons saved from shipwreck used to hang up their clothes in the temple of Neptune, with a picture representing their danger and escape. Soldiers discharged from service suspended their arms to Mars; gladiators, their swords to Hercules; and poets, the fillets of their hair to Apollo. The temple of Æsculapius, however, in which were hung up tablets recording the cures wrought by that god, seems to have been the chief model for the Christian shrine.—*Dict. Christ. Antiq.*, ii. p. 2026; Schaff, p. 432; Middleton, *Letter from Rome*, pp. 146-148.

[2] Mosheim, i. pp. 252, 369; *Dict. Christ. Antiq.*, i. p. 830.

contrary, as we have more than once seen in preceding chapters, the churches, like the persons of the priests, were surrounded with an ever increasing halo of solemn mystery. The temper of the age is shown in the following instance. Two bishops in Libya, about the year 420, quarrelled for the possession of a building which had been used as a stronghold against the incursions of the barbarians. One who desired to secure the spot for a church forced his way in, and causing an altar to be brought, consecrated upon it the sacrament of the supper. By this act, according to general opinion, the building was hallowed, and could no longer be used for the purposes of common life. Happily, however, a few wiser men still lived. Synesius, a philosopher and pupil of the famous Hypatia,[1] had been drawn from his seclusion, to become bishop of a neighbouring see. This man, on hearing of the transaction related above, complained to Theophilus, patriarch of Alexandria, that in this way the holiest ordinances were abused for the vilest purposes. "It is," he said, "not the manner of Christianity to present what is divine, as a thing which can be charmed with magical necessity by certain formulas of consecration, but as something which has its dwelling in the pure and God-like temper of the mind."[2]

---

[1] See *ante*, p. 18, note.

[2] Neander, iii. p. 405, note. It was this Synesius who on his ordination so boldly refused to abandon his wife.—See *Early Church History*, p. 519, note.

Baptistery of S. Giovanni i Fonte, Ravenna.

From an original drawing by Edward Backhouse.

SECTION II. BAPTISM AND THE EUCHARIST.—We drew attention in the former volume to the explicit declarations of John the Baptist, our Lord Himself, and Peter, that whereas John's baptism was with water, Christ's disciples should be baptized with the Holy Ghost; and we at the same time pointed out, how early this grand distinction began to be lost sight of. Even the more thoughtful so identified the spiritual change with the external rite, as to be unable to conceive of the one without the other; whilst in the belief of the multitude, who lost sight altogether of the former, immersion in water removed, as by a magical and instantaneous process, all the defilement of sin, and made them fit for Heaven.

The writers of the previous century, Tertullian, Hippolytus and others, insist so unmistakably on this almost talismanic power as to leave little to be added by those who followed them. Chrysostom clothes the same idea in his own fervid language. "Although a man should be foul with every human vice, the blackest that can be named, yet when he descends into the baptismal pool, he comes up from the divine waters purer than the beams of noon. . . . The baptized put on a royal garment, a purple dipped in the blood of the Lord."[1] Basil urged baptism in his most declamatory style. "Beware lest procrastinating and providing no oil,

---

[1] Isaac Taylor's *Ancient Christianity*, i. pp. 236, 237.

thou should come upon the fatal day. Who in that hour shall administer the rite? It is night; no helper is at hand; death is near. . . . . 'Alas, I neglected to cast off the burden of my sins when it would have been so easy! Miserable wretch! I washed not my sins away in the sweet waters of baptism; and lo, I perish! Even now I might have been sitting in the choir of angels, might have shared the delights of heaven.' "[1] Gregory of Nyssa states that, when alarmed by earthquakes, pestilences or other public calamities, such multitudes rushed to be baptized, that the clergy were oppressed by the labour of receiving them.[2] It was the same superstitious view which induced Constantine the Great to defer his baptism to the latest hour of life.[3]

Each successive age contributed its share towards the conversion of the morsel of bread which the priest had blessed, into an object of adoration and supernatural efficacy, as it is at this day regarded in

---

[1] *Exhortation to Baptism.*

[2] Robertson, i. p. 348. Of the two baptisteries represented in the plates, the more ancient is that of Ravenna. It is believed to be at least as old as Bishop Neon (425-430), the central basin being of the original work. The decorations are later. The niche in which the priest stood to baptize is peculiar. The Verona font is thirty-one feet in circumference, and hewn out of a single block of marble. A frieze of small arches, supported by grotesque heads, runs round the summit. On the eight faces are represented scenes from the New Testament, as the Flight into Egypt, the Slaughter of the Innocents, Angels appearing to the Shepherds. The sculpture is rude. In the midst of the great basin is a smaller one for the priest to stand in.—*Dict. Christ. Antiq.*, i. p. 176; Murray, *North Italy*, 9th ed., p. 287.

[3] See *Early Church History*, p. 433.

Marble Font in the Baptistery of the Cathedral at Verona. *From an original drawing by Edward Backhouse.*

the Romish Church. It is true that the best writers of this period see beyond the external, and dwell upon that inward and heavenly communion with Christ, of which the outward observance, if now of any further service, is only a sign and a memorial. Thus Athanasius, commenting on John vi. 62, declares that the partaking of the flesh and blood of Christ is not there to be understood in a literal sense. "Christ," he says, "mentions on this occasion his ascension to heaven for the very purpose of turning away men's minds from sensuous notions, and leading them to the idea of a spiritual nourishment, inasmuch as He communicates Himself to each after a spiritual manner." And Jerome: "If the bread which came down from heaven is the Lord's body, and the wine which He gave to his disciples his blood, let us go up with the Lord into that great and high room, and receive at his hand the cup which is the New Covenant. He invites us to the feast, and is Himself our meat; He eats with us, and we eat Him. . . . Jesus Christ has given his blood to redeem us, and this may be taken either for his spiritual and divine flesh, whereof He saith Himself, 'My flesh is meat indeed, and my blood is drink indeed;' or for his flesh which was crucified, and his blood which in his passion was spilt with the soldier's lance." So Augustine: "'The flesh without the spirit profits nothing. The inward act of feeding is to be distinguished from the outward. The former is a privilege only of believers; the unbelieving and the unworthy receive nothing but the *sacrament* of the body and blood of Christ."[1]

But the Fathers of the fourth century do not always write thus soberly. Take an example from Ambrose's funeral oration over his brother Satyrus. The vessel in which Satyrus was returning to Italy ran upon the rocks. Unbaptized and uninitiated in the "mysteries," the young man sought amongst those on board for the consecrated elements, which when he had obtained he wrapped in a sacrificial kerchief and tied about his neck. Thus armed, he fearlessly leapt into the sea, believing himself to be so well protected as to need no other help.[2]

SECTION III. VIRGINITY.—Foremost amongst the elements of which the ascetic life was composed is the vow of perpetual celibacy. How the unmarried state came in the fourth century to occupy the place that martyrdom had held during the times of persecution, and how, by its introduction as a rule of devout Christian life, one of the most awful and emphatic predictions of the New Testament was accomplished, has already been shown in the *Early Church History*.[3] From the time

---

[1] Neander, iv. pp. 439–441; Du Pin, iii. p. 105.

[2] Isaac Taylor, i. p. 213.

[3] Pp. 516–521. "God, when he would form a happy and holy world, said, 'It is not good for man to be alone.' Satan, inspiring the apostasy to make the world, and even the Church, unholy and unhappy, said, 'It is

of the Council of Nicæa, the virgin state is the favourite theme with all the great Church writers; and is presented by them sometimes in the very language of the Oriental theosophy. The great object was the mortification of the flesh; and in this exercise, observes Ruffner, Virginity was the most difficult to attain, requiring the aid of all other mortifications. "So to thin the blood, attenuate the flesh, enfeeble the nerves, dry up the marrow, and exhaust the constitution, as to destroy the natural appetite," in this it was considered lay the secret of overcoming "both the demon without and the demon within." Even Origen, so early as the third century, says: "When we abstain from flesh, we do it to chasten the body and reduce it to servitude, in order that we may extinguish our carnal affections, and so put to death our corporeal actions."[1] This kind of teaching was perfected by the writers of the next century.

To begin with Athanasius. "The Son of God has, besides his other gifts, granted us to have on earth an image of the sanctity of angels, namely, Virginity. The maidens who possess this virtue, and whom the Church Catholic is wont to call the brides of Christ, are admired even by the Gentiles as being the temple of the Word. Nowhere, except among us Christians, is this holy

IV.-V. Cent.

---

good for man to be alone; nay, it is *better* for him to be alone.'"—*The Church in the Middle Ages*, p. 174.

[1] Ruffner, *Fathers of the Desert*, i. pp. 222, 223, 225.

profession perfected; so that we may appeal to this very fact as a convincing proof that with us the true religion is to be found." " A great virtue truly is virginity," exclaims Basil, " which, to say all in a word, renders man like to the incorruptible God. For the soul, holding to the idea of the true good, and soaring up to it as on the wing of this incorruptness, and perceiving that by this alone the incorruptible God can be worthily worshipped, brings up the virginity of the body as an obsequious handmaid to assist her in the worship of beauty like her own."[1]

The two Gregorys teem with the same kind of dreamy philosophy. Nazianzen thus addresses a virgin: " Thou hast chosen the angelic life, and hast ranged thyself with those who are unyoked [the angels]; be not thou borne downward to the flesh; be not thou borne downward to matter." Nyssen writes: " In order that we may, with a clear eye, gaze upon the light of the intellectual universe, we must disengage ourselves from every mundane affection;" " that," in the words of Chrysostom, " the soul disengaged from its trammels and all earthly thoughts may wing its way to its home and its native soil." Chrysostom indeed falls into a rhapsody when he contemplates the lustre of virginity. " The virgin when she goes abroad should strike all with amazement, as if an angel had just come down from heaven. All who

---

[1] Isaac Taylor, i. pp. 158, 170.

look upon her should be thrown into stupor at the sight of her sanctity. When she sits at church it is in the profoundest silence, her eye catches nothing of the objects around her, she sees neither women nor men, but her Spouse only. Not only does she hide herself from the eyes of men, she avoids the society of secular women also. Who is it that shall dare approach her? Where is the man that shall venture to touch this flaming spirit? All stand aloof, willing or unwilling, all are fixed in amazement as if there were before their eyes a mass of incandescent and sparkling gold."[1]

<small>IV.-V. Cent.</small>

Between these soaring imaginations however and the actual life of multitudes of those who assumed the vows of celibacy, a great gulf intervened. In the same treatise from which these words are taken Chrysostom thus discloses the reverse side of the picture. "Alas, my soul! our virginity has fallen into contempt. The veil that parted it off from matrimony is rent by shameless hands; the holy of holies is trodden under foot, and its grave and tremendous sanctities have become profane, and are thrown open to all; and that which once was had in reverence, as so much more excellent than wedlock, is sunk far below it. Nor is it the enemy that has effected all this, but the virgins themselves!"[2]

That the monastic vow was very imperfectly kept, both by men and women, is notorious.

---

[1] Isaac Taylor, i. pp. 165, 167, 168, 186, 187.   [2] Id., i. p. 298, note.

Denouncing the practice of the unmarried clergy, who, under the name of spiritual sisters, kept young women, often "consecrated virgins," as housekeepers, Chrysostom exclaims: "What a spectacle it is to enter the cell of a *solitary* brother, and see the apartment hung about with female gear. But it is a greater riddle still to visit the dwelling of a *rich* monk; for you find the *solitary* surrounded with a bevy of lasses, just, one might say, like the leader of a company of singing and dancing girls. What can be more disgraceful! Forbidden by the apostolic precept to meddle at all with temporal matters, he spends his time, not only in mundane but even in effeminate trifles. He is sent to the silversmith's to inquire if my lady's mirror is finished, if her vase is ready, if her scent-cruet has been returned; for matters have come to such a pass that the virgins use more toilet luxuries than those who have not taken the vow. From the silversmith's he must run to the perfumer's to inquire about her aromatics; from the perfumer's to the linendraper's; and thence to the upholsterer's. For the good man is so complaisant that he will perform any errand, however trivial. Add to all these cares the jarrings and scoldings which beset a house full of pampered women! Paul says: 'Be ye not the servants of *men*;' how then shall we be the slaves of women!"[1]

---

[1] Opera, i. pp. 242, 243 (Bened.); Isaac Taylor, i. pp. 294, 295.

Of the 150 extant epistles of Jerome, the greater part have Virginity for their subject, and abound in exhortations, cautions, and rebukes, to these "holy pets of the Church." "Some," he says, in a letter to Eustochium, "walk forth in the most public manner and by sly winks draw after them crowds of young men. They dress in thin purple robes, and tie their hair loose that it may fall over their shoulders, over which a mantle is thrown. They wear short sleeves and thin slippers, and go mincing as they walk. And this is all their virginity." The monks were no better. "Some you may see with their loins girt, clad in dingy cloaks, with long beards, who yet can never break away from the company of women; but live under the same roof, sit at the same tables, are waited upon by young girls, and want nothing proper to the married state except—wives!"[1]

The upholders of celibacy relied upon the example of the Virgin Mary. The dogma of her perpetual virginity was essential to their position. So early a writer as Clement of Alexandria alludes to it, citing as his authority a spurious treatise called the *Protevangelium of James*.[2] The unsophisticated reader of the New Testament is left in no doubt that Mary had children after the birth of our Lord. The language of Matt. i. 25, and of Luke ii. 7, with the mention of the brothers

---

[1] Ruffner, i. p. 237; Isaac Taylor, i. p. 413.
[2] Ruffner, i. p. 219.

of our Lord,[1] is too plain and conclusive to be touched by any authority of Church Father, Council, or pope. "To have admitted," remarks Isaac Taylor, "the plain sense of the intelligible phrase employed by the inspired evangelist would have been tantamount to a betrayal of the whole scheme of religious celibacy. Only let it have been granted that the virtue of the 'mother of God' was nothing better than real virtue, and that her piety was a principle of the heart, and that her purity was the purity of the affections; and only allow that she was a 'holy woman,' and an exemplary wife and mother, such as the Apostles speak of, and commend; only to have done this, would have marred the entire scheme of theology and morals, as fancied and fashioned by the ancient Church. The perpetual inviolateness of the blessed virgin was well felt to be the keystone of the building."[2]

SECTION IV. FASTING.—This observance had been gradually removed from the place which it occupies in the New Testament and in the earliest class of Church writers, into a different sphere. New motives and a new object gave to it a totally new character.[3] The Church at Antioch fasted as

---

[1] Matt. xii. 46; John vii. 5. In this case, as in others, the plainest meaning of words and fullest testimony of Scripture were set at nought by the Church to attain her object.

[2] *Ancient Christianity*, i. p. 83.

[3] The Christian anchorites performed miracles of fasting, but they

they ministered to the Lord, and again when they separated Saul and Barnabas for the work of the Gospel; and Paul shows us how the combat in the spiritual arena is to be waged: "I buffet my body and bring it into bondage, lest by any means after that I have preached to others I myself should be rejected."[1] The widely different place which this observance occupied in the fourth century, and the scrupulous and painful manner in which it was practised, has been repeatedly presented in the foregoing biographies, "What," asks Athanasius, "does Christ require of thee, but a pure heart, and a body unsoiled and brought down with fasting?" "Wouldst thou learn," writes Chrysostom, "what an ornament fasting is to men, what a guard and preservative? Look well to the monastic tribe, blessed and admirable! Men though they are, fasting makes angels of them. God when He made man, instantly committed him into the hands of Fasting as to a loving mother entrusted with his safety.[2] If then fasting were indispensable even in Paradise, how much more so out of Paradise?"[3]

These maxims of Chrysostom's made however but a faint impression on the volatile people of

---

scarcely come up to those of the Hindoo saints. In one of the Brahminical fasts the devotee is neither to eat nor drink for twelve days and nights. In another he drinks only warm water.—Ruffner, i. p. 28.

[1] Acts xiii. 2, 3; 1 Cor. ix. 27.
[2] Does this refer to Genesis ii. 16, 17?
[3] Isaac Taylor, i. pp. 159, 258.

Constantinople. "If," he says, in one of his sermons, "I ask why hast thou been to the bath to-day? thou wilt reply, to cleanse my body in preparation for the Fast. And if I ask why didst thou get drunk yesterday? again thou wilt reply, because I am to fast to-day." "We see," he says again, "nothing but people making merry, and saying to one another, 'Victory is ours; Mid-Lent is over.' ... I know some who, in the middle of Lent, dread already the fast of the next year." The mass of the population indeed alternated between ceremonial observances and sensual excess. The Church fasts, which were observed with superstitious strictness, were succeeded by disgraceful outbreaks of debauchery. Basil gives on one occasion as a reason for protracting his sermon, that although it was in the midst of the fast, many of the congregation, as soon as the service was over, would fly to the gaming-table.[1]

The Fasts were sometimes observed with such scrupulosity that the Church had to interfere. The Council of Neo-Cæsarea, censures the superstition of certain priests who refused to eat herbs which had been boiled with meat.[2] And Timothy bishop of Alexandria was called upon to decide the question, gravely propounded, whether a man who fasted in order to communicate, and who had by chance swallowed a drop of water, ought to

---

[1] Isaac Taylor, i. p. 259; Du Pin, iii. p. 42; Smith, *St. Basil the Great*, p. 70.   [2] Canon 14.

refrain. He replied that he ought so much the more to communicate, because it was an artifice of the devil to hinder him.[1]

SECTION V. ALMSGIVING.—When the fatal maxim was admitted that salvation is to be purchased by good works, the blessed grace of "considering the poor" soon lost its original savour, and was degraded into a matter of barter between the soul and heaven. Chrysostom asks, "What! hast thou not understood from the instance of the ten virgins in the Gospel, how that those who although proficients in virginity yet possessed not Almsgiving were excluded from the mystical banquet? Virginity is the fire of the lamps, and almsgiving is the oil. As the flame unless supplied with a stream of oil disappears, so virginity unless it is united with Almsgiving is extinguished. Now who are the vendors of this oil? The poor who sit for alms about the doors of the church. And for how much is it to be bought? For what thou wilt, for so much as thou hast. Hast thou a penny? Buy Heaven; not indeed as if Heaven were cheap, but the Master is indulgent. Hast thou not even a penny? Give a cup of cold water. Heaven is in the market and we heed it not! Give a crust and take back paradise. Alms

---

[1] Du Pin, ii. pp. 195, 249. One of the charges brought against Chrysostom by the *Synod of the Oak* was that he had eaten a lozenge after Holy Communion.—See *ante*, p. 215.

are the redemption of the soul. As vases of water are set at the church gates for washing the hands, so are beggars sitting there that thou mayst wash the hands of thy soul."[1]

Section VI. Saint-Worship.—The inducement which the martyrs' festivals offered to the heathen to join themselves to the Church, and the evil consequences which ensued from this compromise with idolatry, are fully stated in our former volume.[2]

To the nominal convert, the substitution of the saint for the idol would make but little difference. The old classic mythology may be said to have been replaced by a new Christian Pantheon.[3]

Dr. Middleton, commenting on the idolatry of modern Rome, invites his readers to enter the temples, and see the altars, which were built originally by the old Romans to the honour of their pagan deities. "We shall hardly see any other alteration than the shrine of some old hero filled

---

[1] Du Pin, ii. pp. 218, 219, 260.
[2] *Early Church History*, pp. 498, 499.
[3] The deification of the martyrs naturally excited the mockery of the heathen. "Instead of many Gods," writes the Emperor Julian, "the Christians worship many wretched men." Eunapius the Sardian, one of the last of the pagan authors, exclaims: "These are the gods the earth now brings forth—the intercessors with the gods, men called martyrs, before whose bones and skulls, pickled and salted, the monks kneel and prostrate themselves, besmearing themselves with filth and dust." In like manner the Manichæan Faustus reproves the Catholic Christians: "Ye have changed the idols into martyrs whom ye worship with the like prayers, and ye appease the shades of the dead with wine and flesh."—Maitland, pp. 300, 302; Elliott, *Horæ Apocalypt.*, i. p. 335.

by the meaner statue of some modern saint; nay, they have not always given themselves the trouble of making even this change, but have been content sometimes to take up with the old image, just as they found it, after baptizing it only, as it were, or consecrating it anew, by the imposition of a Christian name. This their antiquaries do not scruple to put strangers in mind of, in showing their churches; and it was, I think, in that of St. Agnes, where they showed me an antique statue of a young Bacchus, which, with a new name, and some little change of drapery, stands now worshipped as a female saint. The noblest heathen temple," he continues, "now remaining in the world, is the Pantheon, which, as the inscription over the portico informs us, having been impiously dedicated of old by Agrippa to Jove and all the gods, was piously re-consecrated by Pope Boniface IV.[1] to the blessed Virgin and all the saints. With this single alteration it serves as exactly for the Popish as it did for the pagan worship for which it was built. For as in the old temple every one might find the god of his country, and address himself to that deity whose religion he was most devoted to, so it is now; every one chooses the patron whom he likes best; and one may see here different services going on at the same time at different altars, with distinct congregations around them, just as the

---

[1] A.D. 608-615.

inclinations of the people lead them to the worship of this or that particular saint."[1]

We have seen how profound in the time of Cyprian was the veneration for the victorious confessors.[2] This feeling gathered rather than lost strength after the Diocletian persecution, and working on the natural tendency of mankind to deify its benefactors and heroes, ended in a universal worship of the saints. Possibly, also, the controversies respecting the Trinity and the nature of Christ may have tended indirectly towards the same result. Although his human nature was in theory as clearly asserted as his divine, yet it was not dwelt upon in the same emphatic manner, and people began to seek out, or eagerly to turn towards, other beings who were supposed to be in closer sympathy with man.[3] These they found in the martyrs. The spirits of the martyrs were believed to hover about their tombs, or even, as Jerome pretended, to be ubiquitous,[4] and prayers were addressed to them as intercessors with God.

Another preparation for saint-worship may perhaps be found in the semi-divine honours which were paid to the Roman Emperors, and which produced a thraldom of the mind extremely favourable to superstitious notions.[5]

---

[1] *Letter from Rome*, pp. 159-162.   [2] *Early Church History*, p. 289.

[3] Milman, iii. pp. 419, 421; Stephens, *Life of St. Chrysostom*, pp. 181, 182.   [4] See below, p. 440.

[5] Schaff, p. 435.   See *ante*, pp. 219, 220. The worship of the Virgin Mary, which sprang up later, will be considered in the next period.

Prayers, thanksgivings, vows, and offerings were everywhere made to the saints. And as in the older mythology there were tutelary gods, to whom the guardianship of special nations and cities, trades and conditions of life, were assigned, so now every country and place, every order and profession of men came to have its patron saint.[1]

The Fathers of the age were leaders in the very fore-front of this superstition. A few specimens out of many, taken from their writings, will suffice. Basil, in an oration delivered on the "birthday" of one of the martyrs, thus appeals to the bystanders: "As many of you as in this place have been assisted by him in prayer, as many as he has brought back into the right way, as many as he has restored to health, or who have had their dead children recalled to life, be ye mindful of the martyr." Again, on the festival of the Forty Martyrs, "Behold a fountain of blessing, a refuge prepared for the Christian! A church of martyrs! Often hast thou laboured to find one who might intercede for thee. Lo! here are forty, emitting one voice of prayer. The wretch bowed down

IV.-V. Cent.

---

[1] Thus James became the patron of Spain; George the Martyr, about whose identity and even existence there has been a voluminous controversy, the guardian saint of England. John was the patron of theologians; Luke of painters; Anthony was venerated as a protector against pestilence; Apollonia against toothache. To Phocas, a gardener at Sinope (through some strange freak of the genius of superstition) was especially entrusted the care of mariners, the ancient office of Castor and Pollux. At the daily meals on shipboard, it was customary to assign him a ration, as to an invisible guest, the proceeds of the sale of such ration being distributed among the poor as a thank-offering for a prosperous voyage. Calendars

with anguish flees to them. O, indissoluble band! Guardians of mankind!"[1]

Gregory Nazianzen thus invokes the great Athanasius, in the oration delivered after his death: "Look down propitiously upon us, and govern this people, who are perfect adorers of the perfect Trinity. If peace should come, preserve me and feed my flock with me; but if war, take me home and place me beside thyself and those who are like thee." Again, in his funeral discourse on Basil, "O divine and sacred head, look down upon us from heaven, and by thy prayers either take away that thorn of flesh which God has given to prove us, or else obtain that we may bear it with fortitude. When we depart this life, receive us into thy tabernacles, that, living together and beholding more perfectly the holy and blessed Trinity we may see the end of our desires. . . . Now indeed he is in heaven, offering up, as I think, sacrifices for us and praying for the people. From him I even now receive counsel, and am corrected

---

of the saints were commenced in the fourth century; and as the number of martyrs exceeded that of the days of the year, many festivals often fell on the same day. The *Lives of the Saints* (Acta Sanctorum) are contained in fifty-eight folio volumes. This colossal work was commenced (or rather sketched) by Rosweyd, before the close of the sixteenth century, was continued by the Bollandists in the seventeenth and eighteenth, and is still in progress. When Rosweyd's prospectus, which contemplated only seventeen volumes, was shown to Cardinal Bellarmine, he asked, "What is the man's age?" "Perhaps forty," was the answer. "Does he," asked the Cardinal, "expect to live 200 years?"—Schaff, pp. 430, 431, 436 note, 445-449.

[1] Isaac Taylor, ii. pp. 174-177; Basil, *Homily*, Boyd, pp. 39-42.

in nightly visions if at any time I fall from my duty."[1]

Gregory Nyssen does not come behind either his friend or his brother. Thus he speaks of the martyr Theodorus. "Last year he quieted the savage tempest, and put a stop to the horrid war of the fierce Syrians. If any one is permitted to carry away the dust with which his tomb is covered, it is to be laid up as a thing of great price. O Theodorus, we want many blessings; intercede for thy country, with the common king. If there be need of more intercession and deprecation, call together the choir of thy brethren the martyrs. Exhort Peter, excite Paul and John the beloved disciple, that they may be solicitous for the Churches which they have founded, that the worship of idols may not lift up its head against us, that heresies may not spring up like thorns in the vineyard; but that by the power of thy prayer, and of the prayers of thy companions, the commonwealth of Christians may become a field of corn."[2]

After reading such rhapsodies we may well exclaim with Bishop Hooper, "What intolerable blasphemy of God, and ethnical idolatry is this!" And these things were not done in a corner. On the occasion of Gregory's oration, the birthday of Theodorus, the people streamed to the shrine in

---

[1] *Church in the Middle Ages*, pp. 131, 132; Roberts, *Church Memorials*, pp. 132, 133.   [2] *Church in the Middle Ages*, pp. 132-134.

such multitudes, that he could compare it to nothing but an ant-hill.[1]

As was to be expected, the fervid imagination of Chrysostom carries him even beyond his brethren. "Let us in this fire of love fall down before the relics of the saints! Great boldness had they when living, but much more now that they are dead; for now they bear the *stigmas*[2] of Christ, and when they show these, they can obtain all things of the King. O wonderful pyre! What a treasure does it hold! That dust and those ashes, more precious than gold or jewels, more fragrant than any perfume." Some relics of the "Egyptian Martyrs" were transported from Alexandria to Constantinople: the city poured itself out to welcome the landing of the inestimable treasure, and to accompany it to the sacred spot where it was to be deposited in gold and marble. The voice of the preacher is lifted up: "Now is our city more securely defended than by ramparts of adamant; now is it walled about with lofty rocks on this side and on that. For these ashes of the saints repel not merely the assaults of visible enemies, or exclude merely sensible evils, but even the machinations of invisible demons, confounding all the stratagems of the devil; and this they do with as much ease as a strong man sweeps down a child's playthings."

---

[1] Isaac Taylor, ii. pp. 181, 183; *Church in the Middle Ages*, pp. 132-134.

[2] Marks of the wounds in the body of Jesus; hence, generally, marks of martyrdom.

He tells too how that once when the harvest was endangered by excessive rain, the whole population of Constantinople flocked to the church of the Apostles and there chose Peter and Andrew, Paul and Timothy, as their patrons and intercessors before the Throne of Grace. Nevertheless Chrysostom, when the evangelical mind was uppermost in him, could say: "A great man can be reached only through porters and parasites, but God is invoked without the intervention of any one, without money, without cost of any kind."[1]

As time goes on, the shades of error deepen. Sulpicius Severus, in his eulogy of Martin of Tours, after lamenting the heavy burden of his own sins, exclaims: "There is a hope, however, left, our sole and last hope, that what we cannot obtain of ourselves we may at least merit by Martin's intercession." And Prudentius thus addresses St. Agnes:—

"O blessed virgin! O new glory!
Noble inhabitant of the celestial height!
Incline thy face with double diadem
To behold our vile impurities.
To whom it has been given by the universal parent
To render pure even the vault of heaven itself.
I shall be cleansed by the brightness

---

[1] Isaac Taylor, ii. pp. 194–198; Schaff, pp. 439, 440. Dr. Pusey observes: "Through volumes of St. Augustine and St. Chrysostom there is no mention of any *reliance* except on Christ alone."—Stephens, *Life of St. Chrysostom*, p. 416.

> Of thy countenance, easy of propitiation,
> If thou wilt fill my heart.
> All is pure which thou pious one deems worthy to look upon,
> Or to touch with thy bounteous feet."[1]

Per. I. Chap. 16.

Augustine, more enlightened, laboured to explain away or to excuse the worship paid to the saints; but his disclaimer is contradicted by facts, and his pleas unwarranted by Scripture. "We do venerate the memory of the martyrs, and this is done both to excite us to imitate them, and to obtain a share in their merits and the assistance of their prayers. But it is not to any martyr that we build altars, but to the God of the martyrs. No one ever says, We bring an offering to thee, O Peter, O Paul, or O Cyprian! Our emotions are intensified by the associations of the place, and love is excited both towards those who are our examples, and towards Him by whose help we may follow such examples. We regard the martyrs with the same affection that we feel towards holy men of God in this life; only there is more devotion in our sentiment towards them, because we know that their conflict is over, and we can speak with greater confidence in praise of those who are already victors in heaven than of those who are still combating here. That which is properly Divine worship, which the

---

[1] Roberts, p. 134. Sulpicius died about A.D. 420; Prudentius flourished about 405.

Greeks call *latria*, and for which there is no word in Latin, we give only to God. To this worship belongs the offering of sacrifices, as we see in the word *idolatry*, which means the rendering of this worship to idols. Accordingly we never offer sacrifice to a martyr, or to a holy soul, or to an angel. Any one falling into this error is instructed either in the way of correction or of caution."[1]

IV.-V. Cent.

SECTION VII. RELICS.—It is not easy for us in this Protestant age and country to comprehend the high value set upon relics, especially from the time when the Empress Helena made the "discovery of the true Cross." No church was complete without the possession of these treasures; no altar was looked upon as truly sanctified, except a bone of one of the Apostles, or the ashes of some distinguished martyr, or a splinter of the Cross itself, was enshrined within it.[2]

In the biography of Augustine allusion was made to his credulity on the subject of miracles.[3] The story there referred to brings out in a salient manner the intense craving for the marvellous of this boasted age. In the year 415, Lucian, a presbyter of the church at Carphagamala,[4] was

---

[1] *Reply to Faustus the Manichæan*, b. xx. c. 21. See also *The City of God*, b. viii. c. 27.

[2] The second Council of Nicæa (A.D. 787) decreed that the presence of relics was indispensable to an altar.—Canon 7.   [3] *Ante*, p. 359, note.

[4] Doubtless the Caphar-salama of 1 Macc. vii. 31. Capt. Conder thinks this may be the present village of Selmeh, near Joppa.

in his bed in the baptistery where he guarded the consecrated vessels. Between sleeping and waking he saw on his right hand an aged man of priestly aspect, with a long white beard, robed in a white stole embroidered with golden crosses, and carrying a golden rod in his hand. The venerable apparition, addressing him thrice by name, charged him to admonish the bishop of Jerusalem to make search for certain sacred remains which had long lain in obscurity, and the discovery of which was peculiarly needed in the perils and disorder of the times. "Who art thou, sir?" asked Lucian. "I am Gamaliel," he replied, "the same who taught Paul the Apostle. He who is buried with me is my master Stephen, who was stoned by the Jews at Jerusalem for the faith of Christ. His body, after it had lain exposed a day and a night, untouched by beast or bird, I directed to be removed by pious men and carried to this place, where I caused a mourning to be made for him forty days, and where at my own charges he was interred. Moreover, Nicodemus, who came to Jesus by night, lies in the same sepulchre; deprived of his rank by the Jews he was nourished by me to the end of his days, and by me honourably buried next to my master Stephen, where also I interred my dear son Abidas." Lucian being slow of belief, the vision appeared again to him, bringing four baskets, three golden, filled with white and red roses, the fourth of silver, with odoriferous saffron, signifying the relics severally of the four occupants of the sepulchre. After two further visions Lucian hastened to Jerusalem, and related what had happened to the bishop, who wept for joy. The inhabitants of the village being summoned by the crier at break of day, search was made at the bishop's command; but it was not until a "simple-minded man," who during the night had been visited by Gamaliel, came to direct the search, that it was successful, and three coffins were found, duly inscribed with the names of the interred. News being carried to the bishop at Lydda, he hastened to the spot, and proceeded to open the coffin of Stephen. As the bones of the martyr were exposed to the light the earth quaked and a fragrant odour was diffused around. "Verily," says the narrator, "we believed ourselves in Paradise." The odour was not only sweet but fraught with healing virtue, seventy-three sick persons, some of them possessed with demons, being made whole.[1]

The bones were carefully gathered up, and dispersed into various lands, some finding their way into North Africa. Here they came under the notice of Augustine, who abandoned himself without hesitation to a belief in the innumerable miracles they were said to have wrought.

---

[1] Isaac Taylor, ii. pp. 319-321.

"I am so pressed," he writes in the last book of *The City of God*, " by the promise I have given of finishing this work, that I cannot record all the miracles I am acquainted with; for if I were even to pass by all the rest, and to relate only those which were wrought in Calama and Hippo by means of the most glorious Stephen, they would fill many volumes."[1]

The epoch we are now reviewing was indeed the very age of wonders and legends. Speaking of Butler's *Lives of the Saints*, which he terms "the fairy-land of unbounded credulity," Isaac Taylor says, "Let any one open the volume at hazard and, without looking at the dates, select a few [narratives] which appear the most ridiculously absurd or on any account peculiarly offensive, and I will venture to predict that they will turn out to be Nicene and not Popish stories. In fact, they will be found to be translations from Athanasius, Basil, Palladius, Jerome, or some of their contemporaries. On the contrary, any lives that may appear to be less objectionable, and in a sense edifying, will be those of modern Romanist saints."[2]

The same passion for relics finds a place in all the great writers of this age. Ambrose is seeking the remains of a predecessor who was banished to Cappadocia; Basil is able to send him the coveted treasure, affirming with great emphasis

---

[1] B. xxii. c. 8.   [2] Vol. i. pp. 347, 348.

the genuineness of the article. The devout sons of the West made pious journeys eastward in quest of the much coveted relics, and not unfrequently the cunning Greeks, who received their genuine coin, sent them home laden with spurious merchandise. Later, as Pope Gregory VIII. tells us, Greek monks came to Rome, to dig up common bones near St. Paul's church for sale in the East as holy Relics. Imperial legislation and the decrees of councils were equally powerless to check this profitable traffic. "Let no one," so runs a law of Theodosius in 386, "remove a buried body; let no one carry away or sell a martyr."[1]

Individuals, no less than churches, coveted the possession of these jewels. We may remember how, so early as the year 311, the lady Lucilla kept by her the bone of a martyr to kiss before she partook of the Bread and Wine.[2] This mania soon became universal. Scarcely any one ventured to go about unprovided with such a talisman. Chrysostom speaks of particles of the True Cross being set in gold and suspended about the necks both of men and women.[3]

---

[1] Smith, *St. Basil the Great*, p. 128; Maitland, *Church in the Catacombs*, pp. 278, 279; Mosheim, ii. pp. 222, 223; Schaff, pp. 455, 456.

[2] *Early Church History*, p. 392. [3] Isaac Taylor, ii. p. 203.

CHAPTER XVII.

THE SPIRIT OF THE AGE (*concluded*).

Per. I.
Chap. 17.

SECTION I. MONACHISM.—We come now to the peculiar feature of the age : the Monastic Life. In the former volume we touched upon the origin of the anchorite's cell and its gradual development into the monastery.[1] The period we are now reviewing saw the new institution spread from Egypt and Syria over all the provinces of the Empire, absorbing into itself the best life of the Church. It will be worth while to examine more closely the features of this singular phenomenon.

Monachism did not spring out of the gospel. Its essential idea has not only nothing in common with New Testament doctrine; it is repugnant to its whole spirit and object. We must go back for the origin of asceticism to an antiquity greater than even Greek philosophy can show, and to countries beyond the Ganges. The elder form of Hindoo superstition,—Brahminism,—was Pantheistic. It proposed to man, as the highest good, absorption into the universal God; and the means by which

---

[1] See *Early Church History*, pp. 178, 523, 533.

this felicity was to be obtained were seclusion from society, mental abstraction, and the mortification of the body even to suicide. The great Brahminical code, the Laws of Menu, written a thousand years before the Christian era, lays down the following rules for the man who would attain perfection: " Let him retire from the world, and gain the favour of the gods by fasting, subduing the lusts of the flesh and mortifying the senses. Let him crawl backwards and forwards on his belly; or let him stand all the day on his toes. At sunrise, noon, and sunset let him go to the water and bathe.[1] In the heat of summer let him kindle five fires about him; when it rains let him bare himself to the storm; in winter let him wrap himself in a wet garment. So let him rise by degrees in the strength of his penances."[2] What have we here but the very type and pattern of the fourth-century asceticism?

In the sixth century B.C., or earlier, the Buddhist reformation took place, by which Nihilism was substituted for Pantheism, and the world not so much despised as bewailed for its emptiness. Less fanatical than the original creed, it yet united self-mortification with contemplation and prayer. The monastery now took the place of the cave or cell, and convents both for men and women were spread over Eastern Asia. The two governing

---

[1] This observance puts to shame the Christian devotees.
[2] Isaac Taylor, i. pp. 178, 179; Ruffner, i. pp. 23-25.

principles of Hindoo philosophy, whether Buddhist or Brahminical, are, first, that matter is essentially evil; and secondly, that happiness consists in exemption from all the affections and influences which spring from matter, in other words, in profound, imperturbable repose, the soul being occupied only with the ceaseless contemplation of the Divine Essence from which it is derived.[1]

Both these doctrines found their way into the Christian Church. With the most famous of the Anchorites, who were held up as the great objects of imitation, the body, instead of being cherished as God's creation, was contemned as "a machine for producing sin, a loathsome prison of the spirit."[2] All earthly things which can afford pleasure to the senses were shunned as a snare. Cities are

---

[1] Schaff, pp. 150, 151; Isaac Taylor, *loc. cit.*

[2] Dorotheus, an Egyptian monk, never gave way to sleep of his own will. It sometimes happened that, utterly overcome with lassitude, he would fall down on his mat. Then he would be sorely grieved, and say in an undertone, "You could as easily persuade angels to sleep as men of the true watchful spirit." He was once asked, "Why do you kill your body in this way?" He answered, "Because my body kills me." Another, an aged man named Benjamin, being afflicted with dropsy, requested those who came to visit him to pray for his soul. "I care little," he said, "for my body; for when it was well it did me no good, and now that it is sick it can do me no harm."—Sozomen, *Eccles. Hist.*, b. vi. c. 29.

Eusebius, a Syrian monk, employed another to read to him from the Gospels. His attention being drawn off by some men ploughing in the neighbouring field, it was necessary to read the passage a second time. To punish himself for his inattention, he fastened an iron girdle round his loins, riveted a heavy collar to his neck, and by a chain drew the two together, so that his head was bent down and he could not look up. This he called foiling Satan by a stratagem. He also made a vow never to tread any path but the narrow one which led from the monastery to the church.—Theodoret, in *Dict. Christ. Biog.*, ii. p. 378.

evil, human society is evil, green fields, shady woods, refreshing streams, balmy breezes, gay and fragrant flowers, the music of speech and the music of nature, all that is sweet to human sense, is poison to the soul. Impressed with this false and miserable estimate of his Maker's works, the Christian seeker after perfection, like the Brahminical, fled into the desert, where amid arid sands and naked rocks, noisome beasts and reptiles, and the fiery sun overhead, he spent his days in punishing his body, fighting with demons, praying to God and dreaming of heaven. It was imagined, moreover, that the more of earthly good the soul renounces and sacrifices for the sake of heaven, the more of heaven's felicity will God bestow upon it.[1]

The Buddhist monasteries, thus originating many centuries before the Christian, have continued to flourish down to this day. They bear a strong resemblance to those of the Romish church. Their vows of celibacy, poverty and obedience, their common meals, readings and religious exercises, correspond so closely with those of the Latin convent, that the Romish missionaries to the East in the seventeenth century were utterly

---

[1] Ruffner, i. pp. 206, 207. The same sentiment is found in the classic poet Horace.
Quanto quisque sibi plura negaverit,
Ab Dis plura feret. Nil cupientium
Nudus castra peto. —*Odes*, b. iii. carm. 16.
The more a man denies to himself, the more will he receive of the gods. Naked I fly to the camp of those who desire nothing.

Per. I.
Chap. 17.

bewildered, and could only suppose that Satan had devised a counterfeit of the true devotion on purpose to plague them.[1] Thus, Borri, one of their number, says: "There are so many priests and monks in that country (Cochin China) that it looks as if the devil had sought to represent among the heathen the beauty and variety of our orders. Some are clad in white, some in black, some in blue and other colours. Some profess poverty, living on alms; others occupy themselves in works of mercy. The priests wear chaplets and strings of beads round their necks, and make so many processions in prayer to their false gods that they outdo the Christians."[2]

The path by which Indian Asceticism travelled

---

[1] Attempts have been made, but without success, to show that the monasteries of Thibet owe their origin to the Nestorian Christians.

[2] Pinkerton's *Voyages and Travels*, vii. pp. 554, 775, &c. The resemblance between the two religions is not confined to the monastic life. Kæmpfer, the historian of Japan (1692), thus describes a Buddhist temple in the Corea. "Before the splendid altar, on which were gilt idols, sweet-scented candles were burning. The whole temple is so curiously adorned that, if it were not for the monstrous shape of the idols, you might fancy yourself in a Roman Catholic church." In Thibet, the country of the Lama, the resemblance was still more astounding. Gerbillon and Grueber, two Jesuit missionaries, remark with wonder the holy water, the prayers for the dead, the dress of the priests, the singing service, fasts and penances, the honour paid to the relics of the saints, processions, convents, even the mass with bread and wine, and extreme unction. Grieved at the multitude of idols which the people worshipped, Borri took pains to set before them the great truth that there can be but one God. To this they readily assented, and defended their practice by an argument, which to a Roman Catholic must have been unanswerable, viz., "that the images placed along the sides of the temples were not intended to represent the Creator of heaven and earth, but holy men whom (says Borri) they honoured as we do the holy apostles, martyrs, and confessors, with the same distinction of greater and lesser sanctity."—Ibid.

into the Church was through Zoroaster, Pythagoras, Plato, Judaism and Gnosticism; and the hotbed in which it was matured was the Alexandrian School. In both cases, in the Christian as in the Buddhist, the monastery was a natural outcome of the Anchorite life.

IV.-V. Cent.

The preceding biographies furnish ample evidence that the monastic profession numbered within its ranks some on whom the choicest gifts of the head and of the heart had been conferred. Doubtless, under the rough cloak and girdle were to be found thousands of sincere and even intelligent Christians, who, although in the darkness of the times they had mistaken the way, yet had their citizenship in heaven.[1] But the monks were for the most part a fanatical, illiterate race. Many were unable to read; the ignorance which would have been despised in the "secular" clergy, was in them admired as a token of sanctity. They were in consequence easily aroused; their partisanship was violent; they denounced every deviation from their own narrow creed and notions as the work of the devil. Beginning, moreover, with seclusion and separation from the world, they came to play the busiest part in all its transactions. "Strange

---

[1] The number of persons of both sexes who during this period followed the monastic rule was prodigious. Palladius speaks of 3000, 5000, or even 10,000 monks under the rule of a single anchoret or abbot; and 10,000 nuns are mentioned as belonging to the religious houses of one city. Nearly 100,000 of all classes were to be found at one time in Egypt.—Isaac Taylor, i. p. 310; ii. p. 114.

Per. I.
Chap. 17.

contradiction of the human mind!" writes Montesquieu; "the ministers of religion amongst the ancient Romans, not being excluded from the duties of civil society, burdened themselves but little with its affairs. And when the Christian religion was first established, the ecclesiastics who were more separated from worldly affairs mingled in them with moderation. But in the fall of the Empire, the monks, bound by a more exclusive profession to flee and even to fear business, embraced every occasion of meddling with it. They ceased not to make confusion everywhere, and to stir up that world which they had left. No state matter, no peace, no war, no truce, no negotiation, no marriage was managed without the help of the monks; the councils of the prince were full of them, and the national assemblies almost entirely composed of them."[1]

Commencing with vows of poverty, the monks soon began to acquire property and even wealth. Jerome says: "Some, when they have renounced the world, increase rather than diminish their estates, and amongst crowds of guests and swarms of servants, claim the title of solitaries." Again: "Some are richer as monks than they were as seculars; and some clericals possess a degree of wealth under the poor Christ, which they did not possess under that rich knave the devil." So John

---

[1] *Grandeur of the Romans*, c. 22.

Cassianus: "We, living in common under an abbot, carry about our private keys, and wear on our fingers the rings with which we seal up our stores. Not boxes and baskets, not even chests and storerooms suffice to hold the things we have collected, or which we received when we left the world."[1]

Much has been said, not by Roman Catholic writers only, in praise of Monachism, and we cannot doubt that the Most High has made use of this institution to subserve his beneficent designs. By means of the monasteries, at some epochs, the wilderness has been reclaimed, the arts of industry have been taught to rude nations, learning has been preserved, a sanctuary provided from rapine and bloodshed, and a fountain opened from which spiritual life and knowledge flowed around. But all this does not prove that the institution was Christian or right; it only shows that which we see continually, that God overrules man's devious methods for the purposes of his own love and goodness. The Israelites did evil when they clamoured for a king, yet the monarchy was made use of in perfecting the divine scheme of man's redemption. It was no real extenuation of the cruel sin of Joseph's brethren, in selling him into Egypt, that he said to them, long afterwards, "Be not grieved that ye sold me hither, for it was not you who sent me but God."[2]

IV.-V. Cent.

---

[1] Ruffner, ii. p. 311.   [2] Gen. xlv. 5-8.

Per. I.
Chap. 17.

Milman has portrayed in eloquent language the evil and the good of the monastic life. "It is impossible," he says, "to survey Monachism in its general influence, from the earliest period of its interworking into Christianity, without being astonished and perplexed with its diametrically opposite effects. Here, it is the undoubted parent of the blindest ignorance and the most ferocious bigotry, sometimes of the most debasing licentiousness; there, the guardian of learning, the author of civilization, the propagator of humble and peaceful religion. To the dominant spirit of Monachism may be ascribed some part at least of the gross superstition and moral inefficiency of the church in the Byzantine Empire; to the same spirit much of the salutary authority of Western Christianity, its constant aggressions on barbarism, and its connection with the Latin literature. . . . Nothing can be conceived more apparently opposed to the designs of the God of nature, and to the mild and beneficent spirit of, Christianity; nothing more hostile to the dignity, the interests, the happiness, and the intellectual and moral perfection of man, than the monk afflicting himself with unnecessary pain, and thrilling his soul with causeless fears; confined to a dull routine of religious duties, jealously watching, and proscribing every emotion of pleasure as a sin against the benevolent Deity; dreading knowledge, as an impious departure from the becoming humility of man. On the other hand, what generous or lofty mind can refuse to acknowledge the grandeur of that superiority to all the cares and passions of mortality; the felicity of that state which is removed far above the fears or the necessities of life; that sole passion of admiration and love of the Deity, which no doubt was attained by some of the purer and more imaginative enthusiasts of the cell or the cloister? Who, still more, will dare to depreciate that heroism of Christian benevolence, which underwent this self-denial of the lawful enjoyments and domestic charities of which it had neither extinguished the desire, nor subdued the regret—not from the slavish fear of displeasing the Deity, or the selfish ambition of personal perfection—but from the genuine desire of advancing the temporal and eternal improvement of mankind; of imparting the moral amelioration and spiritual hopes of Christianity to the wretched and the barbarous; of being the messengers of Christian faith, and the ministers of Christian charity to the heathen, whether in creed or in character?" [1]

We cannot wholly subscribe to these latter sentences. It is true that the only genuine heroism in the world is the heroism of Christian self-denial for the sake of our fellow-men; and it is shameful when those who spend their lives in self-

---

[1] *History of Christianity*, iii. pp. 223-225.

indulgence, forgetful of God and man, affect to despise a simplicity of life, a scorn of ease or a prodigality of unselfish labour, which they can neither imitate nor appreciate. But it can hardly be too much emphasized that the praise which our author is disposed to accord is due to the *motives* only of those who embraced the ascetic life. We would acknowledge in many the excellence of their motive, but we deplore the error of their method. It cannot be said that the cloister is necessary to any of the objects set forth, least of all to the work of the Christian missionary.

Isaac Taylor takes a different view. He wrote at a time when a deluge of semi-popery threatened to overflow this country, a deluge whose waters have not yet altogether abated : " Christianity was just about to work its proper effect upon the Roman world, when the ascetic fanaticism came in ; first to poison the domestic system at the core by its hypocritical prudery, and its consequent separation of the sexes ; and, secondly, to turn off the fertilising current of the most powerful sentiments from the field of common life, and to throw them all into the waste-pipe which emptied itself upon the wilderness. The mighty waters of Christian moral influence, which should have renovated the Roman world and have saved the barbarism of a thousand years, were by the ascetic institute shed over the horrid sands of Egypt and Arabia—there to be lost for ever. . . .

Southern Europe was left for another cycle of centuries, and monkish fanaticism, with its celibacy and its fastings, has continued now these fifteen hundred years to be the grim antithesis of a widespread dissoluteness of manners."[1]

Enough has perhaps been said regarding monkish austerities, but there is one type of self-mortification as yet unmentioned, which confirms in a striking manner the comparison already made between the Indian fakir and the Christian devotee. We mean the Pillar saints.

The first and most celebrated of these was Simeon Stylites, born about A.D. 390. The account of him which has been handed down is as follows: When a youth he entered a monastery near Antioch, where his austerities were so excessive that the abbot begged him to depart, lest the emulation he caused should be dangerous to the weaker brethren. He accordingly withdrew to a place about forty miles from the city, where he lived for ten years in a sort of narrow pen. Afterwards he built a pillar and took up his dwelling on the top of it, which was only about a yard in diameter. He removed successively from one pillar to another, always increasing the height, until at last it reached to sixty feet. In this manner of life he spent thirty-seven years. Day and night he professed to be continually in

---

[1] *Ancient Christianity*, i. pp. 354, 355.

prayer, spreading forth his hands and bending so low that his forehead touched his feet. At three o'clock in the afternoon he addressed the admiring crowd below, heard and answered their questions, sent messages and wrote letters, for he corresponded with bishops and even Emperors.[1] He took only one scanty meal a week and fasted altogether throughout Lent; he wore a long sheepskin robe and a cap of the same; his neck was loaded with an iron chain.[2]

Simeon is said to have converted thousands of Arabs, Armenians, Persians, and heretics; but the conversion seems to have consisted in their being immersed in water and paying divine honour to the saint and his pillar, rather than in any change of spirit or manner of life. At Simeon's death his cowl descended to another monk named Daniel, whose mastery over his body, miracles, and sanctity rivalled those of his predecessor. The two saints found many imitators in the East, but this absurd fashion never got a footing in Europe.[3]

---

[1] When the Emperor Theodosius II. was endeavouring to reconcile the Alexandrians and the Antiochians during the Nestorian controversy, he wrote to Simeon to beg his prayers.—Robertson, i. p. 452.

[2] Evagrius, *Eccles. Hist.*, b. i. c. 13; Theodoret. The chief authority for these marvels is the latter, a contemporary writer, with whom we shall meet again in the Nestorian controversy. His account of Simeon forms one of about thirty lives of the Anchorites contained in a book which he calls "Philotheus." Some of the stories respecting Simeon are considered to be well attested.—Ruffner, ii. p. 234-248.

[3] The pillar was gradually built round with chapels and monasteries, and the figure of the saint as a protecting genius was set up at the doors of the shops in Rome. A German fanatic built himself a similar pillar

SECTION II. THE CHURCH AND THE WORLD.— The Fathers of the fourth and fifth centuries were not blind to the moral condition into which the Church had sunk in their day. "The Church," writes Chrysostom, "is like a woman fallen from her ancient prosperity, who possesses various signs of her former wealth, and displays the little chests and caskets in which her treasure was preserved, but who has lost the treasure itself." Basil likens her to "a ship driven about by the fiercest storms, whilst the crew are quarrelling amongst themselves;" and "to an old garment which tears wherever you touch it, and which it is impossible to restore to its primitive strength and soundness."[1]

By this time, indeed, the distinction between Pagan and Christian had become nominal rather than real. The vile manners of the heathen were still maintained by those who called themselves Christians. Children were by needy parents exposed to perish, boys were sold as slaves for their fathers' debts. Christian parents betook themselves to magicians when their children were sick, and expected a cure to be wrought by hanging a talisman about their necks. The conversation of the market-places was filthy.[2]

---

near Treves, and essayed to live upon it, after the manner of Simeon, but the neighbouring bishops pulled it down.—Mosheim, i. pp. 467, 468.

[1] S. Tuke, Papers on the Fine Arts, in the *Friend* Journal, 1844, p. 248, note; R. T. Smith, *St. Basil the Great*, p. 74.

[2] Ibid., p. 69.

Per. I.
Chap. 17.

The theatre was frequented alike by Christians and heathens, and was, as in the days of Tertullian,[1] the very hotbed of vice. Chrysostom calls it "the seat of pestilence, the gymnasium of incontinence; and a school of luxury, Satan being its author and architect;" and after many unheeded warnings declares he will no longer admit playgoers to the Lord's Supper. By the force of custom, sights were tolerated there which would have been endured nowhere else. Even the celebration of the Eucharist and other rites of the Church were profanely represented.[2]

The circus evoked the pious indignation of Chrysostom even more than the theatre. "The indomitable passion for the chariot-races, and the silly eagerness displayed about them by the inhabitants of Rome, Constantinople, and Antioch, are among the most remarkable symptoms of the depraved state of society under the later Empire. The whole populace was divided into factions, distinguished by the different colours adopted by the charioteers, of which green and blue were the two chief favourites. The animosity, the sanguinary tumults, the superstitions, folly, violence of every kind, which were mixed up with these

---

[1] See *Early Church History*, p. 201.

[2] *St. Chrysostom's Picture of his Age*, pp. 152, 156. "We Christians," complains Gregory Nazianzen, "are brought upon the stage, and made subjects for vulgar laughter in company with the most profligate of men. Nay, there is hardly any gratification so popular as a Christian exposed to mockery and insult in a comedy."—*Life* by Ullmann, pp. 156, 157

popular amusements well deserved the unsparing severity with which they were lashed by the great preacher. 'You applaud my words, and then hurry off to the circus, and sitting side by side with Jew or Pagan, clap your hands with frenzied eagerness at the efforts of the charioteers. You plead business, poverty, want of health, lameness as excuses for absence from church, but these hindrances never prevent your attendance at the hippodrome.'"[1]

Salvian, a presbyter of Marseilles, and a writer of uncommon elegance, has left us a forcible description of the corrupt state of the Church in the fifth century. The biting language in which he declaims is the very counterpart of that in which Cyprian speaks of the heathen world.[2] "What," he asks, " what but fraud and perjury[3] is

---

[1] Stephens, pp. 118, 119.
[2] *Early Church History*, pp. 9–14.
[3] Oaths and the vain use of the Sacred Name were almost universal. A new form of asseveration, *By Christ*, had come into vogue, and a vile superstition had converted the profanity into an obligation of duty. "Salvian was pleading earnestly with some powerful personage that he would not take away from a poor man the last remnant of his substance. 'Already devouring the spoil with vehement desire he shot forth savage glances from his eye against me, and raged at my daring to interfere, and said that it was now his religious duty, and one which he dared not neglect, to do the thing which I besought him not to do. I asked him why; and he gave me the astounding answer, Because I have sworn *per Christum* that I would take that man's property away from him.'"—*Italy and her Invaders*, i. pp. 509, 510. Chrysostom's emphatic condemnation of oaths has been noticed in the *Early Church History*, p. 234. The common habit of interlarding conversation with asseverations by the Sacred Name exceedingly moved his ire. "If," he said, "you hear any one blaspheme in the forum or the streets, smite him on the face; strike his mouth; sanctify your

the course of life of the merchants? What but iniquity that of those attached to halls and courts? What but false accusation that of officials? What but rapine that of all the military? You will say, surely the nobility are free from crime. Not so; for who is there, whether among the noble or among the rich (and it is one of the miseries of these times that none is accounted so noble as he who has amassed the greatest wealth), who is there that shudders at crime? I am wrong. Many shudder at crimes; they are shocked at the vices of others, whilst they themselves practise the same. They execrate openly what they perpetrate secretly. . . . A very few excepted, what else is almost every assembly of Christians but a sink of vices? You will more easily find the man who is guilty of all crimes than him who is guilty of none. But it is the laity only, you will say, who sin at this rate, surely not the clergy. Alas! under colour of religion, men who after a course of profligacy inscribed themselves with a saintly title, have changed their profession only, not their life. They have put off the garment only, not the mind of their former condition. These men well know that what I am saying is true, their own consciences bear witness to every word. . . . The entire mass of the priests is so sunk into this depravity that it has come to be regarded as a

---

hand with the blow; and if any one should drag you before the judge, boldly say, 'The man blasphemed the King of Angels!'"—*St. Chrysostom's Picture of his Age*, pp. 131, 132.

species of sanctity for one to be a little less vicious than the rest. Inasmuch as scarcely any corner is not blotted with the stain of mortal sin, what room have we to flatter ourselves with our name? ... It will, to many, sound insufferable if I should affirm, that we are inferior to the barbarians, who are either heretics (Arians) or pagans. But what if it be so? As to life and conduct, I grieve to say we are worse. ... Ye Romans and Christians and Catholics, ye defraud your brethren, grind the faces of the poor, fritter away your lives over the impure and heathenish spectacles of the amphitheatre, wallow in licentiousness and inebriety. The barbarians, however fierce towards us, are just and fair in their dealings with one another; the impurities of the theatre are unknown amongst them; many of their tribes are free from the taint of drunkenness; and amongst all except the Alans and the Huns, chastity is the rule."[1]

Whatever truth there may be in Salvian's verdict regarding the priesthood, there must have been very many, in all parts of the empire, who

---

[1] *On Providence*, in Isaac Taylor's *Ancient Christianity*, ii. pp. 40-42, 47, 53, 54; *Italy and her Invaders*, i. pp. 506-508. "One must not," observes Thomas Hodgkin, "accept as literal truth every point of the contrast which Salvian draws between Roman immorality and barbarian purity. As the philosophers of last century drew many an arrow from the quiver of the Red Indian to discharge it against the rotten civilization of which France under Louis XV. was the centre, so doubtless has Salvian sometimes used the German chastity, the German simplicity of life, to arouse a sense of shame in his Roman reader."—Ibid.

still adorned the profession of the Christian minister. In support of this opinion we may adduce the unequivocal testimony of an outsider, the heathen historian Ammianus Marcellinus. He has been relating the sanguinary contest between Damasus and Ursicinus for the possession of the Roman See,[1] and thus concludes: "I do not deny, when I consider the pomp and display of the episcopal office in this city, that they who covet such rank are justified in striving with all their might to attain the object of their desires. For when they have gained it, they come into a state of perfect ease and luxury; the offerings of matrons are showered upon them; they ride in chariots, dress with splendour, and feast with even more than royal extravagance. They might be equally happy if, instead, they were to live like some of the provincial bishops, whom rigid abstinence, simplicity of dress, and an humble demeanour commend to the Eternal Deity and his true worshippers, as pure and sober-minded men."[2]

---

[1] See *ante*, p. 64, note.
[2] *Roman History*, b. xxvii. c. 3, §§ 14, 15.

CHAPTER XVIII.

JOVINIAN AND VIGILANTIUS.

SECTION I. From the galaxy of illustrious names, IV. Cent. on which we have been gazing, we turn to that small cluster of obscure men who strove to call back the Church to Apostolic simplicity and truth. The need of reform had become more and more pressing, but the great leaders and teachers of the age had failed to perform their duty; nevertheless the truth was not left wholly without witnesses.

The name of Aërius was introduced in our former work[1] by anticipation rather than in the exact order of time. He flourished about the middle of the fourth century, and may be regarded as the first Protestant after the Council of Nicæa. His teaching on many points anticipated in a remarkable degree that of the most enlightened Protestants of the Reformation.

JOVINIAN. Little is known of the personal history of this monk. As in the case of Aërius, his own writings have perished, his opinions having come down to us only through his op-

---

[1] See *Early Church History*, pp. 551-553.

Per. I.
Chap. 18.

ponents Jerome and Augustine. He received his education in an Italian convent,[1] but his bold and free spirit refused to be shackled by the dead forms which surrounded him, and about A.D. 388 he began to enunciate sounder and more spiritual principles. Especially he denied the superior merit of celibacy;[2] and as just then the popular feeling, consequent on the death of Blesilla,[3] was running against Jerome and Monachism, he made many converts, not only of the laity, but also of monks and nuns; and many of both sexes were induced to marry.[4]

Jerome's friend Pammachius, the husband of Paula's daughter, was one of the first to take alarm at the new heresy. He brought Jovinian's book to the notice of Siricius, the Roman bishop, a blind upholder of celibacy.[5] A synod was convened, A.D. 390, and Jovinian and eight of his adherents were summarily condemned and excommunicated. Jovinian betook himself to Milan, but if he ex-

---

[1] Cave says he lived some years in Ambrose's monastery at Milan.—*Life of St. Ambrose*, § v. 7.

[2] He controverted the perpetual virginity of Mary, a point which was then becoming an article of faith in the Church.

[3] See *ante*, p. 270.

[4] Gieseler, ii. p. 75, note; Robertson, i. pp. 358, 359.

[5] See *ante*, p. 271, note. Siricius decreed by letter that if any bishop, priest, or deacon should marry, he should not look for pardon, "because it is necessary to cut off with the knife those sores which cannot be cured by other remedies."—Schaff, p. 248, note. This was the first *Decretal*, the first *Letter* of the Bishop of Rome which became a rule to the Western Church, and thus laid the foundation of the vast system of ecclesiastical law.—Milman, *Latin Christianity*, i. pp. 75, 76.

pected to meet with indulgence either from the Emperor Theodosius, or the bishop Ambrose, he was grievously disappointed. Siricius had been beforehand with him, and sent three presbyters with a letter of warning addressed to the Milanese Church; and Ambrose hastened to show himself in complete accord with the Roman synod. In conjunction with eight other bishops, he endorsed the sentence of excommunication, and in a letter to Siricius stated that the Emperor also execrated the impiety of the Jovinianists, and that all at Milan who had seen the heretics shunned them like a pestilence. He stigmatizes Jovinian's opinion that there was no difference of merit between the married and the unmarried as "a savage howling of ferocious wolves scaring the flock."[1] The matter did not end here. For, long after, in 412, we find the Emperor Honorius issuing the following edict: "Some bishops having complained that Jovinian assembles sacrilegious meetings without the walls of the most holy city, We ordain that the said Jovinian be seized and whipped, together with his abettors and followers, and that he be immediately banished to the Island of Boa."[2]

---

[1] Isaac Taylor's *Ancient Christianity*, i. p. 346, note.

[2] *Dict. Christ. Biog.*, art. Jovinianus (3), iii. p. 465; Waddington, *History of the Church*, i. p. 338. Boa was a rock near the Illyrian coast. Some historians have thought that the Edict of Honorius was not directed against our monk, but against another heretic of the same name. For this opinion two reasons are assigned, the one that Jovinian, as appears by Jerome, died so early as 406; the other that no such complaint as that on which the edict is founded was brought against him at the synod. The

Per. I.
Chap. 18.

Whilst the merit of the ascetic life was being re-echoed from side to side, and charity was estimated and sins graduated by the outward act, Jovinian stood forth and proclaimed the true doctrine of faith. "There is but one Divine element of life which all believers share in common; but one fellowship with Christ which proceeds from faith in Him; but one new birth. All who possess this, all who are Christians in the true sense, have the same calling, the same dignity, the same heavenly blessings. . . . The labourers of the first, the third, the sixth, the ninth, and the eleventh hour received each alike one penny; and that you may wonder the more, the payment begins with those who had laboured the shortest time in the vineyard. . . . Virgins, widows and married women who have been once baptized into Christ, if their works are right, have equal merit. . . . It amounts to the same thing, whether a man abstain from food, or partake of it with thanksgiving." But when he goes on to say that there are no half-ripe members in the Church, no progression in the spiritual life, we cannot follow him; nor when he declares that he who is once baptized cannot be overcome by temptation; and if any are so overcome it is a proof that they have never received the

---

latter objection is of little weight; with regard to the former, Tillemont suggests that the date of the edict may be erroneous. Moreover, it is not probable there were two Jovinians; if there were, we have one reformer the more, or at least one more instance of a willingness to suffer for conscience sake.—Mosheim, i. p. 366, note.

true baptism. In opposition to the division of sins into mortal and venial (the former only being held to exclude from eternal life), Jovinian took his stand on high and solid ground; he maintained that the Gospel requires and confers a new holy disposition, to which every sin of every kind stands directly opposed, so that all sin, whatever outward appearance it may have, proceeds from the same corrupt fountain, and manifests the same ungodly life.[1]

The publication of Jovinian's book excited, as has been said, considerable attention in Rome. It also aroused the wrath of Jerome in his cell at Bethlehem, and without delay he set to work to extinguish the heretic. "The tone of his reply is that of a man suddenly arrested in his triumphant career by some utterly unexpected opposition; his resentment at being thus crossed is mingled with a kind of wonder that men should exist who could entertain such strange and daring tenets. The length, it might be said the prolixity, to which he draws out his answer, seems rather the outpouring of his wrath and his learning, than as if he considered it necessary to refute such obvious errors." He calls Jovinian's protest against the supposed merit of asceticism, "the hissings of the old serpent, by which the dragon expelled man from Paradise."[2]

---

[1] Neander, iii. pp. 381–390; Robertson, i. p. 358; Augustine, *On Merits and Forgiveness of Sins*, b. iii. c. 13. Jovinian also opposed the excessive veneration for the act of martyrdom.

[2] We take no notice of the charge of gluttony brought by Jerome against

Per. I.
Chap. 18.

So violent was his language that on his reply being sent to Rome, Pammachius and others of his friends attempted to suppress it; but Jerome told them the book had been too much circulated to be recalled. Augustine, who was also opposed to Jovinian, was alarmed at the extravagant terms in which Jerome had extolled celibacy, and depreciated marriage; and to counteract the effect of his tract, wrote a treatise for the purpose of restoring marriage to its true position; although, as was to be expected, he ascribes a still higher degree of the Christian life to the unmarried state, when it is chosen from the right motives. "In this tract," observes Neander, "Augustine distinguishes himself, not only by his greater moderation, but also by a more correct judgment of the ascetic life in its connection with the whole Christian temper. Like Jovinian, he opposed the tendency to set a value upon the outward conduct, upon works as a mere *opus operatum*, without regard to their relation to the disposition of the heart. By giving prominence to the latter, Augustine approached Jovinian, and he would have come still nearer to him, had he not been on so many sides fettered by the Church spirit of the times."[1]

Jovinian. It is probable it had no other ground than that on which the Pharisees rested their accusation against our Lord: "The Son of Man is come eating and drinking; and ye say: Behold, a gluttonous man, and a winebibber, a friend of publicans and sinners."—Luke vii. 34, 35.

[1] Milman, *History of Christianity*, iii. p. 234; *Dict. Christ. Biog.*, iii. p. 465; Neander, iii. p. 392.

The names of two other witnesses of Jovinian's age and country, if not actually his disciples, have also come down to us, Sarmatio and Barbatianus, both of them monks in Ambrose's cloister at Milan. They disputed the benefit of Asceticism and the peculiar merit of the unmarried life. Not being suffered to utter their opinions in the cloister, they renounced their vows,[1] and removed to Vercelli, where they hoped to be able to teach their doctrines unmolested. But Ambrose put the Church in that city on its guard against the heretics. Of the further history of these men we have no account.[2]

IV. Cent.

Thus persecuted by the bishops, written down by the greatest doctors of the age, outlawed by synods, detested by the whole body of the clergy, Jovinian and his adherents were soon forgotten. But though the mouths of the witnesses were closed, the truths they proclaimed were not so easily destroyed. They presently sprang up again in a new quarter.

SECTION II. VIGILANTIUS was born about A.D. 364, at Calagorris, a *mansio* or posting-station, forty-five miles south-west of Toulouse. His father, a descendant of the robbers whom Pompey drove out of Spain,[3] was the inn-keeper of the place, and

---

[1] The monastic vow was not then irrevocable; it was first so made by Benedict of Nursia, A.D. 529.   [2] Neander, iii. p. 391.

[3] *The Book of St. Jerome, the Presbyter, against Vigilantius*, § 4. These

made his fortune by supplying post-horses and refreshment to travellers.[1] Vigilantius assisted him, and it was probably his business to wait on the travellers, drive the cars and act as guide across the Pyrenean mountains.[2]

The ecclesiastical writer Sulpicius Severus, with whom we have already met in the life of Martin of Tours, resided at a villa between Toulouse and Narbonne, and possessed estates on both sides of the Pyrenees. His way from one to the other lay through Calagorris, and the young man attracting his notice, he took him into his service. Here Vigilantius would meet with the best society of which Gaul could boast, and would hear the news of the Christian world retailed, and theological questions discussed. Sulpicius, besides his charity towards the sick and poor, and his care for the maintenance of public and family worship, was occupied in preparing an abridgment of the Holy Scriptures. But in this reasonable and exemplary manner of life he seems to have been disturbed by bishop Martin of Tours, who persuaded him that his benevolent and pious actions were of no value without the practice of austerities. To

---

robbers belonged to the Spanish village of Calagorris, and when they arrived in Gaul they gave the same name to their new settlement.

[1] The posting system was under the direction of the State, and officials or government messengers were carried along at the rate of upwards of eight miles an hour in four-wheeled carriages or light two-wheeled cars, drawn by horses or mules.

[2] Dr. Gilly, *Vigilantius and his Times*, pp. 125-130.

what an extent Sulpicius carried his self-humiliation we see by a letter from his friend Paulinus of Nola. "Thy domestics tell me thou art poor in the midst of wealth, and art living in a state of self-imposed bondage, treating thy servants as thy companions, and thy brethren as thy masters. In fact, that thou art a perfect servant of God, the enemy of riches, the living copy of the holy Martin, an entirely obedient follower of the Gospel."[1]

A.D. 394.

In 394 Vigilantius and a companion were sent by Sulpicius to Nola to visit Paulinus. The reader of our former volume is already acquainted with this enthusiast, who so greatly delighted in his noon-day illuminations;[2] but in view of the protest which Vigilantius was soon to raise against the superstitions of the age it may be well to acquaint ourselves more closely with what must have come under his notice at Nola. The fame of Paulinus was in all the churches. He held a correspondence with Augustine, by whom he was addressed in a style of warm friendship, reverence, and even flattery; and his influence was so great that he was able to set at nought the displeasure of the Roman bishop Siricius.[3]

---

[1] Gilly, pp. 133–140.

[2] See *Early Church History*, p. 481.

[3] Gilly, pp. 166–173. Paulinus was meant for better things. "Rigorous abstinence, periodical fastings, night watchings, coarse vestments, the accumulation of bones and rags of saints, and especially the hourly prostrations at the shrine of St. Felix, absorbed all the capacities of a mind once distinguished by the graces and refinements of the scholar, the poet and the rhetorician."—Roberts, p. 224.

Per. I.
Chap. 18.

Paulinus had fitted up his villa, which stood close to the tomb of his patron saint Felix,[1] as a monastery and a house of reception for strangers. Ample pleasure grounds which had been adorned with fountains, statues and flowerbeds, were transformed into an orchard and a cabbage garden. During Vigilantius' visit, his host began to rebuild the church. The pavement and walls were laid in marble, and on the ceiling of the dome there were wrought in mosaic emblematical representations of the Trinity and the Evangelists.[2] Under the cupola stood the high altar, enshrining ashes of the Apostles, relics of martyrs, and a splinter of the "true Cross." The lofty nave was flanked by aisles, and beyond these were four chapels for private devotion and the burial-places of the faithful. From the church you passed by three latticed arcades to the mausoleum of St. Felix, and from this again in the same manner to his oratory. The building when completed, surmounted as it was by three cupolas and encompassed with walls, had almost the appearance of a little town.[3]

---

[1] A legendary confessor in the Decian persecution, whose life was said to have been miraculously preserved.—Cf. p. 151, note 2.

[2] This is the first mention in the West of allegorical representations or historical pictures in churches. In the East they are spoken of by Gregory Nyssen a generation earlier.—Gieseler, ii. p. 39.

[3] Gilly, pp. 175-178. In imitation of Paulinus, Sulpicius in Gaul built two basilicas, with a baptistery between them, on the walls of which were painted likenesses of Martin and of Paulinus himself.—*Church in the Middle Ages*, p. 141. Paulinus is popularly said to have been the inventor of church bells. It is clear that some sonorous instrument (signum) was

When all was finished, processions were formed, the relics of the saint were displayed, clouds of incense rose, and lights were burned before the tomb, whilst votive offerings were presented by the multitude, who cried aloud "Hear us, holy Felix! blessed Felix!"[1] A festival which took place in honour of the saint whilst Vigilantius was at Nola is described in almost the very words of Prudentius' rhapsody over the pilgrimage to the shrine of Hippolytus in the Roman catacombs.[2] Paulinus himself was somewhat shocked with the prodigal consumption of wine on this occasion,[3] although he is at first inclined to regard the excess with indulgence. "Would they could offer up their vows of joy with more sobriety, and not be quaffing cups of wine within the sacred precincts! Yet I think some allowance may be made for those who indulge a little in these festivals, since rude minds are liable to error, and simple piety is scarcely conscious of the faults it commits." But the sight of an inebriate provokes his wrath: "Thou hast now reason to dread Felix; thou art insulting him by thy drunkenness; wretched creature, thou art making him the witness and the avenger of thy

A.D. 394.

---

first employed about this time to call Christians to worship.—See *Dict. Christ. Antiq.*, i. p. 184, art. Bells.

[1] Paulinus writes to a friend respecting a young man who had been taken ill at Nola: "The Lord permitted his sickness to reach a dangerous point, in order that the virtue of my patron saint's intercession might be made manifest."—Gilly, p. 219.

[2] *Early Church History*, p. 491. [3] Id., p. 498.

revels. I have thought it right," he continues, " to have the walls of the sanctuary decorated with paintings, that in the sacred history, and the pious examples held up to their view, the rustics may forget their wine and become sober." [1]

The rule of the monastery was severe. Paulinus tells us of one of the brotherhood who, after he had been some time at Nola, was much altered; his body grew lean and his face pale; and adds, " He rarely drinks at table, and in such small quantities as is scarcely sufficient to wet his lips, but he does not now complain of an empty stomach or a dry throat." The cloister cooks leaving one after another, Sulpicius sent Paulinus " brother Victor," who proved a rare treasure to his new master. " His dishes," says Paulinus, "are of a kind to destroy the fancies and delicacies of a senator. He thoroughly understands how to dress beans, to make vinegar from beetroot, and to prepare coarse broth for hungry monks. More than this, he seasons his meagre porridge with such salt of grace and such sweetness of charity, that the want of material condiments is not felt." [2]

---

[1] Gilly, pp. 215-217.

[2] Id., pp. 182, 183; Robertson, i. p. 360, note. The monks of the West fell short of the Oriental standard in the discipline of the body as well as the power of abstraction. In one of Sulpicius' dialogues (see *ante*, p. 150), himself and Gallus, a disciple of Martin of Tours, being present, Postumian the pilgrim relates how the ship he sailed in was almost driven on the quicksands (Syrtes), and how, just escaping, he and his companions went ashore to explore the desert country of the African coast. They saw before them a hut shaped like the keel of a ship, and an aged hermit clad in sheepskins and turning a hand-mill. Finding they were Christians, the

Cleanliness and becoming attire were as little regarded at Nola as the delicacies of the table. "Give me," exclaims Paulinus, "the society of those who wear hair-cloth shirts, and whose loins are girdled with a rope. I cannot do with those insolent persons who pride themselves on their well-dressed hair: give me those who for the sake of holy deformity, wear it short and badly cut, such as live in honourable neglect of the niceties of life, who despise personal beauty, and purposely disfigure themselves, that their hearts may be clean."[1]

We must not, however, pass over a redeeming element in the monastic life at Nola, which so long as it remained served as a bulwark against corruption and decay. This was the study of Holy Scripture, a pursuit to which Paulinus devoted himself as ardently as Sulpicius. The difficulties which the Biblical student of that time had to

---

old man received them lovingly, and invited them to join in prayer. "'Laying some skins on the ground for us to recline upon, he set before us a plentiful dinner, half a barley loaf and a handful of a sweet herb. There were four of us and he the fifth. We made a hearty meal.' At this word Sulpicius smiled and said to Gallus, 'How wouldst thou like to dine on a handful of herbs and half a loaf for five men?' Gallus blushed and answered: 'Thou art at thy old tricks, Sulpicius, letting slip no opportunity of taxing us Gauls with voracity; but it is cruel to expect us to live like angels, though for myself I can believe that the angels eat too. As to that half of a barley loaf, I should think it a poor mouthful for myself alone, but that meagre Cyrenian might be well content with it; for hunger belongs to him either by necessity or by nature. Nor do I wonder that half-starved and weather-beaten mariners should think it a good dinner; but for our part, we are far from the sea, in a plentiful country; and what is more, as I have often told thee, we are Gauls.'"—*Dialogues,* i.; Ruffner, ii. pp. 120–122.

[1] Gilly, pp. 180, 181.

surmount, were such as in our day can scarcely be imagined. Books were all in manuscript and took up much room. It was a rare thing to possess the whole Bible in one volume. Origen, Eusebius, and Jerome had introduced into the Scriptures certain divisions,[1] but these fell very short of the chapters and verses which we now possess; and headings of chapters, marginal notes, indexes and concordances were unknown. Paulinus was considered so good a textuarian, that Augustine consulted him, and submitted some of his writings to his correction.[2] The study of the Holy Scriptures by the side of the semi-heathen rites practised at Nola, although it failed to open the eyes of a Sulpicius or a Paulinus, may have been to the more free and inquiring mind of Vigilantius, as a lamp shining in darkness.

On the death of his father in 395, Vigilantius returned for a short time to Calagorris, whence he again set out on a journey to Palestine and Egypt. Revisiting Nola on the way, he was furnished by Paulinus with a letter of introduction to Jerome at Bethlehem. The great recluse received him courteously, and took him to the sacred places, "crossing himself at every step." As Vigilantius appears to have made his visit only three years after Jerome had crushed Jovinian, it is not very unlikely that the opinions of that reformer formed a

---

[1] See *ante*, pp. 129, 130, 134, 135.   [2] Gilly, pp. 195-198.

topic of conversation between them. Another topic was furnished by the Origen controversy, which was then going on, and which seems to have occasioned some interruption to their friendly intercourse. From Bethlehem Vigilantius proceeded to Jerusalem, where he appears to have spent some time with Jerome's opponent, Rufinus, and when on his way home he repeated his visit to Jerome, the suspicious nature and ill-humour of the latter burst forth, and Vigilantius quitted Bethlehem abruptly. On his way back to Gaul he tarried a while in Alexandria, whence, proceeding to the shores of Italy, he made his way home by the Cottian Alps.[1] Wherever he went he seems to have spoken freely of Jerome and his opinions, and to have found many sympathisers.[2]

The recollection of their quarrel rankled in Jerome's mind, and when he heard of the manner in which his late visitor had occupied himself on his journey he vented his spleen in a stinging epistle (A.D. 398). "It would have been just had I given thee no satisfaction by letter, since thou hast given no credence to thy own ears. But since Christ has given us in Himself an example of perfect humility by kissing his betrayer, I intimate to thee in thy absence the same things which I told

---

[1] Some have connected this journey over the Cottian Alps with the early Protestantism which manifested itself in the valleys of Dauphiné and Piedmont, but without, as it seems, sufficient ground.

[2] Gilly, pp. 207, 231, 237, 238, 285; Jerome's *Letter to Vigilantius*.

Per. I.
Chap. 18.

thee when present. . . . Thou hast left Egypt and all the provinces where so many defend thy opinions with effrontery; and hast selected me as an object of persecution, me who reprehend all doctrines contrary to the Church and publicly condemn them. So Origen is a heretic! What is that to me, who do not deny that in many points he is a heretic? If I did not daily anathematize his errors, I should be a partaker of them. . . . I as a Christian, speaking to thee as a Christian, beseech thee brother not to aim at being wise above thy knowledge. From thy childhood thou hast learned another trade, thou hast been used to another kind of training. It is not for the same man to examine both gold coins and the Scriptures, both to sip wines and to understand the Apostles and Prophets. . . . Call to mind I pray thee the time when I descanted on the true resurrection of the body, how thou leaped aside, clapped thy hands and stamped thy feet, proclaiming that I was orthodox. But when thou got out to sea, the offensive odour of the bilge-water struck into thy brain, and thou remembered that I was a heretic. I gave credence to the letters of the holy presbyter Paulinus, not imagining that his judgment of thee could be erroneous; and although I noticed that thy conversation was unpolished, I set it down to rusticity and simplicity rather than to folly. . . . Thy name must have been given thee by *antiphrasis*, for thy whole mind slumbers as in a lethargy.

Thy tongue ought to be cut out and torn to shreds."[1]

Several years may have elapsed before Vigilantius put forth the treatise which has made his name honourable, and which drew down upon him a more severe infliction of Jerome's wrath. As soon as it was published, information of the writer's audacity in attacking the ruling follies of the age was sent to Jerome by Riparius, a priest of the diocese of Toulouse. It drew forth (A.D. 404) a characteristic reply.

"Thou sayest," writes Jerome, "that Vigilantius (he should rather be called Dormitantius) is again opening his foul mouth, and is casting forth the most villainous filth against the relics of the holy martyrs, styling us who receive them 'cinder-gatherers and idolaters,' because we venerate the bones of dead men. . . . I am surprised that the holy bishop[2] in whose diocese he is said to be a presbyter should wink at such madness, and should not with his apostolic rod of iron, dash in pieces the worthless vessel, and deliver him for the destruction of the flesh that the spirit may be saved. . . . If the relics of the martyrs are not to be honoured, how is it that we read 'Precious in the sight of the Lord is the death of his saints'? If their bones pollute those who touch them, how was it that Elisha when dead raised to life the dead

---

[1] *Letter to Vigilantius.*   [2] Exuperius, bishop of Toulouse.

Per. I.
Chap. 18.

man? Were all the camps of the Israelitish host unclean because they carried the bodies of Joseph and the patriarchs in the wilderness? And did they carry unclean ashes into the Holy Land? ... This tongue should be cut off by the surgeons, or rather this mad head should be cured, that he who knows not how to speak may learn sometimes to keep silence. I once saw this marvel and wished to bind the madman with Scripture testimonies; but he went off, he departed, he escaped, he burst away, and has railed against us between the billows of the Adriatic and the Cottian Alps. ... I could have wished to say more did not the brevity of a letter impose on me the obligation to silence, and hadst thou thought it expedient to send me his doggerel books that I might know what I ought to answer. At present I am beating the air, and give proof rather of my own orthodoxy than of his heterodoxy which is manifest to all men. But if thou wishest that I should write a longer book against him, send me his dirges and drivellings, that he may hear John the Baptist announcing, 'Now also the axe is laid unto the root of the tree: therefore every tree which bringeth not forth good fruit is hewn down and cast into the fire.'"[1]

In accordance with this letter, Riparius, and another priest Desiderius, drew up a formal charge against Vigilantius, and sent it with a copy of his

---

[1] *Letter to Riparius,* §§ 1, 2, 4.

tract to Jerome, entreating him to put a stop to the mischief. They represented that the whole neighbourhood was in commotion, and that their own people were infected by the blasphemous doctrines of the heretic. The infuriated monk immediately set to work, and in one night forged the engine which was to "crush the serpent." This was in the year 406.[1]

Vigilantius' treatise is known only through Jerome's answer. It is plain, however, that in his protest against the abuses of the times, Vigilantius takes a wider range than his predecessor Jovinian had done. We have seen that he denied the tombs of the martyrs to be the proper objects of veneration. He calls their relics a heap of ashes and wretched bones, and asks of what use it is to honour and adore and even kiss dust folded up in a linen cloth? He derides the prodigies said to be wrought in the churches of the martyrs, and condemns the vigils performed in them, asserting, as Tertullian and Lactantius had done before him,[2] that the practice of burning tapers by daylight came from the heathen. "How," he asks, "could men think of honouring by the light of miserable wax candles, those martyrs on whom

---

[1] Gilly, pp. 387, 388. Jerome tells us that he wrote his answer "in a single night," because the brother who was to take the letter could not tarry longer.—§ 18.

[2] See *Early Church History*, p. 480.

the Lamb in the midst of God's throne is shedding all the brightness of his majesty?"[1]

In his answer Jerome does not deny that these practices were borrowed from the pagans, but asserts that the same homage, which is to be detested when offered to idols, is to be approved when offered to martyrs. He maintains, further, that Christians are far from intending to pay to creatures the honour which is due to the Creator alone; that their devotion sees in what Vigilantius describes as "wretched bones," something of much greater worth; that they venerate in the tomb nothing which is dead, but through it look up to the saints alive with God, who is in truth not the God of the dead but of the living. In defending the vigils, he could not deny that they often served both as a pretext and an occasion for gross immoralities. To the objection advanced against the lighted tapers, he could only answer that, even though the laity or pious women might be mistaken in supposing the martyrs to be so honoured, yet we are bound to respect such pious feelings, though they may err in the mode of their expression. But the conclusive argument on which he relies is, universal authority. "Was the Emperor Constantius," he asks, "guilty of sacrilege, who transported the holy relics of Andrew, Luke and Timothy to Constantinople, before which the devils

---

[1] Jerome, *Book against Vigilantius*, §§ 4, 5.

(such devils as inhabit Vigilantius) roar, and are confounded? Or the Emperor Arcadius, who translated the bones of the blessed Samuel from Judæa into Thrace?[1] Are all the bishops not only sacrilegious but infatuated, who carried this worthless trash and these loose cinders in silk and gold; and all the people gathered together from Palestine even to Chalcedon, who met them, and received them as if it were the living prophet? Is the bishop of Rome sacrilegious, who offers sacrifice on the altar under which are the venerable bones (the vile dust would Vigilantius say?) of Peter and Paul; and not the bishop of one city alone, but the bishops of all the cities in the world, who enter the church of the dead in which this most worthless dust and ashes are deposited?"[2]

Vigilantius also denied the efficacy of prayers addressed to departed saints. "According to the Holy Scriptures," he says, "only the living pray for one another; the martyrs moreover cannot be everywhere present, to hear men's prayers and to succour them. The souls of the Apostles and martyrs have settled themselves either in Abraham's bosom, or in a place of refreshment, or under the altar of God; and they cannot escape and present themselves where they please. Do they

---

[1] For a description of this magnificent ceremony, see Gibbon, iii. pp. 531, 532.   [2] *Book against Vigilantius*, §§ 5, 8-10.

Per. I.
Chap. 18.

so love their ashes as to hover always round them, lest if any suppliant should happen to draw near they might not hear him?" These opinions are fanciful, but Jerome's reply is no better founded. "If the Apostles and martyrs in this earthly life, before they had yet come safely out of the conflict, were able to pray for others, how much more can they do so, now that they have obtained the victory! and seeing it is asserted of them that they follow the Lamb whithersoever He goes, and the Lamb is everywhere present, we must believe that the faithful are in spirit everywhere with Christ."[1]

Vigilantius spoke lightly of fasting and mortification, and the various austerities of the monks, and even of the hermit life itself. "Should all retire from the world and live in deserts, who would remain to uphold the public worship of God? Who would exhort sinners to virtue? This would not be to fight, but to fly." Especially he denied the merit of virginity, and that celibacy is incumbent on the clergy. It is evident that his teaching had made some converts among the higher clergy, for Jerome declaims against some bishops, who (evidently because they feared the pernicious consequences of a constrained celibacy) would ordain no others as deacons, but those who were married.[2]

---

[1] Id., §§ 6, 7, 9. [2] Id., §§ 16-18.

Another point on which Vigilantius sought to bring men back to Scripture and common sense, was that of the right stewardship of earthly possessions. He showed that those who managed their own property themselves, and distributed their incomes prudently amongst the poor, did better than those who gave away the whole at once; and that it was a more Christian act for a man to provide for the poor of his own neighbourhood, than to send his money to Jerusalem for the support of the monks in that city who lived on charity. On these as on some other points, Jerome has nothing to oppose but flimsy sophistry. What he lacks in reason, however, he makes up in abuse. Thus he opens the letter in these words: "Many monsters have been born into the world, centaurs and satyrs, owls and bitterns, Cerberus, the chimera and the many-headed hydra, and the three-formed Geryon. Gaul alone has had no monsters, but has always abounded in brave and eloquent men. Suddenly Vigilantius has arisen, who, in his unclean spirit, fights against the spirit of Christ."[1]

A.D. 406.

From this time we almost lose sight of the reformer. According to some, the bishop Exuperius, who refused in the first instance to take part against Vigilantius, and was even said to favour him, was eventually induced by the invec-

---

[1] Id., §§ 1, 14.

442   THE *GOLDEN AGE* OF THE CHURCH.

Per. I.
Chap. 18.

tives of Jerome, and the influence of Innocent I. of Rome, to have him banished from Aquitaine. One historian records that he served a church in Barcelona, and this may well agree with the statement just related. It is thought that he may have perished about the year 409, in that great hurricane of the Northern barbarians, which after desolating Gaul, broke over the Spanish peninsula, and converted it into a desert.[1]

SECTION III. The Catholic worthies whose lives we have endeavoured to portray are the men to whom the Romanists of the present day, and many who bear the name of Protestant, look up, as to the Fathers of the Church; and the century in which they flourished is regarded as its golden age. No constellation of luminaries so bright and so numerous is to be met with again until we come to the Reformation. At the same time how far all these celebrated churchmen were as individuals, true Witnesses for Christ, is a question on which there may well be a difference of opinion. Few of the readers of this volume are likely to follow Cardinal Newman in the reasons he gives for honouring Jerome. "I do not scruple to say, that were he not a saint, there are words and ideas in his writings from which I should shrink; but as he *is* a saint, I shrink with greater reason

---

[1] Gilly, pp. 470, 473, 476.

from putting myself in opposition, even in minor matters and points of detail, to one who has the infallibility of the Church pledged to his saintly perfection. I cannot, indeed, force myself to approve or like these particulars on my private judgment or feeling; but I can receive things on faith against both the one and the other. And I readily and heartily do take on faith these characteristics, words, or acts of this great Doctor of the Universal Church; and think it is not less acceptable to God or to him to give him my religious homage than my human praise."[1] To argue in this manner is to impose on one's self a slavery worse than that of Egypt. Many of our readers will agree with Newman in his private opinion regarding Jerome, and some will perhaps go further, disposed, like Isaac Taylor, to challenge the claim of that extraordinary man to any place at all amongst the true Witnesses for Christ.[2]

It is clear that these renowned Fathers of the Church have not earned our gratitude in some essential matters. They found the episcopal authority already inordinately great; they left it absolute. They found the system of celibacy and monkery and the worship of saints and relics a young and sturdy plant; they left it a great tree overshadowing the whole land. They found the

---

[1] *Church of the Fathers*, pp. 300, 301. These views are indeed sufficiently refuted by Jerome's own words.—See *ante*, p. 298.

[2] Ibid.

Church half resolved to employ force in compelling men's consciences; they left her fully embarked on this fatal course. Down to their time, schismatics (not to say heretics) were regarded with some symptoms of charity, and treated with some show of consideration; but after the time of Augustine all this has vanished: it is, "Recant, or die; return to the bosom of Holy Mother Church, or perish like a malefactor." Such from this time forward was the only alternative. At the same time the dogma of one Catholic Church, beyond the pale of which there is no salvation, became fixed and universal.

In passing judgment however upon the Church teachers and rulers of this age we must bear in mind that men are to be weighed in the balance of their own times, and not in that of any other. The degree of light which prevailed in their day must always be taken into account. The fourth and fifth centuries formed an age not only of rank superstition, but of profound moral corruption. The social and political sores went on festering until they became intolerable, and had to be cut out by the swords of the barbarians.

In estimating, on the other hand, the motives and characters of the Reformers, Aërius, Jovinian, Vigilantius, two important considerations present themselves. They are men almost unknown to history. Despised and proscribed by nearly the whole Church, no friendly biographer has traced

their course or drawn their portrait; or if this was
done, envy and bigotry have effectually effaced the
record. And as the story of their life has perished,
so it is with their writings; these have either been
designedly destroyed or have become buried in
oblivion. Not a fragment of all that proceeded
from the pens of these three Witnesses has come
down to us, except in the quotations made from
their books by those who undertook to refute
them.[1] No man, it is needless to say, would ever
consent to be judged on the evidence of extracts
from his writings made by an adversary. The
meaning of quoted words may be greatly modified,
or even neutralised, by the unquoted context.
Other writings of the same author, or other chapters not referred to, may set his object or his
motive in a totally different light, and in the place
of distrust, awaken sympathy and admiration.
Lastly, the extracts themselves may be garbled.
And if all this is true as a general rule, it is
emphatically so when the antagonist is a Jerome.
Hence we draw our estimate of the character of
these reformers from slender material. We know
not whether they possessed the true spirit of love
and faith which is able to disarm or to rise above
the persecution of man. We do know that they

---

[1] The monks were the only librarians during the Middle Ages, and they admitted none but orthodox books. Thus the works of such writers as Vigilantius and Jovinian, even if not purposely destroyed, would soon disappear.

saw clearly some things in respect of which the eyes of the leading churchmen of the age were blinded.

If the warning voice raised by these just men had been heeded, and the Church had happily retraced her steps out of the labyrinth of error into which she had wandered, with what affection would their names have been embalmed! Their writings would have been preserved with as much care as those of Athanasius or Chrysostom, and we might have constructed biographies of them as worthy of our attention and even as full of incident as those of the champions of orthodoxy. But if their known deeds be fairly weighed and duly considered, they will be found to deserve the title of Christian heroism. The whole Christian world was rapidly sinking into an easy and fatal slumber. They lifted up their voices to utter the warning cry. They were almost alone; they could hope for no inspiring echo from any other quarter. The courage of Chrysostom has been much extolled when he ventured from the fastness of his pulpit to attack the Empress Eudoxia; and of Basil and Ambrose, when they confronted Valens and his minister and the Emperor Theodosius, with a spirit as haughty as their own; but the breach into which Jovinian and Vigilantius threw themselves was one of far greater danger and for a far nobler prize. If any men ever played a part which should entitle them to the gratitude of posterity, surely it was these. And carefully must we note that, although their opponents, in order to weaken their influence, seek in every way to blacken their memory, yet no tangible accusation is made against them, either as to the honesty of their motives or their moral life.[1]

---

[1] The opinion of Du Pin lends support to the above. "It is a misfortune that Jovinian's and Vigilantius' books are lost; and there is reason to believe from those other disputes wherein St. Jerome was engaged, that if we knew what they said for themselves, instead of thinking them heretics, we should esteem them illustrious defenders of the Christian religion, against that superstition, which an immoderate zeal for a monastical life did at that time introduce into the Church. . . . Since obstinacy is necessary to make a man a heretic, it would be rashness to call Jovinian a heretic, of whom we know nothing but what we have from his enemies."—*Hist. of Eccles. Writers*, iii. p. 89, note.

www.ingramcontent.com/pod-product-compliance
Lightning Source LLC
Chambersburg PA
CBHW031956300426
44117CB00008B/785